RESEARCH METHODS IN GENERATIVE SECOND LANGUAGE ACQUISITION

This timely text provides a comprehensive overview of the research methods used by the Generative Second Language Acquisition framework.

The authors lay out the history and state of the art in the field, explain the theoretical underpinnings of this work, and offer practical hands-on guidance for developing, conducting and understanding studies related to L2 grammatical competence—using a rich array of techniques and advancing key insights into the rationale and circumstantial pros and cons of each method.

With useful features in a consistent chapter structure, including diverse case studies and discussion questions, the book will be an invaluable resource to students and researchers of SLA, applied linguistics, theoretical linguistics, education, and related areas.

Roumyana Slabakova is Professor and Chair of Applied Linguistics at the University of Southampton, UK. In addition, she is Adjunct Research Professor at UiT The Arctic University of Norway. She is a Founding Co-Editor of *Linguistic Approaches to Bilingualism* and is currently Co-Editor of *Second Language Research*.

Tania Leal is Assistant Professor of Spanish Linguistics at the University of Arizona, USA. In addition to this role, she serves as a faculty member in the Graduate Interdisciplinary Program in Second Language Acquisition and Teaching (SLAT). She is Associate Editor for *Linguistic Approaches to Bilingualism* and contributes to the editorial board of *Second Language Research*.

Laura Domínguez is Professor of Linguistics at the University of Southampton, UK. She is a member of the editorial boards of *Second Language Research*, the *Journal of the European Second Language Association* and the *International Journal of Spanish as a Heritage Language*. She was also a board member of *Studies in Second Language Acquisition*.

Second Language Acquisition Research Series
Susan M. Gass and Alison Mackey, Series Editors
Kimberly L. Geeslin, Associate Editor

The *Second Language Acquisition Research Series* presents and explores issues bearing directly on theory construction and/or research methods in the study of second language acquisition. Its titles (both authored and edited volumes) provide thorough and timely overviews of high-interest topics, and include key discussions of existing research findings and their implications. A special emphasis of the series is reflected in the volumes dealing with specific data collection methods or instruments. Each of these volumes addresses the kinds of research questions for which the method/instrument is best suited, offers extended description of its use, and outlines the problems associated with its use. The volumes in this series will be invaluable to students and scholars alike, and perfect for use in courses on research methodology and in individual research.

Researching Incidental Vocabulary Learning in a Second Language
Edited by Mark Feng Teng and Barry Lee Reynolds

Second Language Speech Processing
A Guide to Conducting Experimental Research
Isabelle Darcy

Research Methods in Generative Second Language Acquisition
Roumyana Slabakova, Tania Leal and Laura Domínguez

For more information about this series, please visit: www.routledge.com/Second-Language-Acquisition-Research-Series/book-series/LEASLARS

RESEARCH METHODS IN GENERATIVE SECOND LANGUAGE ACQUISITION

*Roumyana Slabakova, Tania Leal,
and Laura Domínguez*

NEW YORK AND LONDON

Designed cover image: © Getty Images | ktsimage

First published 2025
by Routledge
605 Third Avenue, New York, NY 10158

and by Routledge
4 Park Square, Milton Park, Abingdon, Oxon, OX14 4RN

Routledge is an imprint of the Taylor & Francis Group, an informa business

© 2025 Roumyana Slabakova, Tania Leal and Laura Domínguez

The right of Roumyana Slabakova, Tania Leal and Laura Domínguez to be identified as authors of this work has been asserted in accordance with sections 77 and 78 of the Copyright, Designs and Patents Act 1988.

All rights reserved. No part of this book may be reprinted or reproduced or utilised in any form or by any electronic, mechanical, or other means, now known or hereafter invented, including photocopying and recording, or in any information storage or retrieval system, without permission in writing from the publishers.

Trademark notice: Product or corporate names may be trademarks or registered trademarks, and are used only for identification and explanation without intent to infringe.

Every effort has been made to contact copyright-holders. Please advise the publisher of any errors or omissions, and these will be corrected in subsequent editions.

Library of Congress Cataloging-in-Publication Data
Names: Slabakova, Roumyana, author. | Leal, Tania, author. | Domínguez, Laura (Linguist), author.
Title: Research methods in generative second language acquisition / Roumyana Slabakova, Tania Leal and Laura Domínguez.
Description: New York, NY: Routledge, 2025. |
Series: Second language acquisition research series | Includes bibliographical references and index. | Summary: "This timely text provides a comprehensive overview of the research methods used by the Generative Second Language Acquisition framework"— Provided by publisher.
Identifiers: LCCN 2024016919 (print) | LCCN 2024016920 (ebook) | ISBN 9780367750220 (hardback) | ISBN 9780367750206 (paperback) | ISBN 9781003160762 (ebook)
Subjects: LCSH: Second language acquisition. | Generative grammar.
Classification: LCC P118.2 .S577 2025 (print) | LCC P118.2 (ebook) | DDC 418.0072/1—dc23/eng/20240523
LC record available at https://lccn.loc.gov/2024016919
LC ebook record available at https://lccn.loc.gov/2024016920

ISBN: 978-0-367-75022-0 (hbk)
ISBN: 978-0-367-75020-6 (pbk)
ISBN: 978-1-003-16076-2 (ebk)

DOI: 10.4324/9781003160762

Typeset in ITC Galliard
by codeMantra

CONTENTS

List of figures   *vii*
List of tables   *viii*

PART I
Methodological preliminaries and issues   1

1 Introduction   3

2 Research issues   13

3 The life cycle of an experimental design   26

4 Designing experiments in GenSLA   38

PART II
Methods typically used in GenSLA   53

5 Acceptability tasks   55

6 Interpretation tasks   70

7 Speech tasks   84

8 Latency-based measures	100
9 Eye-tracking	119
10 Event-related potentials	136
11 Production tasks	149
12 Learner corpora	168
References	*185*
Author index	*211*
Subject index	*214*

FIGURES

6.1	Picture representing Meaning 1 (one person stroking every cat) reproduced with permission from Marsden (2009)	76
6.2	Picture representing Meaning 2 (every cat being stroked by a different person)	77
7.1	Percentage correct identification of Polish stress by different groups of speakers	92
8.1	Self-paced reading trial	105
8.2	A Latin Square presentation of a study with four conditions and eight total items/lexicalizations	109
9.1	Example of eye movements during reading the phrase. The knight attacked the windmill on his donkey	122
9.2	Example of foveal, parafoveal and peripheral regions	123
9.3	Sample display (determiner + same condition) (yellow objects have the same gender; green object is a distractor and a different gender)	128
10.1	Hypothetical ERP waveform in response to a stimulus	139
11.1	Pictures used in the elicitation task in Bayram (2013)	156
11.2	Prompt: "My little daughter, why _____ (to scare)" from García-Tejada, Cuza and Lustres Alonso (2023)	158
12.1	Sample of a CHAT transcript from TalkBank	175
12.2	Access to the CLAN programs in the commands window	177

TABLES

2.1	Form and meaning relationships in two similar sentences	14
2.2	Paradigm of *was/were* agreement in Buckie English	17
4.1	L1–L2 feature mismatch	45
6.1	Story–test sentence combinations in a TVJT	72
8.1	Self-paced reading task design with predictions for RTs, Leal and Hoot (2022), critical region	107
8.3	Felser and Robert's (2007) cross-modal priming task design	116
9.1	Experimental design in Roberts et al. (2008)	132
10.1	Experimental design (for ERP experiment) in Gabriele et al. (2021)	146
12.1	Types of tasks used in SPLLOC 1 and SPLLOC 2	181

PART I
Methodological preliminaries and issues

1
INTRODUCTION

This book provides a detailed and comprehensive overview of the main research methods employed by researchers investigating second language acquisition (SLA)[1] within the generative framework. This introductory chapter offers an overview of the main themes covered in the book, starting with an introduction to I-language, the main object of study in generative SLA (GenSLA). The chapter explains some of the main theoretical assumptions, theories, and hypotheses assumed by generative researchers over the past 40 years. It also highlights some recurrent themes that will be explained in detail throughout the book and finishes with a short summary of each of the parts into which this book is divided.

1.1 I-language and the role of Universal Grammar in SLA

GenSLA is interested in investigating I-language, the abstract and unconscious linguistic system held by native and L2 speakers. I-language is a system of rules (what we call a "grammar") which is internal and individual to each speaker. This contrasts with what is known as E-language,[2] which is an actual manifestation of I-language and refers to how language is used by communities of speakers.

Apart from being individual and internal to each speaker, I-language is characterized as being intensional in the sense that it specifies a set of "rules" generating *all and only* acceptable expressions and sentences (see details in Isac & Reis 2013). For instance, speakers of German do not have to memorize every single instance of a plural noun that exists in this language (this would take a lot of memory and resources in a speaker's brain);

DOI: 10.4324/9781003160762-2

instead, their I-language includes a rule that can generate every instance of a plural noun in German. Native speakers unconsciously make use of this rule when constructing sentences that include plural nouns.

I-language, which is an abstract and unconscious linguistic system, is constrained by principles of Universal Grammar (UG). In a key article describing the GenSLA enterprise, Rothman and Slabakova (2017: 3) describe UG as:

> [I]t is argued to be a genetically endowed blueprint to the most generalizable facts about language; that is, it contains the linguistic information that is common to all human languages, labeled principles […] UG also identifies and restricts the parameters of grammatical variation between languages.

What exactly UG is and what it contains continues to be a topic of discussion. Over the past 20 years of research in linguistic theory, the tendency has been to simplify the contents of UG and start paying more attention to the role that the input and general cognitive mechanism play in language acquisition (see Biberauer 2019). Although the debate around the content of UG continues, the consensus is that UG constrains the grammars that can be entertained by speakers (both native and non-native). That is, learner I-grammars, which are the object of study in GenSLA, are limited in the options they can entertain, as they have to fit the linguistic requirements imposed by UG.

L2 grammars, also known as interlanguage grammars, although still developing, are considered I-languages with the same characteristics as grammars of native speakers (i.e., they are individual, internal, and intensional). They are the mental grammars entertained by learners at different stages of development and specify what learners know as acceptable or unacceptable in the language they are acquiring. As an example, an L2 speaker of English needs to learn how reflexive pronouns work in this language, and, in particular, that they can only refer to subjects already mentioned in the same clause (as shown in 1a) and cannot refer to someone else (as in 1b).

1. [Mary] looked at [herself] in the mirror.
    a. Herself = Mary
    b. *Herself = Sarah

Native speakers possess implicit knowledge of how reflexive pronouns work in their first language and use that knowledge, also unconsciously, as a first approximation when they construct L2 sentences to communicate with others. Over time, they build an L2 mental grammar that crucially includes both what is grammatical/correct/allowed and what is not (i.e., they need to know about 1a and 1b together).

1.2 Choosing the right method to investigate underlying grammars

The purpose of this book is to explore the tools and methods that generative researchers use to study learner grammars. For this reason, the main question that we aim to answer is *What research methods are appropriate to investigate I-language?*

The first step toward answering this question is to accept that, in fact, it is not possible to completely access I-language, as any data that researchers collect will always be tapping performance and not the actual knowledge that speakers have about grammatical constructions (such as those shown in example (1)). The lack of access to a speaker's competence has been recognized by GenSLA researchers for some time now (see White 2003). It is, thus, agreed that the main (linguistic) tasks which have been developed by researchers are designed to reveal key insights into what speakers (unconsciously) know about the underlying grammars they are learning, but they are limited by the fact that what the tasks collect is ultimately the learners' judgment or evaluation or interpretation, which is as a type of language performance. As Schütze (1996, 2016: 24) explains, "Judgment is a product of performance and intuition is part of competence," where intuition refers to the ability that native speakers have *to get a sense* of whether a sentence is grammatical or not.

Nevertheless, important gains have been achieved in the GenSLA field thanks to good-quality data collected by well-designed judgment and interpretation tasks. Traditionally, the tasks that are preferred in GenSLA research have been those which are carefully designed, controlled (i.e., they are constructed according to a set of pre-defined variables), and inspired by theoretical questions in (linguistic) theory. These tasks are often used to collect evidence to support or refute hypotheses on how grammars develop and get to be acquired. Due to the highly experimental nature of these tasks, a control group is often needed as a baseline for comparison with the learner or experimental group. Who is selected as the control group, or baseline, for these studies depends on the specific research questions and assumptions of each study, so it often varies (i.e., native speakers, bilingual speakers, and L2 speakers can all be appropriate controls in specific contexts). Researchers must pay careful attention to the design of the tasks to ensure their validity and appropriateness for collecting the correct type of data, which are then used to explain the specific phenomenon under investigation (see discussion in Domínguez & Arche 2021).

Traditionally, the preferred task for many researchers working on generative issues has been the Grammaticality Judgment Task, better described as an Acceptability Judgment Task (AJT), since speakers do not have direct access to their grammatical unconscious knowledge. In an AJT, participants are asked for their introspective linguistic judgments on a series of

6 Methodological preliminaries and issues

constructions or sentences, some grammatical and some ungrammatical. AJTs have played an important role in GenSLA research because they can be easily adapted to investigate a wide range of linguistic phenomena (e.g., knowledge about pronouns, grammatical gender, word order, tense, and aspect) but also because they can elicit judgments on ungrammatical constructions, something which is not possible with other type of tasks, such as uncontrolled oral production tasks. For instance, researchers investigating the acquisition of English reflexive pronouns (as shown in example (1)) will find it useful to ask learners whether they think that (1a) is possible, as well as whether they think (1b) is not possible. One evaluation without the other is not sufficient. A task that elicits this kind of direct evidence (about what is correct and what is incorrect in a grammar) can be useful to obtain key insights into I-language. AJTs have some limitations, as will be explained in Chapter 5 of this book, but they can provide the sort of evidence that is useful to researchers interested in investigating underlying grammatical representations. For instance, how can we know whether learners of English know that reflexive pronouns can refer only to the subject of a sentence and not to another subject not present in the discourse?[3] This kind of evidence, concerning referential properties of pronouns in this case, will be very difficult to obtain by using other tasks, such as an interview or a film retelling.

Early on, many studies usually employed AJTs on their own. As we will show in this book, this is no longer the case, as researchers currently make use of a variety of task types, often eliciting different types of data, including behavioral tasks (e.g., fill in the blanks, acceptability tasks, controlled story-retell tasks, and picture-verification tasks), online tasks (e.g., self-paced reading tasks), and data elicited using tools from other cognitive sciences (e.g., data elicited using an eye tracker or data measuring brain activity).

1.3 A field in motion: parameters, features, and the role of UG

We have already pointed out that GenSLA researchers are interested in investigating the underlying representation of grammatical knowledge held by speakers. Over the years, these researchers have proposed learning theories and hypotheses inspired by the latest advances in linguistic theory (see summaries in Rothman & Slabakova 2018; Slabakova 2016; Hawkins 2018). The field has benefited from the many studies designed to test the validity of those theories across different populations and learning contexts. The main assumptions adopted by GenSLA were proposed by the linguist Noam Chomsky in a succession of publications spanning over five decades. His views on how language works, how languages vary, and how languages are learned have shaped the research questions that GenSLA researchers have focused on and investigated over the past 40 years.

1.3.1 Early on: the "Principles and Parameters" era

In the 80s and early 90s, the main questions centered on the notion of UG and its accessibility during the process of acquiring a second language. At the time, there was a special interest in investigating whether L2 speakers would be able to have access to UG, as Chomsky had proposed for L1 acquisition, and whether they would be able to eventually achieve targetlike representations.

The prevalent view of language at the time was based on Chomsky's "Principles and Parameters" theory (see Chomsky 1959, 1965, 1975, 1980, 1981a, 1981b, 1986b; Chomsky & Lasnik 1993). Chomsky had proposed that UG contained all aspects of language that were common across languages, what we know as *principles*. Principles refer to the abstract knowledge of the grammar which does not need to be learned. For instance, a principle of UG is that sentences must always contain an element that can be identified as the *subject*, most often the person or thing that performs the action of that sentence and which represents what the sentence is about. In linguistic theory, subjects can be easily identified because they appear in prominent positions in the syntactic structure of a sentence.

Crucially, languages can choose whether to not pronounce the subject in certain contexts, as when the subject can be clearly identified by the context. The languages which allow subjects to be null, or not pronounced, are known as pro-drop or null-subject languages. The fact that this choice exists (i.e., whether a particular language is pro-drop or not) shows that principles of UG are subject to parametrization (an option exists regarding how the principle can be satisfied). Each *parameter* consists of a set of two options known as settings or values. Like principles, parameters are also part of UG, which means that the learning task assumed for children is minimal: children just need to set each parameter to the right value based on the input available to them. This explains why German, French, or English children eventually set the parameter to the [–] option as these are [–pro-drop] languages, whereas Italian, Spanish, or Hindi children set it to the [+] value as these are [+pro-drop] languages. This parameter-setting view of language acquisition was seen as desirable because it could explain why children could acquire their native language fast and with seemingly minimal effort[4] as it simplified the learning task quite considerably.

The Principles and Parameters theory was quickly adopted by GenSLA scholars, as it could explain differences across languages in a straightforward manner and could make specific predictions for acquiring languages with different settings of the same parameter. For instance, English learners of Italian would need to reset the value of the pro-drop parameter from [–] to [+]. Successful resetting of this parameter was taken to mean that learners could still access UG in adulthood. Moreover, SLA researchers were also interested in proving that interlanguages also respected the properties of natural languages (e.g., French, Arabic, and Warlpiri), as they are constrained by the principles and properties of UG.

A parameter-setting view of language acquisition was also useful because it assumed that all syntactic properties linked to the same parameter could be acquired together and with minimal effort (Chomsky 1981b). For instance, the null-subject or pro-drop parameter comprises a cluster of properties, the licensing of null subjects being just one of them. Once learners figured out the correct setting for this parameter, all the linked properties in the cluster could be learned in a kind of automatic fashion (again, this makes learning a language a much easier task).

After years of research, the available evidence pointed to the conclusion that L2 grammars do, indeed, respect the properties of UG and that parameters can be reset, at least in some contexts. However, some other expected findings were not attested, such as the automatic acquisition of the cluster of properties linked to a parameter. Also, whereas some parameters could be reset fairly easily (e.g., the null-subject parameter), other parameters took much more effort (e.g., the parameter responsible for the interpretation and use of articles). This finding could not be easily explained. Furthermore, some aspects of the grammar were not easily linked to specific parameters and were persistently difficult to acquire (e.g., grammatical gender). The focus on ultimate attainment (i.e., whether L2 speakers could achieve full grammar) left other important questions unanswered, such as how the actual resetting happens and on what basis.[5]

The Principles and Parameter framework was useful in answering some early questions on accessibility to UG, but the switch-like nature of parameters proved to be ultimately unhelpful when the research questions became more sophisticated. What the field needed was a change in the theoretical paradigm, which would allow the decomposition of parameters into smaller units. This came about in the mid-90s when Chomsky introduced the Minimalist Program (Chomsky 1995) and radically changed the way that cross-linguistic differences were conceptualized. Minimalism moved the focus from binary-type parameters to how features are specified in lexical items (e.g., nouns, verbs, and adjectives) and functional categories[6] (Holmberg 2010; Gallego 2011).

1.3.2 *The role of features in the Minimalist view of language and acquisition*

In the previous section, we saw how, early on, UG was assumed to contain the principles and parameters (and their possible values) that learners would be able to access during the language acquisition process. However, one of the goals of the Minimalist Program (Chomsky 1995) was to make UG as bare and minimally specified as possible. This meant moving the mechanisms that could explain differences across languages out of UG. Following work by Borer (1984), Minimalism saw cross-linguistic differences as arising from differences in the features (e.g., number, gender, case, and tense) that could be found encoded on lexical items and functional categories. For instance, the feature [+past] when referring to events in the past tense is mapped onto the morpheme [-*ed*] in English. In some contexts, a verb in the past also conveys habituality (i.e., an action that used to take place on many occasions), as in *I played tennis when I was a child*. In this context, the [-*ed*] morpheme attached to the verb carries (at least) two syntactic features, [+past] and [+habitual]. This mapping is specific to English and may not be shared by any other language, as [+past] and [+habitual] may be mapped onto other forms or, even, to no form at all in other languages. This illustrates that languages differ in the way that each specific syntactic feature is mapped onto specific forms (Berwick & Chomsky 2011).

This new focus on features dispensed with parameters in the classical sense and could still account for differences across languages in a specific and principled manner. Crucially, it provided a new framework for investigating language acquisition, one in which the main tasks for children are (a) to select a set of features from a universal inventory (this selection being specific to each language) and (b) to assemble them onto the appropriate words or categories. In SLA, researchers also turned their attention to the role that features played in explaining the properties of interlanguage grammars. Some researchers proposed that L2 features that are not already present in the L1 may not be acquired in adulthood so L2 grammars would never be completely targetlike. For instance, the "Representation Deficit Hypothesis" (Hawkins 2001; Hawkins & Chan 1997; Franceschina 2001, 2005; Hawkins & Liszka 2003) and the "Interpretability Hypothesis" (Tsimpli 2003; Tsimpli & Dimitrakopoulou 2007; Tsimpli & Mastropavlou 2007) proposed representational deficits caused by the inability to acquire L2 features with the correct specifications.

On the other hand, other researchers argued that acquiring new L2 features is possible, and that the difficulty lies in accessing the appropriate morphological form which expresses those features. Under this view, English learners would be successful in acquiring the [+past] and [+habitual] features but may find it difficult to map these two features onto [-*ed*]. In this respect, the Missing Surface Inflection Hypothesis (Haznedar & Schwartz 1997; Prévost & White 2000), Feature Reassembly (Lardiere 2000, 2009), and the Bottleneck Hypothesis (Slabakova 2008, 2013) have investigated problems in the mapping between fully acquired syntactic features onto their corresponding morphological forms. Other researchers have also argued that the problematic mapping is between the syntactic component and discourse-pragmatics (Hulk & Müller 2000; Müller & Hulk 2001; Sorace 2005; Sorace & Filiaci 2006; Tsimpli et al. 2004). Key evidence to illuminate these debates has been achieved by means of sophisticated methodological designs often using a combination of different tasks (oral production, acceptability judgment tasks, etc.).

Further refinement in the methodological designs used in studies to test existing hypotheses has been achieved in the past few decades. Optionality (using and omitting the same form in the same discourse) is now accepted as a common feature of L2 grammars, and so tasks that seek participants' intuitions often include the possibility that L2 speakers show optionality in their responses, typically by allowing responses to be recorded on an acceptability scale (from less to more acceptable). Other researchers have also argued that some grammatical constructions are not suitable to be tested by Grammaticality Judgment Tasks, as they are subject to gradient acceptability (they can be more or less acceptable in certain contexts rather than strict grammatical/ungrammatical) (see Sorace 1996; Sorace & Keller 2005; Sprouse et al. 2018).

As the field continues to debate these issues and more, the methodological design has become more rigorous and more sophisticated, often including a combination of tasks that elicit behavioral (strictly linguistic) and online (processing) evidence. New links between SLA and other related fields, mainly psycholinguistics and neurolinguistics, have also proven to be successful in illuminating existing debates and opening new lines of inquiry.

1.4 Organization of the book

In this book, we provide a comprehensive overview of the research questions, designs, techniques, and instruments used by generative scholars investigating SLA and other areas of multilingualism. Our goal is to make the reader aware of the rich choice of research methods available to generative researchers while advancing key insights into the rationale and usefulness of each method, based on factors such as the property to be acquired, the linguistic module(s) involved, learners' native language, the learning task, linguistic complexity, or the acquisition context. The book comprises 12 chapters and is divided into two parts.

Part I (Chapters 1–4) briefly introduces the field of GenSLA, describing its key assumptions and highlighting some of the main theoretical trends over the past 40 years. This first part also introduces the key terminology used throughout the book, as well as central issues regarding methodological design and data analysis in SLA experiments. Other topics covered include how to design research questions in the generative framework, what kinds of questions can be answered, and how.

Part II (Chapters 5–12) includes eight chapters covering individual methods used in SLA research. Each chapter includes an accessible description of the method covered and a brief history outlining its use in acquisition studies. The focus is on how the tasks described measure implicit knowledge of the L2 property under investigation (construct validity), linking theoretical considerations to methodological design. We illustrate each of the methodologies described in each chapter with examples from existing studies where each task has been used successfully. These chapters also survey best practices in experimental design, including the design of tokens and stimuli. To assist researchers in choosing a proper methodology for their research questions, we also include a descriptive listing of the advantages and disadvantages of each method. At least one exemplary case study is featured in each chapter using the method in question. Finally, a few discussion questions to aid with comprehension of the material are included in each chapter.

1.5 Discussion questions

1 Generative researchers are interested in studying the development of mental grammars, which we have described in this chapter as part of I-language. Consider what this means in terms of learning the following structures: English present tense, third person singular [–s] as in *My brother speak-s Urdu*, and Spanish gender marking on determiners, nouns, and adjectives as in *La casa azul* "the blue house." First, consider the features and properties involved in the acceptable construction of these structures and then think of what type of task would be suitable to investigate the acquisition of these two constructions.

2 For decades, there has been much debate around the question of whether UG is fully accessible during the process of acquiring a second language. In your view, what could constitute key evidence for the (in)accessibility of UG? Think about what structures L2 speakers could produce/accept which, although not completely targetlike, are compatible with UG.

Notes

1 These researchers investigate SLA and other areas of multilingualism such as child bilingual acquisition, heritage language acquisition, third language acquisition, and native language attrition. Throughout this book, we use the term "SLA" as an umbrella term to cover additional language acquisition.

2 The notion of I-language overlaps with what is known as "competence," broadly defined as the unconscious knowledge that speakers have of the grammars of the languages they speak. Similarly, "performance" refers to what speakers actually produce, which is not always a true reflection of their competence. This is similar

to E-language. In this book we use both I-language and competence to mean the underlying and unconscious grammatical knowledge within a single speaker.
3 Another type of judgment task, called a Truth-Value Judgment Task (Crain & McKee 1985; Crain & Thornton 1998), is used to investigate whether participants know the correct interpretation of a sentence in a particular context. The target sentences are ambiguous (i.e., they can have more than one interpretation), so a context used for disambiguation is required. See Chapter 6 for an extended discussion.
4 The fact that children can acquire a complex grammar with seemingly minimal effort and with the available input (which does not contain all the evidence to deduce the rules of that grammar) is an argument in favor of a "Poverty of Stimulus" in child language acquisition. A similar case has been proposed for adult second language learners as well. This is fully explained in Chapter 2.
5 This is particularly important since generative researchers assume that initial full transfer of the native grammar applies in the early stages of L2 acquisition. Learners are able to recover from this massive transfer and acquire an L2 grammar thanks to access to UG (see Schwartz and Sprouse (1994)'s "Full Transfer-Full access" Hypothesis).
6 Functional categories are elements which have no real semantic content and have purely grammatical functions. For instance, the definite article "the," the preposition "on," and the conjunction "and" are all examples of functional categories.

Further reading

Roberts, I. (Ed.). (2017). *The Oxford Handbook of Universal Grammar*. Oxford: Oxford University Press.

Roberts, I. (2019). *Parameter Hierarchies and Universal Grammar*. Oxford: Oxford University Press.

Rothman, J., & Slabakova, R. (2018). The generative approach to SLA and its place in modern second language studies. *Studies in Second Language Acquisition, 40(2)*, 417–442.

2
RESEARCH ISSUES

This second background chapter takes up where Chapter 1 left off. We will delve further into some seminal ideas without which the GenSLA framework cannot be understood properly. The first issue to be explored briefly is the *Poverty of the Stimulus* (PoS), the argument that some knowledge that learners possess does not come from the input. The chapter also presents *variability* from two perspectives: that of *individual differences* and that of *linguistics-based variation*. Next, we tackle the important distinctions between *input, exposure* and *experience*, following Carroll (2017). We briefly compare research methods from different frameworks (usage-based, neurolinguistics, etc.). Finally, this chapter problematizes control groups and what they are for, native speakers used as controls and the construct of the native speaker in second language acquisition (SLA) research.

2.1 Poverty of the stimulus

The PoS refers to "the enormous gap between the input available to the child (primary linguistic data) and the system of knowledge acquired, a system that includes what is possible but, crucially, excludes what is impossible" (Schwartz & Sprouse 2013: 138). Children acquiring their native language create a complex grammatical system in their mind/brains, only some of which is modeled by the ambient language. In this sense, the input that children are exposed to is "impoverished" but only with respect to what can be gleaned from it inductively. Using those two sources, Universal Grammar (UG) and the input, children acquire extremely complex and subtle properties of the community language at a relatively young age. Numerous such

DOI: 10.4324/9781003160762-3

14 Methodological preliminaries and issues

learning situations can be described, but the most convincing ones, called *the bankruptcy of the stimulus*, obtain when negative knowledge is involved, that is, knowledge of the *unacceptability* of a certain construction in the target grammar. This knowledge cannot come from observing the input since unacceptable sentences would never appear in the input in the first place; thus, the ungrammaticality will never be modeled.

In what follows, we present an extended example of the argument that a learner cannot safely assume that an alternative to the construction she has acquired *has to* be available or unavailable in that same language. This learning situation is implicated in the PoS cases as described by Crain and Thornton (2000).

1   The Ninja Turtle$_1$ danced while he$_{1/2}$ ate pizza.
2   He$_1$ danced while the Ninja Turtle$_2$ ate pizza.

In sentences such as (1), the pronoun *he* can refer both to the matrix subject, *the Ninja Turtle*, or to someone else in the discourse. The notation adopted here is to use the same subscript (1 or 2) when pronoun and antecedent co-refer. In example (2), on the other hand, *he* may not refer to the individual called the Ninja Turtle. Note that these two sentences have almost the same word order but quite different interpretations, one of them being ambiguous. We can visualize this situation in Table 2.1.

The lack of one interpretation as in the top right-hand corner is called a "negative constraint." It presents a critical argument for PoS situations, since learners are not exposed to the unavailable form–meaning mapping. You might consider performing an experiment to find out whether children acquiring English as their native language know the facts in Table 2.1. An act-out task would be appropriate, where the experimenter produces the test sentences and asks the child to mime actions with toy figurines. If the child shows sensitivity to the absence, for example, by not acting out or rejecting one interpretation in an act-out task, one could maintain that knowledge of something unmodeled by the input is accessible.

This logical problem of acquisition has different dimensions when a second or additional language(s) is being acquired. What could be a PoS property for children need not be the same for adults acquiring that same language

TABLE 2.1 Form and meaning relationships in two similar sentences

The NT$_1$ danced while he$_{1/2}$ ate pizza	*He$_1$ danced while the NT$_2$ ate pizza*
He = the Ninja Turtle	X
He = someone else	He = someone else

as an L2, just because their native language may have already modeled that property. For that reason, as Schwartz and Sprouse (2013: 152) argue, the best demonstration of PoS in action is when the lack of a certain construction is involved. For example, the native language of the learners makes available two options for a certain meaning or a certain form (construction), while the L2 grammar allows only one meaning or form. The second grammar is in this sense "restricted." No positive evidence is available for the lack of meaning or form, as it will not appear in the input, but the absence of evidence is not evidence of absence. If L2 learners demonstrate knowledge of the restricted L2 grammar, then this knowledge has to come from UG and not from the input. As Rothman and Slabakova (2018: 426) point out, every PoS case in L2 acquisition may rise or fall on its own merit, but collectively they argue for the involvement of some innate knowledge.

How can this line of arguments be disputed or supported? To demonstrate that UG is available in L2 acquisition, on its own and not just through the native grammar, research has to obey two conditions: (a) The linguistic phenomenon under investigation should constitute a learnability or PoS problem, in that it cannot be readily induced from the L2 input or learned on the basis of instruction; (b) the universal principle under investigation should not operate in the L1, or the L1 and L2 should differ with respect to parameter settings.

Numerous researchers have investigated such situations in SLA, starting from White (1985b, 1988) (Marsden 2009; Martohardjono 1993; Montrul & Slabakova 2003). Let us illustrate with a recent study by Heil and Lopez (2020) which meets the requirements mentioned above. The authors tackle a well-known distinction in English, shown in (3) and (4).

3 Mary persuaded John to be honest.   Object Control
4 Mary believed John to be honest.   Raising to Object

These two sentences are superficially similar, differing in just one verb, but their meanings are strikingly dissimilar. In (3), John is being persuaded to be honest after the moment of speech; in (4), John already has the quality of honesty, according to Mary. The second construction, Raising to Object, is not available in Spanish, the native language of the learners tested in the study. It is also exceedingly rare in the input, according to corpus counts: less than 0.05% of all instances of the verb *believe* (British National Corpus) and 0.00144% of raising verbs in a corpus of news on the web (NOW). Among other properties, Heil and Lopez tested a curious aspectual restriction: Raising to Object constructions can take a stative predicate as in (4) but not a dynamic predicate as in (5a) in the non-finite clause. The embedded predicate has to be either perfect (5c) or progressive (5d). The Object Control construction

16 Methodological preliminaries and issues

does not exhibit this restriction, as we can ascertain in (5e). In addition, Raising to Object has an alternative way of expressing the same message, with a finite embedded verb as in (5b).

5   a. *John believes Mary to run.
    b. John believes that Mary runs.
    c. John believes Mary to have run.
    d. John believes Mary to be running.
    e. John persuaded Mary to run.

After the researchers ascertained that this aspectual restriction (among other properties) was not taught in language classrooms, is impossible to observe in the input, and is not available from the mother tongue, they tested Spanish learners of English on their knowledge of it. The L2 learners exhibited monolingual-like knowledge of the restriction on the non-finite complement (5a). The authors argued that the learners had successfully acquired the full spectrum of English infinitival constructions and that the PoS learning situation had been overcome using innate knowledge provided by UG.

For more examples, we refer readers to a review of such properties by Schwartz and Sprouse (2013), which elaborates on five different types of PoS properties. An important point to keep in mind is that the existence of PoS learning situations is no longer a theoretical necessity but a matter of observation and ultimately of empirical evidence. Every PoS case must be defined, defended and tested on its own.

2.2 Variability and gradient acceptability

Variability is a hallmark of language and hence of linguistic knowledge. In the broadest sense, variation refers to differences in linguistic form and interpretation. A trivial level of variation is that among languages, which clearly differ in their lexicons, phonology, morphology, syntax and semantics. Within the same language, where changes of form cannot be explained by changes in meaning, we invoke the linguistic context. For example, the English regular plural morpheme -s is pronounced [s] after voiceless consonants, [əz] after sibilants, and [z] elsewhere. In addition, languages sometimes allow two forms with the same meaning. The possible omission of the complementizer *that* in English provides an example. Whether we drop the complementizer or not, the meaning does not change in this particular linguistic construction exemplified in (6a) where the embedded or subordinate clause (in square brackets) has the function of an object in the main clause. Note, however, that this is not the case in (6b), where the subordinate clause is subject.

6   a. Everyone knows [(that) the Earth is round].
    b. [*(That) the Earth is round] is indisputable.

Variability is also intimately connected to the PoS problem we discussed in the previous section. The gist of the issue is this: can a learner assume, having acquired one construction through positive evidence, for example, (5b) above, that an alternative construction with the same meaning will be unavailable, in this case (5a)? In other words, is there always a one-to-one relationship between form and meaning? In the examples of finite and non-finite complementation in (5), this assumption is warranted because (5b) is acceptable while (5a) is not. However, that assumption is not supported by sentences such as the one in (6a). More generally speaking, this assumption is patently false in language. Examples abound of constructions with alternative forms but the same meaning, two more of which are exemplified below in (7) and (8).

7   a. Who did you speak with?   (Preposition Stranding)
    b. With whom did you speak? (Pied-piping)

8   a. I looked his address up.   (Particle Shift)
    b. I looked up his address.

In a nutshell, no learner can safely assume that any linguistic form has only one meaning, and vice versa, one meaning can be expressed by one form only.

In addition to pervasive linguistic variation, variation manifests among individual speakers. Abstracting away from the ideal speaker–listener invoked in Chomsky (1965), there are lexical and grammatical differences between varieties of English, e.g., those spoken in the USA, Canada, the UK, New Zealand and Australia. Regional variation is also widely attested. Take, for example, the variable pronoun agreement with the past copula in Buckie English, spoken in Scotland (Adger & Smith 2005). Compare the forms in Table 2.2 with the ones in standard English. Notice that optionality abounds even within this paradigm itself.

TABLE 2.2 Paradigm of *was/were* agreement in Buckie English

	Singular	*Plural*
First	I was	we was/were
Second	you was/were	you was/were
Third person	(s)he was	they were

Adapted from Adger and Smith (2005).

18 Methodological preliminaries and issues

Register variation is also widely attested; for instance, the utterance in (7b) is likely to be used in a formal register while the one in (7a)—in an informal situation. We cannot do justice here to the enormous literature on language variation, and we should not try. The point we are making is that variation in language is pervasive and on many levels: grammatical, lexical, regional and socially based. Hence, variation is also ubiquitous in the input to which L2 learners are exposed.

Furthermore, it is well known that sentences have gradient acceptability, as noticed and discussed by Chomsky (1965) (Sprouse et al. 2018). Examples in (9) from Francis (2022) illustrate that, between the completely unacceptable and completely acceptable, there are some sentences of intermediate acceptability. These are usually marked with one or two question marks.

9. a. Sincerity may frighten the boy.   Acceptable
   b. ?Sincerity may admire the boy.   Less acceptable
   c. ??Sincerity may elapse the boy.   Even less acceptable
   d. *Sincerity may virtue the boy.   Unacceptable

Chomsky (1965) considers both formal syntactic explanations and semantic explanations for the gradient judgments. While (9a) contains a regular transitive verb *frighten*, the verb *admire* in (9b) is also transitive (so syntactic requirements are not violated), but its selection is semantically flawed because only sentient beings can admire, not feelings. (9c) illustrates a clause with the intransitive verb *elapse* containing an object, while (9d) does not even have a main verb since *virtue* is a noun. The latter two examples violate syntactic requirements for well-formedness. Over the years, many explanations of gradient acceptability have been discussed in the literature, in addition to these above, including pragmatic, prosodic and processing accounts. The point we want the reader to notice here is that acceptability is not black and white and it may have many sources, sometimes working together.

In this section, we paid close attention to the variability of the linguistic signal. Variation exists among languages of the world and among speakers of the same language; for the same speaker, some sentences may have gradient acceptability. Experimental methods should be sensitive to this variation and its representations.

2.3 Input, exposure and experience

In the previous sections, we considered the ambient input, arguing that true PoS properties will not be demonstrated in it. We also recognized the great variability of words, phrases and constructions in the input. It is high time to offer a working definition of what "input" is. One should be careful in reading the literature on language acquisition, where "input," "exposure," and "experience" are often used interchangeably. However, it is worth thinking about how they are different.

Carroll (2017), for one, argues that it is important to distinguish between the two. Exposure refers to "what is observable and measurable in a particular learning context" (Carroll 2017: 4), for example, what is observable in a classroom interaction recording or in second language textbooks. The input, on the other hand, refers to the whole target grammar and to the speech signal that the language processor has to analyze and interpret. In Carroll's definition, it amounts to "constructs which are relevant to the solution of a particular learning problem" (Carroll 2017: 5). For example, a passive construction exists in English (e.g., *I was offered some tea*), and so it constitutes part of the input. However, the passive may not be prominently, or not at all, exemplified in some L2 English learner's experience; hence, the input and exposure for that particular construction and for that particular learner might diverge.

Whenever learners, all learners, are exposed to language, the speech signal goes to the parser for analysis and comprehension. This is what Fodor (1998a, 1998b) regards as input to language processors. If the existing learner grammar cannot parse a certain string, say passives, this could be because some construct in the input is not represented in the grammar yet or represented incorrectly. This parsing failure becomes what for Fodor is input to the language acquisition mechanisms. Something appears in the input that cannot be parsed yet and hence has to be learned. The extralinguistic context and situation, knowledge of the world and linguistic knowledge in one area of grammar, say semantics, can aid or "bootstrap" new knowledge of morphosyntax (Morgan & Demuth 1996; Naigles 1990). Our understanding of these acquisition mechanisms is still imprecise, but there is no doubt that they exist, since people learn language.

Furthermore, research in bilingualism has demonstrated that cumulative (length of exposure) or relative (language X versus language Y percentages) input quantity predicts rates of linguistic development (e.g., Chondrogianni & Marinis 2011, among many others). More exposure certainly leads to better outcomes in SLA. One could take this as proven, although individual variation is inevitable. Means of quantifying a learner's language exposure include observation, questionnaires, parental reports and self-reports. For example, a recent study by Torregrossa, Andreou, Bongartz and Tsimpli (2021) wanted to calculate dominance scores for their bilingual participants. The property under investigation was reference use. They used scores from a questionnaire probing home language history, early literacy, current language use and current literacy in each of the two languages.

The dependent variable was proficiency as reflected by a vocabulary test score. Not all independent factors contributed equally to the dependent variable variation; home language history and current literacy were the two most important factors. In the end, these scores were entered into a calculation of a dominance index. The authors concluded that language experience played a significant role in determining bilingual outcomes.

In summary, language experience is a crucial factor contributing to language development, and scholars are using sophisticated measures and statistics to quantify it. Next, we look at other research that puts a premium on language experience.

2.4 Research methods from other frameworks

Usage-based approaches are theoretically opposed to generative approaches to SLA. This does not mean that usage-based and generative scholars disagree about everything in the process of language acquisition. Quite the opposite, there is qualified agreement on how vocabulary, some functional morphology and visible syntactic processes are acquired. It is acknowledged by both families of approaches that a relatively small set of cognitive processes, such as categorization, analogy and chunking, can explain quite a lot in language structure and function (Ibbotson 2013). In other words, as we argued in the last section, the importance of language experience should by no means be underestimated. Nor should it be overestimated, for that matter.

What are the research methods that highlight the importance of experience in SLA? The usage-based position is closely allied with that of cognitive linguistics where the fundamental linguistic unit is the construction: a meaningful assembly of symbols in a specific order, used to signal communicative intentions (Goldberg 2006). Hence, syntactic schemas and idioms are very important in this framework. However, it is not sufficient to show that these cognitive units are acquired with some priority. In usage-based theory, analogy should also operate in a more abstract sense to extend the prototypical meaning of constructions. Thus, research is looking for evidence at these two levels of acquisition: one more specific and exemplar-based and the other more abstract and analogy-based.

It makes sense that corpus studies are the first port of call for this research program. Indeed, statistical distributions and frequencies in corpora (written and oral) are the foundation on which usage-based scholars build their experimental methods. For example, within verb–argument constructions, Ellis and O'Donnell (2012) studied the type–token distribution of locative constructions (e.g., *The boy dragged the toy across the floor*) in a large corpus of English usage. They discovered that the most frequent locative verb *types* account for the lion's share of the *tokens*; in other words, locative verbs presented a Zipfian distribution.[1] The researchers also established that there is a very high contingency between verbs and constructions, in the sense that some verbs appear selectively in one type of locative construction and not in another. Finally, the most frequent verbs were also the most prototypical in that they exemplified best the construction semantics.

Representative usage-based studies use free association tasks and training tasks. In one such study by Ellis, O'Donnell and Römer (2014), German, Spanish and Czech advanced learners of L2 English were given a number of locative patterns, such as "V *across* N" (as in the example above) and were asked to fill the V slot with the first word that came to their mind. Their responses were analyzed for frequency, contingency and prototypicality effects, based on the native data elicited by Ellis and O'Donnell (2012). Advanced learners were found to have lexical associations as rich and strong as those of native speakers.

In another representative study by Ellis and Sagarra (2011), three groups of learners were tested on L2 Latin sentences. They had not studied Latin before the experiment. One group was exposed to Latin adverbs, another to verb forms and the third did not receive any pre-training. In the second phase, all participants were shown legitimate adverb plus verb combinations. Finally, a receptive test asked them to identify the temporal reference of Latin sentences, again containing adverbs and verbs. Not surprisingly, the lexical cues learners were pre-trained on proved to be decisive in their temporal choice. Thus, the adverb group paid attention to adverb cues and not verbs; the opposite was true for the verb group, while the control group fell in between.

In conclusion, usage-based research methods are well placed to uncover the effects of exposure on lexical and grammatical knowledge in a second language. In addition, they pay more attention than generative studies to the effects of shared attention on cognition. However, they have a hard time explaining the acquisition of patterns that are not attested in the input and the successful acquisition of meanings that are unavailable in a language.

2.5 Control groups

We have already mentioned "control groups" several times in this chapter. It is time to define and explore them more fully. Generative L2 researchers aim at uncovering, describing and explaining the underlying grammatical competence of L2 speakers. L2 speakers are learning language, and it is inevitable that they make errors in their development. These learner errors have been acknowledged as a vital source of knowledge on exactly how learner grammars are developing (Domínguez & Arche 2021). Ever since

Lado talked about "transfer errors" and "developmental errors" in his Contrastive Analysis Hypothesis (Lado 1957), investigators of second languages have known that how the native language works and how the target language works have to be systematically compared to identify where potential pitfalls to acquisition lie. This practice of comparing the specific features, morphemes and constructions of the two languages involved survives to the present day. It is an indispensable part of language acquisition research.

Let us take an extended example of a linguistic *contrast*. In an English *wh*-question, the question words (*who, when, what, where, how much*, etc.) have to appear at the left-most edge of the sentence, as exemplified in (10a). The same is true of Bulgarian *wh*-questions (11a). However, multiple wh-questions in English and Bulgarian differ in structure and even in surface word order. Bulgarian allows more than one wh-words to pile up at the top of the sentence. Example (10b) asks information about two variables, with respect to a certain dinner (three wh-words are also possible): who came and when they came. The sentence in (11b) has the same interpretation, but the two question words are next to each other.

10 a. **Who** came to the dinner?
    b. **Who** came to the dinner **when**?

11 a. **Koj** dojde na večerjata?
      who came to dinner-DET
      'Who came to the dinner?'

    b. **Koj koga** dojde na večerjata?
      who when came to dinner-DET
      'Who came to the dinner when?'

It is logical to expect that Bulgarian learners will have no difficulty with acquiring single wh-questions in English, but they might have more difficulty with multiple wh-questions because that is what their native language does not model. How can we know about these distinctions between English and Bulgarian without asking a group of native speakers about their intuitions? Generally speaking, first, if we *only* look at learners' behavior, we cannot predict where they might encounter difficulties. In other words, scholars cannot discuss learning tasks and make predictions about acquisition without establishing the facts of the two languages. And for that we need control groups.

Second, and very importantly in a book on research methods, scholars are not always secure in the research instruments they create: say, Truth-Value Judgment Tasks or Acceptability Judgment Tasks. Some test sentences might not work as expected, or some task instructions may be unclear to test takers. To validate the test instruments, we need a control group of speakers of the target language. This is particularly important because native judgments are not just variable but gradient, as we discussed in Section 2.2. Gradient acceptability of target language judgments is indicative of how native speaker grammars are structured and constrained. We can expect the same to be true of the second language grammars learners are building. An early generative L2A study documented one such case of gradient acceptability. Martohardjono (1993) set out to examine how English learners with Italian, Indonesian and Chinese as native languages would evaluate two types of wh-movement violations, termed *strong* and *weak* violations, exemplified in (12) and (13), with the underline showing the original position of the moved wh-phrase.[2]

12   ??Which neighbor did John spread the rumor that ____ stole a car?
13   *Which man did Tom fix the door that ___ had broken?

The exact account of the gradient unacceptability is not so important anymore; what is important is that the control group of native speakers rejected sentences as in (12) 79% of the time, while those in (13) were rejected 94% of the time, a significant difference. We mentioned this study in our section on PoS, since these are both unacceptable sentences and learners would never have been exposed to them. This study makes a convincing case for UG engagement by showing that L2 learners of English were as sensitive to gradient unacceptability as the control group, albeit with some L1-based differences. Without testing a native control group on the distinction proposed by linguistic theory, Martohardjono (1993) would not have been able to make her persuasive case. The same point is forcefully made recently by Domínguez and Arche (2021).

2.6   The construct of the native speaker

The founder of generative grammar, Noam Chomsky, characterized language as a mental entity, taking the form of implicit knowledge in the mind of the speaker/hearer (Chomsky 1965). He referred to this mental entity as I-language or *competence*, to be distinguished from actual language use, E-language or *performance* (see Chapter 1). In the first years of the generative framework, the "ideal native speaker" was an abstraction introduced to get at competence without the distraction of performance.[3] To delineate, describe and explain why sentences as in (10) are acceptable and why sentences as in (12)–(13) are unacceptable to different degrees, descriptive accuracy was based on speaker intuitions taking the form of acceptability judgments. This is because only acceptability judgments can evaluate contrasts such as the ones mentioned above, as sentences are matched head-to-head. In comparison, data from spoken or written discourse cannot as cleanly address the generative research question: to uncover the structure of language as a mental construct. Using acceptability tasks, generative scholars have achieved remarkable success in describing multiple individual languages and language in general.

However, the original data collection methods were also criticized for being informal and non-controlled (Labov 1972), sometimes dependent on the intuitions of the researchers themselves. It was difficult to adjudicate data disputes. Since the works of Schütze (1996) and Cowart (1997), it has been widely acknowledged that judgment data have to be collected rigorously, using well-controlled experimental methods. The present volume is a testament to the rich variety of experimental methods used in generative SLA nowadays, judgments as well as psycholinguistic and neurolinguistic methods. Our knowledge of language in the mind of the speaker has come a long way indeed.

There is absolutely no doubt that language is not just a mental but also a psychological and a social entity. Processing as well as sociolinguistic variables, well studied by the respective branches of linguistics, undeniably impact on the mental, or cognitive, construct of language knowledge. The native speaker as envisioned by Chomsky (1965) is relevant only to the discovery of the mental rules in the mind of the language speaker, including a healthy disregard for speaker variation in the interest of maximal generalization. In this sense, the original concept of the ideal native speaker may have outlived its usefulness, since well-controlled experimental studies are as common in generative syntax now as in psycholinguistics, sociolinguistics and neurolinguistics. Every discipline of linguistics employs a slightly different concept of the relevant speaker, according to its own research questions. No branch of linguistics is capable of covering the whole language experience, nor should they pretend to be able to. For instance, variation linguists interested in regional varieties test groups of speakers from these varieties, maybe in different age groups to track development.

While the construct of the native speaker may be useful in generative syntax, semantics and phonology, is it justified in generative SLA? In the previous section, we discussed two compelling reasons for including native speaker control groups in GenSLA studies: to validate the property under investigation and to validate the test instrument. What kind of native speakers are appropriate, for those functions of control groups to be met? That decision should depend on the specific research questions of each study. For instance, a monolingual and a bilingual control group are used in some heritage language studies (Leal Méndez et al. 2015). Bilingual controls might also be appropriate in processing studies, where speed and accuracy likely depend on the mind operating with one or two languages. Monolingual controls may be more appropriate when subtle semantic or syntactic properties of language are tested offline. Most importantly, as necessitated by good experimental design, control and experimental groups should be matched as much as possible on education, literacy, age and other experiential variables. The bottom line is that researchers should not preclude using native speaker controls based on non-scientific considerations (Domínguez & Arche 2021). At the same time, they should be sensitive to native speaker variables not distorting the non-native comparisons.

2.7 Discussion questions

1 In the first section of this chapter, we argued that PoS learning situations involve acquiring linguistic properties to which learners have not been exposed. Is there an individual-level PoS? What do we have to show in order to argue that an individual learner was not exposed to a certain construction?
2 Discuss variability that you have observed among speakers of your own native linguistic variety. Do you think this variability is acquirable by additional language learners? What would the conditions be for a successful acquisition?
3 Imagine that you want to exploit the adult L2 acquisition of Bulgarian multiple questions, as exemplified in (11). How are you going to choose participants for an experimental group? How about a control group? Is it important that the participants in the control group are bilingual?

Notes

1 It has been established that, across all languages, the frequency of words follows a Zipfian distribution, showing a peculiar relation between a word's frequency and its rank (Zipf 1949). Intuitively, this distribution reflects the fact that languages have relatively few high-frequency words and many low-frequency ones and that the decrease in frequency is not linear (the most frequent word is twice as frequent as the second-most frequent word, and so on).
2 The strongly unacceptable sentences contained violations of Subjacency and the Empty Category Principle, while the weak ones violated Subjacency only.
3 Since Chomsky (1986b), the ideal native speaker idea has been supplanted by I-language and E-language, the former standing for internal(ized) language (the grammatical system in the brain), while the latter standing for public external languages used by populations. These are the terms we introduced in Chapter 1.

3
THE LIFE CYCLE OF AN EXPERIMENTAL DESIGN

Linguists and non-linguists alike all have questions about capital-L Language. We might be curious as to why a second (or additional) language is so difficult to learn, while children seem to effortlessly and quickly acquire the one to which they are exposed. Or, given headlines in the news, we could wonder whether the most advanced of Google's AI could show evidence of understanding the meaning of sentences. Yet, although language scientists may share common interests and inquiries with most of the population, they usually go about finding out the answers in different ways—in other words, they differ in the *methods* they use. While experience might be the source of knowledge non-linguists use to make determinations about language, most generative linguists use the scientific method.

This chapter explores how generative linguists engage with the empirical research process while introducing some basic concepts of experimental design.[1] We will start with the basic tenets of the scientific method, which is the foundational system that generative linguists use to conduct experimental work. After discussing the basic steps of the scientific method and some guidelines behind the generation of hypotheses, we discuss basic principles in experimental design, including the definitions of variables and conditions, along with some participant-selection sampling practices. We round off the chapter by discussing the notion of (internal and external) validity and reliability: two foundational concepts when determining the quality of experimental designs.

DOI: 10.4324/9781003160762-4

3.1 The scientific method

Although the "scientific method"—a rather broad overgeneralization meant to demarcate a wide set of research practices—is not the only way researchers obtain knowledge about language acquisition, in this book we will concern ourselves with research that aims to test generalizations prompted by observations made by researchers (hypotheses). Hence, we do not cover many descriptive and qualitative methods that use different approaches to explain the acquisition of additional languages. Although these can certainly be appropriate for the study of myriad aspects of the acquisition of additional languages, they are outside of the scope of our endeavor (see, however, Davis 2011; Duff 2012; Gabryś-Barker & Wojtaszek 2014).

As we have seen, research said to follow the scientific method starts with a creative conjecture that intends to explain an observation or a series of observations with a generalization—a hypothesis. For instance, if you notice that two seeds from the same fruit, planted in neighboring yards, grow at different rates, you can surmise that certain factors are behind this difference. You could conjecture that one seed grows faster because it receives more water or perhaps more sun. In other words, you could propose that the amount of water or sun are factors that affect a given plant's development. Alternatively, you could conjecture that the composition of the soil in the yard is behind this differential growth, along with any number of other potential factors.

To find out whether your conjecture is accurate, you could be a passive observer of these yards and the farmers who tend to them, scrutinizing their practices for days on end, to confirm your conjectures. However, that could take an impossibly long time, and you would be at the mercy of the neighbors' whims and schedules. Another possibility is that you could conduct an experiment yourself, precisely measuring the amount of water, sun, or nutrients in the soil to (empirically) test the validity of your hypotheses. The latter approach brings about a host of advantages (beyond saving time and maintaining good relations with your neighbors). If you conduct a series of experiments where you can control each factor under study, you can rule out multiple factors and draw connections between seemingly unrelated phenomena. Even if you don't have *the* answer to your question after conducting your experiment, you may be able to discard a potential explanation and generate even more hypotheses to explain differences in growth.

3.2 Formulating hypotheses

In Chapter 2, we proposed using an experiment to determine whether children show knowledge beyond what is modeled in the input. Specifically, we proposed an act-out experiment to find out whether children had knowledge that certain pronoun interpretations are not available (i.e., the pronoun "he" in a sentence such as "He$_1$ danced while the Ninja Turtle$_2$ ate pizza" cannot refer to the Ninja Turtle, only to another male entity). If children were to reject this interpretation via our proposed experiment, we would find support for the notion that children can acquire linguistic knowledge *beyond* what the input can directly offer. That is, we can produce convincing experimental evidence that agrees with our Poverty of the Stimulus hypothesis.

3.2.1 Sources of hypotheses

Where do hypotheses come from? Formulating hypotheses to explain language phenomena within the generative study of second language acquisition (SLA) is typically based on *knowledge of extant theories of language* and *theories of language acquisition and development*. For instance, you might wonder why it is so difficult for speakers of a grammatically genderless language, such as English, to acquire languages like Spanish or French, which can mark gender with a functional piece of morphology attached to the end of nouns. To explain difficulties with the acquisition of gender agreement, one could propose all sorts of wild conjectures. However, without the knowledge of how gender agreement works in French or Spanish, it is unlikely that our conjectures will amount to much of an explanation. In this regard, generative linguistics has much to bring to the table in terms of understanding SLA because it offers an independent theoretical framework from which we can study linguistic behavior (Slabakova 2019a, 2019b). If what we are acquiring in SLA is *language*, we need a theory of language. Similarly, if we disregard what we know about language acquisition generally and SLA particularly, it is unlikely that our speculations will be on the right track.

SLA, a field rich with different perspectives, has seen extensive interdisciplinary growth in the past decades; however, not every framework studying SLA explicitly avails itself of a theory of language. The transdisciplinary framework proposed by the Douglas Fir Group (2016), for instance, proposes that L2 learning is a process that occurs at three levels of influence (micro, meso, and macro levels). At the micro level, individuals use "their neurological mechanisms and cognitive and emotional capacities" (p. 24) to engage with others, availing themselves of myriad resources, among them linguistic resources. At the macro level, this framework places the "large-scale, society-wide ideological structures with particular orientations toward language use and learning (including belief systems, and cultural, political, religious, and economic values)" (p. 24). It makes sense that a theory of language would not necessarily be needed at a macro level but might be at the micro level, which is where linguistic resources are proposed to be used.

Because generative SLA concentrates on linguistic representations, it heeds Gregg's (1993) perspective that to account for the process of how second languages are acquired, researchers need a *property theory*, which explains how language is represented in the mind of a speaker, and a *transition theory*, which explains the causal mechanisms that account for the linguistic representations explained by the property theory. Within the generative study of L2 acquisition, we have several hypotheses that aim to explain the process, such as Full Transfer/Full Access (Schwartz & Sprouse 1996), the Bottleneck Hypothesis (Slabakova 2016), and the Interpretability Hypothesis (Tsimpli & Dimitrakopoulou 2006).

Although we can formulate hypotheses based on existing theories about language and language acquisition, the *personal experiences* of researchers can also inspire research questions and predictions. Take Donna Lardiere, for example, whose experience with an end-state L2 learner of English whose native language was Chinese led to a formal and systematic examination of her naturalistic longitudinal production data. This analysis, in turn, led Lardiere to propose the hypothesis that learners can show knowledge of syntactic restrictions despite showing deficiencies in the production or the related morphology (Lardiere 1998).

3.2.2 Types of hypotheses

By now, you will have noticed that many hypotheses consist of assertions that predict that changes in a particular factor (e.g., the amount of water that a plant receives) will produce measurable changes in the object of our observation (e.g., the rate at which a plant grows). In this type of hypothesis, the researcher is predicting a relationship of the type *cause-and-effect*, such that if the hypothesis were to be true, we could argue that change in plant growth is the *effect* of watering practices. The converse would also be accurate: We could assert that watering practices *cause* changes in plant growth.

Let us move on to an example related to SLA testing of an extant hypothesis. The Feature Reassembly Hypothesis (Lardiere 2009), of which we will learn more in Chapter 4, proposes that difficulties with the acquisition of functional morphology stem from (*are an effect of*) the complexity of re-configuring (*re-assembling*, in Lardiere's terminology) the organization of features in lexical items. When learning a second language, learners already have a blueprint of how their first language works. If the first language differs from the second language in terms of formal features, learners must reconfigure the features that are assembled to L1 specifications to match the specifications of the L2. In this case, Lardiere hypothesizes that feature incongruity will result in (*cause*) greater difficulty in L2 acquisition. Note also that, by extension, if the feature matrices of the first and additional languages match, the Feature Reassembly Hypothesis suggests that acquisition should be straightforward, because the first language is not standing in the way.

Not all hypotheses test causal relationships, however. We could, instead, predict that two things have something in common, and we could attempt to determine how much these two things are related to each other (within the same set of observations, of course), typically using a descriptive statistical tool such as a correlation. An example used in a psychology textbook to describe correlations involves the relationship between word length and the length of the definition of each word (Abdi 2009). We could start by taking a random sample of 20 words from the Oxford English Dictionary (OED). Then, we could count the number of letters forming each word, as well as the number of lines that the OED uses to describe said word. If we were to do that with several random samples, we would find a relationship between word length and number of lines because shorter words tend to be polysemic, hence needing more lines to accurately define them. But this is not to say that word length *causes* longer definitions—we can only say that these things are related. (As linguists, we could have an interesting conversation about why functional words tend to be shorter, but we will leave that for another day!)

Because we are focusing on (quasi-)experimental design and methods, we will be concerned with the first type of hypothesis, which aims to uncover causal relationships. Before we move on to different elements of experimental design, let us note that hypotheses used in experimental designs should also be transparent, precise, and parsimonious. The importance of such characteristics should soon be clear, once we explore this topic in more detail.

3.3 Elements of experimental design: variables and conditions

3.3.1 *Variables and types of variables*

Given that the scientific method has been around for a long time, it should be unsurprising that conducting a reliable and valid experimental study must follow a series of practices and guidelines, some of which we will briefly discuss here. In the previous section, we were concerned with hypotheses that predicted causal relationships between things. Because *things* is hardly a scientific term, we will use the term used in experimental research, which is *variable*—an appropriate term, since we predict change.

Variables can be of different types. One way to classify variables involves the range over which they can vary. In our water-plant-growth hypothesis, we predicted that a change in the variable "amount of water" would cause a change in growth. Water can be measured very precisely, such that we can vary the amount in fine degrees. These types of variables are known as *continuous* variables. To give a language example, a variable like "number of days of study abroad" would qualify as a continuous variable. Other variables cannot be manipulated in such ways. For instance, if we are interested in "country of birth" as a variable, we can choose only discrete values, such as "Mexico," "Spain," or "Bulgaria." These types of variables are known as *categorical* (or discrete) variables.

While these examples (amount of water, country of birth) are relatively straightforward, some variables commonly used in L2 studies can pose dilemmas. "Days of study abroad," for instance, can be easily identified as a continuous variable, but that does not mean that this label is exclusively reserved for things that can be measured in units such as duration, weight, volume or length. One such example is linguistic *proficiency*, which in the field is often treated as a categorical variable, even when we manipulate it to be measured continuously by using a proficiency test. Leal (2018) found that, within a three-year period (2013–2016), nearly all of the experimental L2 studies in the journal *Studies in Second Language Acquisition* treated proficiency as a categorical variable, dividing learners into discrete categories such as "beginner," "intermediate," or "advanced." Yet she argued that the distinction between these categories is usually arbitrary and problematic, in both theoretical and statistical terms. For this reason, whenever possible, variables that measure behavioral outcomes should be treated as continuous, with a few caveats, such as when our data include imprecise measurements.

Another taxonomy divides variables into dependent or independent variables—categories that are directly related to the aims of the study and, crucially, the hypothesis guiding the experiment. To return to our water example, we proposed to manipulate the amount of water to determine its impact on plant growth, and, for obvious reasons, not the other way around (how much plants grow does not have an impact on the amount of irrigation they receive). When we deliberately plan to manipulate a variable and measure its (predicted) impact, we call this an *independent* variable. It is called independent because its value cannot be attributed to other variables—it is directly changed or manipulated by the researcher. *Dependent* variables, then, are those whose change we predict will depend on the levels of our independent variables. In our example, the dependent variable would be the length (in units) of plant growth.

3.3.2 Conditions

Our basic plant experiment aimed to understand why two plants, despite growing out of seeds from the same fruit, displayed differences in how much they grew. We said that, if we were to systematically investigate the effects of factors such as the amount of water, sun, or nutrients, we would need to control them exactly. Now we know that these factors would be the independent variables in our study, while the length (in inches, centimeters, or whichever unit we chose) would constitute the dependent variable.

Let's now investigate the amount of sun as a potential factor behind plant growth. Let's say that we set the experiment up so that one plant will receive exactly six hours of full sun each day. After six hours, we would cover the plant up. Now let's agree that we would expose the second plant to only two hours each day, ensuring that all other potential factors (which are outside the scope of this particular experiment) remain the same, such that the conditions of the soil and irrigation would be exactly comparable. We would then say that our study has two *conditions*: a six-hours-of-sun condition and a two-hours-of-sun condition. For short, let's call them high-sun and low-sun conditions. Let's say that we chose these particular sun-exposure times because we know that plants in the region typically receive six hours of sun per day, such that two hours would be a lower amount of sun than what plants typically receive. In this case, we would call the six-hours-of-sun (high-sun) condition the *control condition* because we didn't change anything from what the plant would already receive, on average, if we had not intervened. However, our two-hours-of-sun (low-sun) condition would have been intentionally manipulated. For this reason, we could call this the *experimental condition*. While not all experimental studies have an experimental condition, SLA studies typically do. In both cases, however, it is useful when researchers label their conditions clearly so that readers can determine precisely what is meant. If it is not clear which condition would be the "experimental" condition, we would unnecessarily confuse our readers. In fact, reporting clearly every aspect of our design, especially as it concerns the variables, conditions, and levels, is of paramount importance for methodological transparency—a lack that can have a host of negative consequences for research outcomes (see Marsden 2019, for discussion).

While we have deliberately kept our experiment very simple, a study can be much more intricate, involving multiple independent variables (amount of sun, *and* water, *and* soil nutrients) and more than two levels per condition (e.g., high sun, medium sun, and low sun). Determining how many conditions a study can have depends on a variety of factors, including the number of participants in each group and the number of items in each condition, among many other considerations. While these are outside the scope of our discussion, many books address these more specifically (e.g., Mackey & Gass 2005, 2012).

3.4 Quasi-experimental research

After discussing some basics of experimental design, we must draw an important distinction that has characterized research in generative SLA and, more generally, most research in applied linguistics. Scientists typically draw a distinction between experimental studies and quasi-experimental studies. Importantly, both experimental and quasi-experimental research can uncover cause-and-effect relationships between variables, where we expect that a given change in an independent variable will cause a change in the dependent variable. However, there are limitations in language research that typically mean that our research is quasi-experimental rather than experimental.

One reason is that some of the independent variables cannot be manipulated by the experimenter, such that we cannot talk about a "true" experiment but a "quasi" experiment (Sani & Todman 2006). Take country of birth, for instance. While we can decide to recruit people from Argentina or Bolivia, we cannot make a participant change their country of birth (there are no "Argentinean" and "Bolivian" versions of a single person in the way that we manipulate the amount of sun to determine a high- or low-sun condition). Sani and Todman (2006) note that one of the difficulties with this type of research is that it complicates our interpretations because it is harder to unveil a direct causal relationship between the variables. Maybe there is something special about our Argentinean group or our Bolivian group, such that some of the differences could come from some of the country-specific experiences (maybe to do with the educational system, maybe with family dynamics and language experience, etc.) that play a role without us taking it into consideration. Thus, although our plant example can help us understand the notion of a variable, it is not one that can be directly analogous to linguistic research.

A second reason most applied linguistic experiments cannot be considered truly experimental is the lack of random assignment when sampling participants.[2] Sampling decisions are crucial and inevitable because, in nearly all cases, unless we are doing a *census* study (Riazi 2016), we are not interested in or cannot have access to every member of a given group (think of the number of people that comprises the group "second language learners of English" and how impossible it would be to reach every single one of them). Thus, the logic behind sampling is relatively practical and simple: we study the behavior of a sample so that we can make inferences about the behavior of the population of interest. Yet for this to be a sound practice, our sample should be *representative* of the population—if the sample closely resembles the characteristics of the overall population, we can say that it is more representative of the population (Dörnyei 2007). Thus, although a goal of generative SLA is to understand and account for the mental representations in the minds of *all* second language learners, we have access to only certain types of learners, which might not be representative of the population for many reasons—a fact to which researchers must pay close attention.

Random assignment is not the norm in language studies. For instance, in classroom studies, researchers typically use what is known as *convenience* sampling, meaning they study an intact group of participants because the groups are already formed and we have access to them (e.g., a specific section of Spanish 101 meeting at a certain time, enrolled in university X). For obvious reasons, this intact group could fail to resemble other groups of L2 learners of different ages, L1/L2 combinations, different socioeconomic and educational backgrounds, instructional settings, etc. On the flip side, convenience samples can reflect "authentic learning environments using genuine class groups" (Dörnyei 2007: 120) such that the possibility that we end up with unrealistic, somewhat "sterilized" environments is not as large a threat. Researchers also use convenience sampling when they are selecting participants because they meet certain criteria related to the purpose of the investigation (Dörnyei & Csizér 2012), such as the first and additional languages of the participants or their L2 proficiency. Thus, although researchers must take into consideration the drawbacks of quasi-experimental designs, these can deliver dependable results.

Although this discussion is necessarily abbreviated, it is crucial to remember that the inferences we make about the data we collect must take into consideration the type of design we are using, with special attention to our sampling practices. In what follows, we provide an overview of two basic notions that have been used to determine the quality of (quasi-)experimental designs: validity and reliability.

3.5 The quality of (quasi-)experimental design: validity and reliability

3.5.1 *(Internal and external) Validity and threats to validity*

At a basic level, (quasi-)experiments hypothesizing about causal relationships aim to determine whether these relationships are either true or false in the real world. In other words, they aim to be sound: a valid representation of the state of things. Following Cook and Campbell (1979), *validity* is "the best available approximation to the truth or falsity of propositions, including propositions about cause" (Cook & Campbell 1979: 37). In simple terms, validity indexes the degree to which an experiment measures what it purports to measure. Although there are many types and classifications of validity, we will examine both internal and external validity—notions proposed by Donald Campbell and his colleagues. For more definitions and discussion of other types of validity as used in SLA, see Mackey and Gass (2005, 2012).

According to Cook and Campbell (1979), internal validity refers to the "validity which we infer that a relationship between two variables is causal or that the absence of a relationship implies the absence of cause" (Cook & Campbell 1979: 37) such that our results can be considered a true reflection of the causal relationship *within* the population sample in our study and not the consequence of some type of error, methodological or otherwise. To determine internal validity, we are seeking the answer to the question: to what extent can we assume that the changes in the independent variables, as manipulated by the researcher within our study, are the cause of the measured changes in the dependent variable?

External validity, on the other hand, refers to the degree to which we can generalize the results of our experiment *beyond* the sample, to the population that our sample purports to represent. In the case of external validity, we seek the answer to the question: to what extent can the results of our study be generalized to the population of interest? The relationship between internal and external validity is an important one. If a study is devoid of internal validity, the results are meaningless because we cannot draw conclusions from them. In this case, external validity is also irrelevant, because the results do not constitute true findings in the first place. However, a study can have internal validity and no external validity. For instance, the results of a medical trial could hold for a particular group of people, but these could not be generalized to patients who differ in non-trivial ways from those included in the sample in a given medical trial (Patino & Carvalho Ferreira 2018).

One of the reasons (quasi-)experimental design is complex is that there are myriad ways in which validity can be threatened. Cook and Campbell (1979), for instance, note that low statistical power, violated assumptions on statistical tests, lack of reliability of measures and treatment implementation, random irrelevancy in experimental settings, or random heterogeneity in respondents can all pose threats to validity. Indeed, as Rogers and Révész (2019) rightly note, "any aspect of the experiment that raises doubts as to whether the results have led to accurate and meaningful interpretations threatens the validity of the research" (Rogers & Révész 2019: 134).

3.5.2 Reliability

If validity indexes the extent to which an experiment measures what it aims to measure, reliability indexes the consistency of the measurements. Say, for instance, that we decide to measure proficiency using a written test such as the International Test of English Proficiency. Naturally, we would expect that the same learner would earn comparable scores if they were to take the test in different testing sessions. If the learner gets wildly different scores, we would say that the test is not reliable. Importantly, "consistency" can refer to the consistency of the instruments used in data collection (*instrument reliability*) but also to consistency in the reporting of the study (Riazi 2016). In certain types of research, we are also concerned with *rater reliability*, which seeks to determine whether the scores provided by raters are consistent with other raters doing the same job (Mackey & Gass 2005).

As with internal and external validity, threats to reliability can severely restrict the conclusions that we can draw from the data. High reliability also has additional benefits, as some researchers have argued that increased reliability allows for decreased sample sizes (Abate et al. 1995). To avoid threats to instrument reliability, in particular, researchers can use different methods. These techniques include test–retest, parallel forms, and internal consistency checks (see Rienzi 2016). Researchers can also report an index of reliability using tools such as Cronbach's alpha.

The relationship between validity and reliability has evolved throughout the years within several frameworks in SLA research. Chapelle (1999) notes that early in language testing research, where validity and reliability are foundational notions, these two concepts were seen as distinct. However, most testing researchers acknowledged that reliability was a prerequisite for validity. Later on, researchers noted that reliability could be seen as one type of evidence of validity, further advancing the notion that the two cannot be seen as entirely distinct.

In this chapter, we have tackled foundational notions of (quasi-)experimental design so that we can move forward to more direct operationalizations within generative SLA studies. We have discussed the generation of hypotheses and identified foundational notions such as variables and conditions, as well as constructs such as validity and reliability. While this introduction is necessarily brief and selective, it is illustrative of the way in which generative SLA researchers go about answering research questions. In the next chapter, we focus on how to design experiments in the generative SLA framework more specifically.

3.6 Discussion questions

1 You have probably heard the phrase "Correlation does not imply causation," which is used in a variety of contexts. Based on the discussion in the chapter, can you articulate what you believe are the main differences between (quasi-)experimental designs and correlational designs?
2 We have discussed several threats to the validity of (quasi-)experimental designs, but these are not the only ones. Can you think of other potential

threats to validity that are important to consider in L2/Ln acquisition research?
3 In this chapter, we have briefly discussed some issues related to sampling for linguistic studies. We mentioned that researchers search for a representative sample of the population of interest while also touching upon some difficulties that this poses for behavioral studies. One issue we did not mention is related to self-selection: because most studies rely on participants *agreeing* to take part in an experiment (i.e., they are volunteers), we have unwittingly sampled a population that might have specific characteristics. Can you think of what characteristics might be different in a group that volunteered for a study, as opposed to a group that did not? How might this affect the data that we obtain? What studies are more affected by this sampling conundrum?

Notes

1 As we will see shortly, most experiments in L2 studies are considered quasi-experimental designs because they either involve an independent variable that cannot be manipulated (e.g., gender and native language) or lack of random assignment to groups (Sani & Todman 2006).
2 Rogers and Révész (2019) also note that quasi-experimental research does not require a control group, although most include a comparison group of some sort. In a strict sense, although the presence of a control group is not required in experimental research, it does pose threats to internal and external validity (Cook & Campbell 1979).

Further reading

Dörnyei, Z. (2007). *Research methods in applied linguistics: Quantitative, qualitative, and mixed methodologies.* Oxford: Oxford University Press.

Mackey, A., & Gass, S. M. (2005). *Second language research: Methodology and design.* Mahwah, NJ: Lawrence Erlbaum Associates.

McKinley, J., & Rose, H. (Eds.) (2019). *The Routledge handbook of research methods in applied linguistics.* New York: Routledge.

4
DESIGNING EXPERIMENTS IN GenSLA

This chapter takes up the issues presented briefly in Chapter 1 and delves deeper into them with an emphasis on research questions (RQs) and design. Armed with the knowledge of the scientific method presented in Chapter 3, we consider how to formulate RQs in the generative framework, what kinds of questions can be answered and how, the hypotheses we use to address these, etc., taking into consideration factors such as the property to be acquired, the linguistic module(s) involved, learners' native language(s), the learning task, linguistic complexity and the acquisition context. This chapter will also address the currently debated issue of proficiency tests: why measuring proficiency independently is important and what options GenSLA researchers have.

4.1 Investigating Universal Grammar principles and parameters

4.1.1 The research questions in the 1980s and 1990s

From its inception in the 1980s, GenSLA has always focused on describing and explaining the system of implicit second language knowledge and, more specifically, how it is represented in the mind/brain of the L2 learner. Throughout the 1980s and 1990s, the main emphasis was on Universal Grammar (UG), containing the knowledge that is common to all human languages. At the same time, GenSLA scholars were sensitive to the constant interplay between UG and two other sources of L2 knowledge: the mother tongue (L1) and information that comes from exposure to the target language.

DOI: 10.4324/9781003160762-5

What is UG, again? And what is contained *within* UG? To reiterate from Chapter 1, UG is argued to be an innate blueprint of what every language learner has access to. In this respect, it is compared to other mental systems that need external stimuli to be activated (e.g., vision). UG contains the linguistic information that is common to all human languages, labeled *principles*. This information mediates between what is learnable based on input and domain-general cognition alone. In light of this understanding of UG, the general research question of the classical GenSLA period included variations on "Do second language learners have access to UG?"

Answers ranged from "learners have full access to UG" (the Full Transfer Full Access Hypothesis: Swartz and Sprouse 1996, but also White 1989) through "learners have only partial access" (the Failed Functional Features Hypothesis: Hawkins & Chan 1997; the Minimal Trees Hypothesis: Vainikka & Young Scholten 1996) to "learners have no UG access" (Clahsen & Myusken 1989). What kind of research findings could inform this debate? For example, if learners were shown to successfully acquire properties not available from their native grammar, then they were deemed to have access to UG. This demonstration was particularly effective if it referred to early (Grüter 2005/2006) or uninstructed (Slabakova 2003) L2 knowledge.

Learning principles were also considered to be part of UG, representative of the third factor in language design (i.e., principles of general cognition; cf. Chomsky 2005). For instance, the Subset Principle (Berwick 1985) stipulates that whenever there are two competing grammars generating languages, of which one is a proper subset of the other, the learning strategy is to select the subset one. In other words, learners are conservative—they only assume a grammar sufficient to generate the sentences they hear, expecting positive evidence to show them that the superset parameter setting is valid.

A specific RQ in the classical GenSLA framework, narrowing down the general RQ (see above) could be: "Is there evidence that parameter X can be reset in SLA?"

4.1.2 *L2 knowledge of principles*

In the classical period of GenSLA, research on UG principles took a somewhat indirect approach, for the following reasons. If scholars investigated a true, exceptionless language universal such as all languages have consonants and vowels or all languages have verbs and nouns, the bar would be set too low. In addition, even if it was established that this information were available to learners, one wouldn't be able to make the claim that it came solely from UG and not from the native language. Therefore, researchers tackled universal information that was nevertheless dependent on some parametric choice. One example we saw in Chapter 1 referred to the Pro-Drop Parameter. Another example comes from the so-called Overt Pronoun Constraint (OPC; Montalbetti 1984) which is dependent on that parameter. In Japanese and Spanish, both null subject languages, overt and null embedded subjects can refer to a referential antecedent, someone mentioned in the discourse or even in the main clause. In example (1) from Japanese, no matter whether the embedded subject is the overt pronoun *kare* 'he' or the null pronoun *pro*, both can refer to Mr Tanaka, the main clause subject. Mr Tanaka is a referential subject, one individual identified by the discourse.

1 Referential antecedent context:

　a. Tanaka-san$_i$ wa [kare$_{i/j}$-ga kaisya de itiban da to] itte-iru
　　 Tanaka-Mr Top he-Nom company in best is that saying-is

　b. Tanaka-san$_i$ wa [*pro*$_{i/j}$ kaisya de itiban da to] itte-iru
　　 Tanaka-Mr Top pro company in best is that saying-is
　　 'Mr Tanaka is saying that he is the best in the company'
　　 He = Mr. Tanaka or
　　 He = someone else mentioned before

2 Quantified antecedent context:

　a. Dare-ga$_i$ [kare-ga$_{*i/j}$ kuruma o katta to] itta no?
　　 Who-Nom he-Nom car Acc bought that said Q
　　 #He = which person
　　 He = someone else mentioned before

　b. Dare-ga$_i$ [*pro*$_{i/j}$ kuruma o katta to] itta no?
　　 Who-Nom *pro* car Acc bought that said Q
　　 'Who said that he bought a car'
　　 He = which person or
　　 He = someone else mentioned before (Kanno 1997)

However, compare the binding indices in (2). When the main clause subject is the question word *who*, a quantified antecedent, *kare* can no longer refer to that entity. In other words, the (2a) reading cannot ask about which male person said that he, that same person, bought a car. This reading is available if the embedded subject is a null pronoun as in (2b), so Japanese can certainly express that meaning but not with the structure in (2a). Thus, we see that overt pronouns in null subject languages are constrained in their possible interpretations, hence the name Overt Pronoun Constraint. Both pronouns can refer to someone else mentioned in the discourse, for example, Mr. Osuke.

Now, everyone can appreciate that this is a difficult contrast to acquire from exposure alone, because clarifications about possible and impossible readings are rarely, if ever, provided to learners. The contrast is almost certainly not taught in language classrooms. But there is one more reason why this property was widely researched in the 1990s. Knowledge of this property could not be transferred if the native language was not a null subject language, such as English. Since English does not have null pronouns in embedded clauses, if L2 speakers showed sensitivity to the OPC, they would only be able to thank UG for it and not help from their native language. Both Kanno (1997) and Pérez-Leroux and Glass (1999) found evidence for such a conclusion. In summary, the main research question of these studies probed whether a universal constraint was functional in learner grammars, but only if it did not come directly from the native language.

4.1.3 L2 parameter knowledge

Parameters were the stars of the classical GenSLA period. The premise of parameter resetting was as follows. Equipped with UG, child learners can narrow down the search space by limiting their hypotheses to only the settings that UG allows. For instance, languages can either have null subjects or not allow them (the pro-dro parameter). The fact that only two choices are logically possible makes this parameter a no-brainer, hence not that interesting to investigate. However, null subjects themselves were just the beginning. Almost every parameter that was discussed in the classical GenSLA period came with a parametric cluster of superficially unrelated constructions that were nevertheless dependent on a common syntactic explanation and were purportedly learnable if only a salient, unifying piece of structure was acquired. In the case of the Null Subject Parameter (NSP, also known as the Pro-Drop Parameter; Rizzi 1982), here are the constructions argued to be related within the cluster (after Rothman & Iverson 2007):

3 a. Yo/*pro* vivo en Miami. (null subjects)
   I /*pro* live in Miami
   'I live in Miami.'

   b. *pro* Llueve mucho. (no expletive subjects)
   pro rains a lot.
   'It rains a lot.'

   c. Llegaron ellos. (postverbal subjects)
   came they
   'They came.'

d. Quién crees **que** habla español?   (that-trace effect)
   who think.2sg that speak.3sg Spanish

e. *Quién crees ___ habla español?
   who think.2sg speak.3sg Spanish?
   'Who do you think (*that) speaks Spanish?'

The specific RQ then would be: "Can L2 learners reset all of the parametric clusters?" Presumably, learners only need to converge on one of the syntactic properties in (3), null subjects, lack of expletive subjects, etc. to attain knowledge of the rest, since each property in the cluster is hypothesized to be linked to an underlying unifying analysis. The properties linked to the Verb Movement Parameter cluster (White 1991) were adverb placement and main verb movement in questions and negation.

The premise of parametric clusters, where a number of properties come into the L2 grammar for free, just in case one acquires the crucial piece of morphosyntax responsible for parameter restructuring, was very attractive to scholars in the classical GenSLA period. An even more far-fetched prediction was that of instantaneous parameter resetting: that the whole cluster of a certain parameter would be activated in the L2 grammar at once. As it happened, research findings on the Pro-drop (or the Null Subject) Parameter (White 1985a, 1986; Phinney 1987; Liceras 1989) and on the Verb Movement Parameter (White 1991) were not kind to these predictions. Later on, Rothman and Iverson (2007) examined the whole NSP cluster, including the OPC from example (1), and concluded that only null subjects, lack of null expletives and the OPC clustered in the interlanguage of their intermediate learners of L2 Spanish. However, their learners were 75% accurate on postverbal subjects, which was comparable to their OPC accuracy. Five months of study abroad in Spain made no difference to any of the cluster properties for those learners. Hence, this study supported the earlier conclusion that the that-trace effect was not acquired as part of the NSP.

Why might that be? A superficial inspection of the cluster in (3) would yield the observation that there is much evidence in the input for null subjects, lack of expletive subjects and even postverbal subjects. On the other hand, learners are much less likely to be exposed to sentences as in (3d–e), as this construction is much less frequent and more complex than the rest of the cluster. Yet, the careful reader might object at this point that the OPC sentences in (4), comparable to the Japanese examples in (2), are as complex as and even less frequent than the that-trace effect examples. Arguably, the OPC presents a Poverty of the Stimulus situation (see Chapter 2).

4 a. Quién₁ dice que él ₊ᵢ/ⱼ tiene mucho dinero?
      who says that he has much money

   b. Quién₁ dice que *pro* ᵢ/ⱼ tiene mucho dinero?
      who says that has much money
      'Who says he has much money?'

And the careful reader would be right. Why are intermediate learners of Spanish sensitive to the contrast in (4a–b) but not to the one in (3d–e)? Answers to this question cannot come from frequency alone. Perhaps, as argued at the time by Jaeggli and Safir (1989) and Safir (1985), the NSP has a smaller cluster than the one originally proposed by Rizzi (1982).

4.2 Features encoding parametric variation

In the 21st century, the change of orientation in GenSLA RQs was prompted by an evolving view of parameters. White (2003) and Lardiere (2005) discussed the acquisition of *functional features* as the new focus of formal L2A research. The refocusing was complete with the publication of the Feature Reassembly Hypothesis (FRH) by Lardiere (2009).

4.2.1 What are functional features?

Before delving further into the new GenSLA approach, let us look at an extended example of nominal features as encoded in English pronouns. We will work these out from a set of sentences as in (5).

5 a. **He** likes chocolate.
   b. **She** likes chocolate.
   c. **They** like chocolate.
   d. **It** is chocolate.
   e. She likes **them**.

In these particular sentences, we can identify the following features or grammatical meanings. *He* in (5a) expresses the following: [third person], [singular], [masculine], [human] and [Nominative]. In other words, the feature bundle expressed on *he* has values for all the features in (6).

6 $\begin{bmatrix} \text{Person} \\ \text{Number} \\ \text{Gender} \\ \text{Animacy} \\ \text{Case} \end{bmatrix}$

To underscore the terminology linguists use, [Person] is a morphosyntactic feature with values [1, 2, 3]; [Number] is a feature with values [singular, plural] in English. See if you can work out the feature values for the bolded pronouns in (5b–e). They have to be values of the bundle in (6), but they also have to *uniquely* identify each different pronoun bolded in (5).

Furthermore, notice that some feature values are dependent on other feature values being present. Lardiere calls these dependencies "conditioning environments." For instance, the [gender] and [animacy] feature is expressed only on three-person singular pronouns. Thus, when we say "she," we are referring to a female person, but when we say "they," we may be talking about female or male people or about inanimate objects. Of course, the context will disambiguate these values. The FRH argues that the more reassembly is needed in adjusting the feature bundles in the L2, including the conditioning environments, the harder L2 acquisition is.

4.2.2 How can we test feature reassembly?

The general and specific RQs have changed subtly in the feature environment. In their general form, they ask: "Can feature bundles be readjusted in SLA?" Note that for the readjustment to proceed, learners still need knowledge about the possible features and the possible feature values. For example, the feature [Number] has two values in English but three values in some Slavic languages such as Slovenian: [singular], [dual] and [plural]. For some scholars, features and their values are provided by UG, but for others, parameters are emergent, in the sense that categories and formal features are constructed on the basis of language-specific positive linguistic data (Biberauer & Roberts 2015).

Furthermore, a crucial continuation of the specific RQ is now possible: Do all features of a specific feature bundle reset at the same time, and, if not, what factors modulate the process? We will look at these factors in the next section. The essential requirement in testing for feature reassembly is that researchers have a very clear idea what the exact features are in the L1 and the L2 so that they can specify the learning task as an (re-)assembly task. How do novice researchers find out about features and bundles? The safe route is to access the syntax or semantics literature for concrete published proposals. However, keep in mind that features are mappings of form and meaning, so even if you don't find a published study, you are likely to detect the different meanings in the two languages. The following study described in Box 4.1 provides a clear example.

> **Case Study Box 4.1: Shimanskaya and Slabakova (2017)**
>
> ***Property:*** Pronoun features in French and English. As we saw in Examples (5)–(6), English pronouns express a bundle of features, of which the relevant ones here will be [Gender] and [Animacy]. French marks gender on all nouns, not just pronouns, but does not mark animacy. *I see him* can only refer to a male human, while *I see it* can only refer to an object. In French, both are rendered as *Je le vois* 'I see him/it.' Thus, we can designate gender in French as a grammatical category but a semantic category in English. The English–French contrast is summarized in Table 4.1.
>
> TABLE 4.1 L1–L2 feature mismatch
>
> | *English* | *French* |
> |---|---|
> | Him [+human]
 Semantic gender [masculine] | Le [±human]
 Grammatical gender [masculine] |
> | Her [+human]
 Semantic gender [feminine] | La [±human]
 Grammatical gender [feminine] |
> | It [−human]
 No semantic gender | |
>
> *General Research Question:*
> Can learners reassemble features in the L2 from the way they are assembled in the L1?
> *Specific Research Question:*
> Can learners acquire that the feature [±human] is not contrastive in French, but that gender is a grammatical feature?

4.3 Other factors to take into account

4.3.1 *The native language*

In formulating RQs, this is perhaps the first factor or variable (see Chapter 3) that one should consider. As already argued in this chapter, we do not want the property under investigation to be present in the L1 and the L2, because there is nothing to learn with respect to that property, except the lexical items. However, language groups with similar settings for a property can be used effectively. If a research design contains two L1 groups learning the same L2, with contrasting starting settings, the demonstration of a learning task and acquisition process can be that much more cogent.

Take, for example, Slabakova's (2000) study, where a Spanish-native and a Bulgarian-native groups were tested on knowledge of English telicity marking (roughly, when can we interpret an event as complete). English and Spanish mark telicity by combining a dynamic verb with a certain type of object (e.g., *eat a sandwich*), while Bulgarian signals the same meaning with verbal prefixes but objects do not play a role. In the event, only the English controls and the Spanish learners, but not the Bulgarian learners, demonstrated a significantly different evaluation of telic and atelic sentences. This research design can mitigate criticism that GenSLA studies unfairly compare bilinguals and monolinguals. If the two bilingual groups at the same level of proficiency behaved differently, the only reason could be their native grammar.

4.3.2 Linguistic complexity

We already touched on the issue of linguistic complexity when discussing the Null Subject Parameter. Linguistic complexity is actually quite hard to define and has to be distinguished from task complexity and from the linguistic complexity of learner writing, both topics discussed in the applied linguistics literature. When is a linguistic structure complex? Although a few linguistic proposals are on offer, in this chapter we assume the definition of Pallotti (2015). According to Pallotti, the construct of "complexity" is used with three distinct meanings in linguistic research. A construction can be typologically or **structurally complex**, for example, wh-questions are more complex than declarative sentences because they involve movement of syntactic constituents (covert or overt). A construction can be **cognitively complex** or difficult to process. For example, object relative clauses are well known to be harder to process than subject ones, at least in English. Finally, a construction can be considered complex because it is **difficult** to acquire or is acquired late. These three views refer to different aspects of complexity and often are not correlated.

Pallotti assumes "a simple view of complexity," based on linguistics principles that we can use. Morphological complexity is calculated on word class (nouns, verbs, etc.) and counts the number of exponents of various grammatical categories and functions. Thus, English nouns are marked for number, while German nouns are inflected for gender, number and case, making the latter more complex. Syntactic complexity depends on the number of constituents and the syntactic operations they participate in. The lexical complexity of a text refers to the wide variety of lexemes used. A text which uses 200 different words is more complex than one which employs only 100.

How can we take linguistic complexity into account when articulating our RQs? In a parameter cluster, for example, it is unrealistic to expect more and less complex structures to be acquired at the same time. In a feature bundle, it is similarly unrealistic for all features of a functional category to be reset at the same time. Varying complexity in the L1 and the L2 should be given careful consideration and can be used to make predictions for ease or difficulty of acquisition. For instance, German nouns which express three grammatical categories morphologically, can be predicted to be harder to acquire than English nouns with one marked category. Gender on nouns (e.g., French in Box 4.1) is a highly complex feature to acquire because it is idiosyncratic: all nouns in a language with grammatical gender are randomly assigned to gender classes and have to be learned one by one, with some help from sound regularities perhaps. Linguistic complexity can be turned into an RQ itself. It is possible to inquire whether more complex structures are *always* acquired with more difficulty. The reader already suspects that the answer is No, because there will always be other factors involved.

4.3.3 The acquisition context

The learning context can have a marked influence on acquisition. The first main division in this respect is whether acquisition happens in the country where the L2 is spoken or in the learner's native (or indeed a third) country. The terms "second language learning" and "foreign language learning" are used to designate these two contexts. Acquisition can be *naturalistic* (in society) or *instructed* (in a classroom). Clearly, acquiring a language in the classroom, but in the country where the language is spoken widely, provides both naturalistic and classroom exposure. Researchers should be careful to consider this factor together with the other factors discussed in this section.

Classroom exposure to a property may include *explicit* instruction or not; it may include *negative evidence* or not. In this respect, the study by White and Juffs (1998) is enlightening. These scholars compared the performance of two groups of Chinese learners of English on knowledge of *wh*-movement constraints. One group of participants had never left China, while the other group of learners was studying in Canada. Participants in the former group were mainly exposed to classroom input, while the latter group was exposed to naturalistic English input as well.

However, both groups of learners presented judgments that were highly accurate. In addition, there were no statistical differences in their performance on this complex property, in spite of differences in their context of acquisition. The authors concluded that the intricate *wh*-movement constraints were "activated" without explicit knowledge or instruction. Another, and a negative example, is one that we mentioned earlier. In the Rothman and Iverson (2007) experiment, study abroad provided the participants extended exposure to natural Spanish, but did not lead to their improved performance on the constructions in the NSP cluster. In summary, one should keep input and exposure, closely dependent on acquisition context, in mind when one formulates RQs and designs studies.

4.3.4 Evidence in the input, including lexical and construction frequency

In discussing evidence in the input, let's refresh our memory for some concepts we discussed in Chapters 1 and 2. We considered "input" to be the whole second language, including *forms* that the learner can hear or read, mapped onto *meanings* that she can uncover from linguistic knowledge, the context, world knowledge and the previous discourse. "Exposure," on the other hand, is the portion of input that individual learners have been exposed to; input and exposure may not overlap completely. Consider the previous section on acquisition context in this respect.

If certain words, functional morphemes, phrases, sentences or discourse functions are present and readily observable in the input, we say that there is "positive evidence" for them. If a certain linguistic property is not freely discoverable from the input, we call it a negative constraint; its acquisition may be possible through UG or parameter values already set. Importantly, "negative evidence," or explicit correction of errors in form or meaning, may not always lead to acquisition (Slabakova et al. 2020). Generative SLA theory argues that negative evidence cannot alter grammatical knowledge states because it is not reliably provided to all learners to an equal degree and because, even if it is provided, learners do not attend to it (White 1989).

Consider the following example.

7 In a restaurant:

Last week I had the sole here. It was delicious. The salmon I haven't tried (***it**) yet.

The pronoun *it* in bold is not acceptable in English, hence the star inside the brackets. It is called a resumptive pronoun because it "resumes" the noun *the salmon* which has moved to the top of the structure in a topicalization construction. Many languages, including Arabic and Spanish, allow such pronouns. How can an L2 learner acquire the fact that resumptive pronouns are not allowed in English? If the learner produces the wrong sentence *The salmon I haven't tried it yet*, some interlocutor needs to say: "No, you don't need the pronoun in English" or something explicit along these lines. It is very unlikely that such an overt correction is ever provided, and, even if it is provided, it is not offered reliably to all learners. This explicit correction is what we call "negative evidence." When creating experimental designs, we must carefully consider whether there is positive evidence for our property, and, if not, where the knowledge of it comes from. The answer to the latter question is usually found in linguistic theory.

Even if there is positive evidence for a certain property, it is quite relevant *how much* evidence there is. We are talking about *frequency* in the input here. Frequency can be calculated for lexical items, for morphemes and for grammatical constructions. The calculations are based on large corpora of written or spoken speech. The Corpus of Contemporary American English, known as COCA, contains over a billion words and is made up of different corpora. You can search for words and phrases in many other ways, so check it out. The rule of thumb would be that a frequent word, morpheme or construction would be encountered more often in the input, would be more highly activated in the lexicon and would be used with greater accuracy.

However, frequency does not have magic powers. There are many frequent items that still give rise to difficulty. Take the extremely frequent subject–verb agreement morpheme in English. All verbs in the present tense that have a third-person singular subject have to appear with this form:

8   John eat-s in the cafeteria every day.

The agreement ending appears in 37.5% of all present tense lexical verbs (Jensen et al. 2020: 25), which amounts to many millions of occurrences. It is regularly taught explicitly. At the same time, it is rarely supplied in free production by speakers of languages that do not have such agreement. Just one example would suffice: Patty, Donna Lardiere's research participant, who is a fluent English speaker with many years of experience living in the USA, produces the *-s* agreement morpheme just 4.5% of the time (Lardiere 2007).

4.4 Language exposure and global proficiency

It is customary in GenSLA research to measure proficiency independently of the properties they investigate. What is the rationale for this? We are interested in the developmental dimension: is it the case that, with increased proficiency in the second language, research participants are more accurate on the property? Or is it the case that learners do not demonstrate knowledge of this property, even at advanced proficiency levels? Maybe proficiency makes no difference to implicit knowledge of the property? We have already encountered examples of all these situations in this book. Extensive research too numerous to cite here has established that language proficiency affects spoken word recognition, lexical access, language processing, sentence-level and discourse-level comprehension, as well as qualitative and quantitative variation in language-related neurocognitive activity. We cannot provide an accurate understanding of language acquisition and bilingualism without taking general language proficiency into account; hence, proficiency evaluation is a crucial part of GenSLA studies.

Including a *language exposure questionnaire*, together with the proficiency measure, has also become an important part of GenSLA research. This is because it has been established, as frequently mentioned in this book, that experience determines not only specific linguistic knowledge, say, functional features, but also general proficiency. One excellent questionnaire that can give the reader a good idea of the range of questions to be asked of research participants is the LEAP-Q questionnaire (Marian et al. 2007), which can be found in https://bilingualism.northwestern.edu/leapq/. It is freely available to the research community and is translated into many languages. Although this questionnaire includes self-ratings of proficiency, the authors recommend that researchers use an independent measure of proficiency and do not rely on self-evaluation (Kaushanskaya et al. 2018).

What are some common measures of proficiency? Among the many measures available to researchers, we will focus here on ones that are easy to administer and do not take an inordinate amount of time and effort in experimental studies. Whole or portions of standardized tests can be used, but pride of place among proficiency tests belongs to *cloze* and *C-tests*. Both tests' results are highly correlated with results from standardized proficiency scores, suggesting that these two tests offer a reliable shortcut to proficiency estimation. The cloze test (Brown 1980; Tremblay 2011) provides participants with a connected text of 300–400 words on a topic of general interest, such as global warming. The text has to be accessible to an average reader with a high school education. Here is an example from Tremblay (2011: 369).

9 The world economic growth ___(1)___ created an increase in ___(2)___ level of ___(3)___ dioxide (CO_2) in the atmosphere much ___(4)___ rapidly than anticipated, according to a study ___(5)___ on Monday in the reports of the United States ___(6)___ Academy of Sciences.

There are two important things to consider in creating a cloze test: the deletion and the scoring methods. How do we decide which word to delete, so that when provided by the participant, we can evaluate their understanding of the text, grammatical and lexical knowledge? One approach is to delete every seventh or every ninth word in the text, whatever it may happen to be. Another approach is the so-called rational deletion method used in the example above so that a balanced proportion of content and function words could be elicited from L2 learners. With respect to the scoring method, researchers also have choices: to accept as correct only the word that appeared in the original text (called "the exact scoring method") or to allow all words acceptable in that slot, for example, synonyms (see Brown (1980), for a comparison of these scoring methods). The latter scoring method involves creating a bank of acceptable answers, which may be cumbersome and imprecise. For that reason, some researchers opt for a multiple-choice presentation, which reduces the average testing time and simplifies scoring (Luchkina et al. 2021).

C-tests are similar to cloze tests, except that the first half of the deleted words is provided to the test takers. In a paragraph-length reading passage, half of every second word is deleted, from the second sentence onward. This manipulation creates a lot of blanks, typically 75–125 in three short paragraphs.

10 This is an example C-test passage. Starting wi___ the sec_____ word o__ this sent_____, the la___ half fr___ each consec_____ word h__ been del_____. (Norris 2018: 12–13).

Although slightly different, both cloze and C-tests are excellent instruments for establishing global language proficiency. Some validated tests are available at the end of published research or in research repositories; if they are re-used, permission has to be sought and proper attribution must be made to the original creators. Finally, proficiency tests that are entirely online have been created in recent years. The LexTALE (Lemhöfer & Broersma 2012) is a short and easy-to-use lexically based proficiency test. A disadvantage at this moment is that it does not have versions in many languages, but such versions are being created.

4.5 Conclusion

In this chapter, we developed our understanding of research design, discussing general and specific RQs in the classical GenSLA framework of parameters and in the 21st-century approach using formal features. Some seminal characteristics of research design are reliance on linguistic analysis for establishing contrasts that exist in the L2 and may or may not be manifested in the L1, careful consideration of variables and participant groups, taking into account additional linguistic variables such as linguistic complexity, the context of acquisition and the evidence that the input provides for a certain property. We discussed participant questionnaires and independent proficiency measures as indispensable ingredients of the GenSLA research design.

4.6 Discussion questions

1. How are parameters and features different?
2. How are acquisition contexts (SLA versus foreign language acquisition (FLA)) related to language input and exposure? Give examples from your own experience.
3. Consider study abroad among university college students. Rothman and Iverson (2007) established that a five-month stay in a Spanish-speaking country did not change students' knowledge of the constructions making up the Spanish Null Subject Parameter. Does this mean that the NSP is not a valid parameter?

Further reading

Pallotti, G. (2015). A simple view of linguistic complexity. *Second Language Research*, *31*(1): 117–134.

Marian, V., Blumenfeld, H. K., & Kaushanskaya, M. (2007). The Language Experience and Proficiency Questionnaire (LEAP-Q): Assessing language profiles in bilinguals and multilinguals. *Journal of Speech, Language, and Hearing Research*, 23: 945–950.

Slabakova, R., Leal, T., Dudley, A., & Stack, M. (2020). *Generative second language acquisition*. Cambridge: Cambridge University Press.

PART II
Methods typically used in GenSLA

5
ACCEPTABILITY TASKS

5.1 What are Acceptability Judgment Tasks?

From the beginning of the generative linguistics enterprise (Chomsky 1965, 1981a), native speaker judgments of grammatical acceptability (Acceptability Judgment Tasks, AJTs) have been of primary methodological importance. This is because generative syntactic theory takes native speakers' judgments of (un)grammaticality as a manifestation of linguistic competence: A sentence which is judged as grammatical (acceptable) by a native speaker of a certain language makes part of that speaker's mental grammar of the language, while a sentence which is judged as ungrammatical violates some linguistic rule of that grammar. Generative syntactic theory has historically relied on introspective AJTs rather than controlled experiments, on the assumption that the judgments of an individual native speaker are representative of those of other native speakers. However, this assumption has been challenged and criticized by many (Cowart 1997; Schütze 1996). The use of controlled AJTs with a good number of native speakers is now the norm, particularly after the appearance of crowdsourcing testing platforms (e.g., Amazon Mechanical Turk, Prolific).

5.1.1 Advantages

Language acquisition researchers have traditionally relied more on production data, in both child and L2 acquisition. However, judgments provide indispensable data in such investigations because they uncover information not readily available from production. For instance, an advantage of AJTs is

DOI: 10.4324/9781003160762-7

the avoidance issue: if learners do not produce a certain structure, say, past tense marking, the researcher cannot be confident that they do not know it. It could still be a part of their grammar but optional or hard to pronounce, so learners may just be avoiding it. Judgment tasks can provide a better snapshot of the learner grammar, because evaluating sentences is cognitively easier than producing them.

Another point of interest is that AJTs focus on form, not on meaning. In other words, the researcher is not so much interested in what interpretation the participant attributes to the target sentence but whether its form is an acceptable rendition of the meaning that most speakers would attribute to that target sentence. Let us take some examples. Most fluent speakers of English would be able to interpret sentences as in (1) and (2), although they will be aware that there is something wrong with the form, the agreement morpheme in (1) and the word order in (2).

1 My brother work in the library.
2 My brother his homework did yesterday.

How about second language acquisition? From its outset, GenSLA researchers inherited this reliance on AJTs to discover a learner's competence at a particular interlanguage stage. Learners could recognize sentences in (1) and (2) as English sentences with a clear message, just as native speakers. However, the verb in (1) is missing the -*s* morpheme of subject–verb agreement and could be accepted by a learner who has not acquired that morpho-syntactic feature of English reliably (see Jensen et al. 2019 for Norwegian learners who make this error). The sentence in (2) could seem acceptable to a learner whose native language uses a Subject–Object–Verb word order, e.g., Japanese or Hindi. Acceptance of sentences such as (1) and (2) in an AJT suggests specific gaps in the learner knowledge at that particular interlanguage stage.

5.1.2 Factors affecting AJTs

A Grammaticality Judgment Task is another name for an AJT, and many scholars use the two names interchangeably. However, Cowart (1997) argued that AJT is the more appropriate name, since grammaticality is established within linguistic theory; that is, linguists evaluate the grammaticality of a sentence (which is unobservable) based on whether it is acceptable to speakers (which is observable and measurable). Also from the outset, it was recognized that sentences might have degrees of acceptability. A sentence as in (3) is considered less unacceptable than the one in (4) because we can understand the proposition while we feel there is something wrong with the form, while the latter is completely incomprehensible and also known as "word salad." Interpretation and form can interact as well. In (5), the unacceptability of the form leads to the sentence not having a plausible interpretation.

3 Who what brought to the party?
4 To brought who party the what?
5 I helped themselves to some cake.

Most linguists nowadays would agree that acceptability judgments do not rely on a single and homogeneous grammar representation but depend on a range of factors, including ambiguity and frequency of the participating lexical items. Most prominent among these factors, however, are sentence processing and pragmatics. If a clause is difficult to process because computationally complex, some speakers would consider it unacceptable. A case in point is provided by the examples in (6), where the sentence in (a) involving movement in the main clause is computationally simpler than the one in (b) involving movement over a clause boundary. Think about whether these two sentences are equally acceptable to you. If an interpretation is not plausible or feasible in the context, its acceptability is degraded, compare examples in (7) and your evaluation of them (Dąbrowska & Street 2006)

6 a. Who ___ thinks that Mary wrote a book?   (less complex)
   b. What do you think that Mary wrote ___?   (more complex)

7 a. The man bit the dog.   (implausible)
   b. The dog bit the man.   (plausible)

5.2 Description of the method

AJTs (Sprouse 2011, 2018, 2023) typically target specific linguistic contrasts or properties that have been selected for investigation in the research design. They address the research questions of GenSLA studies, such as whether learners have reset a certain parameter or have acquired a specific expression of a meaning. Researchers who use AJTs have a number of methodological choices to make, which we tackle one by one below.

5.2.1 Mode of presentation

The test sentences in an AJT can be presented aurally or in a written form or both at the same time (bimodal presentation). An aural presentation is more natural, as it approximates speech. A possible hurdle, specifically for lower proficiency learners, could be speech perception in the L2. On the other hand, long convoluted sentences presented in the written mode rely on reading skills. With the aim of investigating this difference, Murphy (1997) presented learners with declarative sentences with embedded questions and wh-questions that violated Subjacency. Participants were slower when sentences were presented aurally, and, even more importantly, they were less accurate when they heard the test sentences. The researcher emphasized the importance of considering the methodology when interpreting research results. At the same time, Plonsky et al. (2020), which presented a synthesis of the use of AJTs and a meta-analysis of the effects of task conditions on learner performance, reported that modality was not found to have a strong or stable effect on learner performance.

5.2.2 *Timed or untimed AJTs*

AJTs can be presented as untimed, where the participants have no time limit for making the decision, versus timed, where the participants have to make the decision under pressure. From the point of view of the "construct validity" of AJTs (see Chapter 3) or what exactly they measure, researchers have argued that imposing a time window in AJTs makes them a better measure of implicit knowledge than explicit knowledge. This is probably because research participants have no time to engage in explicit metalinguistic knowledge or prescriptive norms and provide their judgments based on linguistic intuitions or "gut feeling." Furthermore, timed judgments may replicate the natural conditions of speaking a second language, namely, having to express oneself in real time (McDonald 2006).

What is the procedure for timing AJTs? The experimental setting in Hopp's (2010) Experiment 3 with L2 learners of German went like this. Testing was entirely online. Each trial sentence was preceded by a fixation point in the center of the screen. When the participant pressed the "Go" key, the test sentences were presented word-by-word in the center of the screen. The rate of presentation was set to 250 ms per word plus 17 ms per letter, to offset the effect of longer words. Sentences were presented without punctuation. After the final word of each sentence, the screen changed color and the participants made an immediate binary decision (acceptable or unacceptable) by the press of a button. In Experiment 4, Hopp presented the same stimuli to native speakers of German, using successively lower speeds for each word: 155 ms, 105 ms, 88 ms and 71 ms. The findings suggest that both non-native and native speakers made more errors when the AJT presentation became more and more time compressed.

5.2.3 AJT with corrections

Since AJTs focus on form rather than meaning, the simple collection of binary responses or even responses on a scale does not guarantee that participants are rejecting target sentences for the right reason. For example, an experimental condition can be created around subject–verb agreement as in (1), but a participant may reject a target sentence not because she has noticed the omission of *-s* but because she does not recognize a certain lexical item. The researcher is getting the right result for the wrong reason. One way to rectify this is by asking participants to correct the sentences they deemed unacceptable. As Ionin (2021) points out, there are at least two problems with this option. If participants are asked to correct the sentence immediately after taking the "unacceptable" decision (as in Falk & Bardel 2011), the task becomes considerably more explicit and may be influenced by prescriptive norms and instruction. Furthermore, participants may tend to avoid the "unacceptable" response to avoid the extra work. If, on the other hand, corrections are left for the end of the task (as in Gass & Alvarez Torres 2005), then learners may not remember why they marked a certain sentence as wrong. In both cases, corrections are not conducive to participants accessing their linguistic *intuitions*.

What can be done to ameliorate the right-response-for-the-wrong-reason problem? One solution is to use a high number of target sentences, at least 8 or 10, per condition. If the number of target sentences becomes too high, several item lists can be created, where some participants see a subset of target sentences and the rest are evaluated by other participants. Another solution is to use a high number of participants, since it is unlikely that individuals might reject target sentences for the same wrong reason.

5.2.4 Response types

There are several types of tasks that participants can be given in an AJT. They can be asked to (a) provide a Yes–No answer; (b) choose a rating on a Likert scale; (c) make a Magnitude Estimation (ME) choice; and (d) choose which of two target sentences they consider more/less acceptable. We will now unpack what kind of information those choices yield.

In a Yes–No task, participants are presented with one sentence at a time and asked to categorize it as either acceptable (Yes) or unacceptable (No). This choice is suited to eliciting judgments of categorical acceptability.

8 Example of a Yes–No response

	Acceptable	Unacceptable
What did you think whether John bought?	☐	☒

The same one-sentence-at-a-time presentation, but paired with a Likert scale, asks participants to consider relative acceptability on a scale from 1 to 5 or 1 to 7, where 1 usually stands for unacceptable ("This does not sound natural in my language") and the higher number for acceptable ("This sounds natural in my language"). Typically in GenSLA experiments, instructions include "anchor" sentences that exemplify the lower and higher end of the scale.

9 Example of a Likert scale response:

What did you think whether John bought?

1	2	3	4	5
Completely unacceptable				Fully acceptable

In ME (Bard, Robertson & Sorace 1996), participants are presented with a reference sentence (called the standard), which is assigned a numerical acceptability level (called the modulus). They are then asked to rate target sentences (one at a time) as multiples of the acceptability of a reference sentence.

10 Example of a ME response

Standard: Who thinks that my brother was kept tabs on by the FBI?
Acceptability: 100
Target: What did you think whether John bought?
Acceptability: ____

For example, with a standard of 100, participants may rate the target sentence in (10) as 50. Both Likert scales and ME are more suited for detecting gradient acceptability. Finally, the forced choice presentation is not commonly utilized in GenSLA; it is well-suited to questions about differences between related constructions but does not tell us much about how acceptable the target sentences are on an absolute acceptability continuum.

Through the years, all of the response types have been examined and critiqued. For example, the forced binary choice (Yes or No) task is considered not very sensitive to exactly where a sentence is located on the acceptability scale, presenting a rather crude judgment. It could be appropriate for evaluating sentences like the one in (1), where a functional morphology error is immediately noticeable by expert informants. Scales have also attracted a lot of research attention. At issue is whether informants perceive scales as ordinal or interval. An *ordinal scale* does not require the points on the scale to be equidistant from one another, hence measurable in statistics. An example of a four-point ordinal scale could include the values "fully acceptable," "quite acceptable," "quite unacceptable," "fully unacceptable." There is no way of knowing that the distance between scale points is equal. For instance, for some research participants "quite acceptable" may be very close to "fully acceptable" and far away from "quite unacceptable." Furthermore, one can easily insert an additional scale point such as "neither acceptable nor unacceptable" between the points "quite acceptable" and "quite unacceptable," making it a five-point scale. Therefore, ordinal scales should not be quantified; thus, we cannot calculate a mean score for a participant or for an item.

An *interval scale*, on the other hand, has equidistant points as inches on a ruler, and its values can potentially be used in statistical analysis. It is common practice in GenSLA research to label the values of an interval scale in the instructions to participants, as in (9). Schütze and Sprouse (2014) point to another hazard:

> [B]ecause participants can only use the limited number of response points (i.e., there is no 3.5 on the scale), it is impossible to ensure that the intervals are truly uniform—that is, that subjects treat the difference between 1 and 2 the same as the difference between 4 and 5. This problem is compounded when aggregating across participants in a sample.
>
> *(p. 33)*

This risk can be minimized by using anchoring examples. However, it is worth keeping in mind that no response type is without its limitations.

Needless to say, the choice of response type in a research design should depend on the type of target sentences investigated and the type of evaluation expected (categorical versus gradient). Researchers should carefully consider response types and scales, taking into account the literature that has tested the property under investigation. But, in the end, all response types may be the same at the fundamental conceptual level. The cognitive task for the participants is to provide their estimation of acceptability. If what we are after is detecting differences between conditions (see next section), the data provided by each task are likely to be similar.[1]

5.3 Task design

5.3.1 Instructions

AJT should be preceded by explicit instructions, making it clear to the participants what they are expected to do (check a box, circle an answer, press a button, etc.). Sometimes GenSLA researchers specify in the instructions that participants should not think about prescriptive or instructed grammar rules. Instead, participants are invited to share their "feeling" for the sentences provided. Unless dictated by the research questions, instructions should also specify that researchers are not interested in comprehensibility, as unacceptable sentences are often perfectly comprehensible. Box 5.1 provides an example of AJT instructions, modified from Slabakova (2006).

5.3.2 Practice items

It is not common to include extensive practice items in an AJT, unlike in other psycholinguistic tasks (such as self-paced reading). This is because the instructions already provide anchoring sentences exemplifying the Y and the N response (as in Box 5.1) or the scale extremes, in a Likert-scale response type. These anchoring examples serve as practice items. Note that the anchor sentences should not demonstrate the phenomenon tested so that the participants are not primed. It could be a good idea to exemplify one lexical and one grammatical contrast, as in Box 5.1.

Box 5.1 Example of AJT instructions, modified from Slabakova (2006)

Learners develop a feeling for sentences in the second (or third or fourth) language that they speak. For example, learners feel that the following sentences are not good sentences in English:

1. Mike was probable to win the game.   A (U)

2. Sally were eating breakfast when I saw her.   A (U)

We would mark those sentences as unacceptable by circling the letter U as above. On the other hand, these other sentences sound perfectly fine. We mark them as acceptable by circling A.

1. Mike was likely to win the game.   (A) U

2. Sally was eating breakfast when I saw her. (A) U

Please read the sentences below and mark them as acceptable or unacceptable according to your intuition about them. Do not worry about their truth or falsity. Can you show what is wrong with the sentences that you marked as unacceptable? Write the acceptable sentence next to the U circle.

5.3.3 Factorial design

If an experimental design contains one independent variable (say, Group: native speakers and L2 learners) and one dependent variable (say, Accuracy on an AJT, from 0 to 1), we call this a unifactorial design. For example, one could be interested in the past tense marking in English by native speakers of Chinese. The AJT will minimally contain sentences as in (11):

11 Acceptable: You work**ed** until very late last night.

   Unacceptable: You work until very late last night.

While perfectly respectable, this design is perhaps too minimal. We are usually interested in examining a richer slice of grammar, as linguistic properties influence each other. Tsimpli and Dimitrakopoulou (2007), for example, were interested in how long-distance wh-movement sentences with a gap or resumptive pronouns were accepted by Greek-English bilinguals. They predicted that this acceptability may be affected by the following four factors: whether the wh-word was subject versus object, whether it was animate versus inanimate, whether it was discourse-linked and whether the complementizer *that* was present. In (12), we illustrate what test sentences are needed to examine how discourse-linking (*which X*) affects gaps or resumptive pronouns. But, first, let us explain gaps and resumptives. A wh-word is semantically linked to the constituent it questions. In (12a, c), *who* is asking about the object of *like* (Jane likes some person; who is it?). When *who* moves to the top of the structure, it leaves a gap in the object position of the embedded clause, as in (12c). Some languages like Arabic, but crucially not English, fill that position with a pronoun, called resumptive pronoun. That is why (12a) is unacceptable.

12 a. *Who do you think that Jane likes him?
    b. *Which student do you think that Jane likes him?
    c. Who do you think that Jane likes ____?
    d. Which student do you think that Jane likes ____?

Now, we would like to know whether a wh-word linked to some previous discourse (*which X?*) affects resumption. If we start by comparing (12a) and (12b) and we find that (12b) is the more acceptable of the two, can we claim that d-linking makes sentences with resumptives less unacceptable? Not really. We also need to examine (12c) and (12d). The difference between (12a) and (12b) may be smaller, equal to or larger than the difference between (12c) and (12d). This will tell us whether d-linking improves only wh-movement sentences with resumptives or all wh-movement sentences.

The four sentences in (12) form a factorial design with two factors: wh-type with two levels [±d-linking] and resumption with two levels [±resumptive pronoun]. A factorial design is the best way to isolate the effect of each factor and their interaction.

5.3.4 Conditions

Factorial designs cannot be implemented with single test sentences. Researchers have to create *experimental conditions,* containing at least five or six, but ideally eight, lexicalizations of the exact same construction (cf. Section 3.3.2). For instance, all four examples in (12) should become separate conditions in a test design. Conditions with different lexicalizations are crucial because the choice of words may affect the acceptability of the test sentences or their plausibility or both. It could also be the case that individual participants might have lexical gaps. But lexical choice is not the only factor that affects acceptability. There might even be factors that we do not know about. For that reason, experiments typically involve multiple items instantiating the same structure. In this way, unsystematic influences cancel each other out and judgments center on a "true" value for the corresponding structure.

Let us look at an extended example from a recent study, Tang, Fiorentino and Gabriele (2023). Following Choi, Ionin and Zhu (2018), the researchers investigated whether L2 learners rely on transfer from their native language or the universal semantic distinction of atomicity or both, in the acquisition of the count/mass distinction. They examined L1-French and L1-Chinese learners of English. Atomicity refers to whether a noun contains "atoms," or minimal elements, that retain the property of the noun, such as *furniture,* whose components are also pieces of furniture. The design involved the following factors, hence, conditions: count versus mass nouns, atomic versus non-atomic mass nouns and concrete versus abstract nouns. Since atomicity is relevant only among mass nouns but abstractness cuts across all nouns, there are six conditions as in (13):

13 Conditions in Tang et al. (2023)
    a. Count concrete
    b. Count abstract
    c. Mass atomic concrete
    d. Mass atomic abstract
    e. Mass non-atomic concrete
    f. Mass non-atomic abstract

Furthermore, the test should comprise acceptable and unacceptable sentences in equal proportion. Tang et al. included six acceptable and six unacceptable test items in each condition. To illustrate different lexicalizations (wording), we reproduce their test items from the mass atomic concrete condition (13c). Note that, in all test items, the quantifiers *a lot of* and *more* pointed to more than an atom being included in the mass noun.

14 Acceptable items
   a. I dumped a lot of mail into the trash when I was cleaning up.
   b. Mary brought a lot of luggage on her trip to Europe.
   c. The police chief purchased more equipment for officers in the community.
   d. Alicia carried a lot of cash when she traveled.
   e. Lauren bought more furniture for her new house.
   f. The soldier packed a lot of clothing before his departure.

15 Unacceptable items
   a. The child saw more lightnings last night than ever before.
   b. Peggy bought a lot of underwears at the department store.
   c. The company proposed a lot of infrastructures as a solution to the problem.
   d. The singer wore more jewelries than his dancers at the concert.
   e. Pam gave a lot of stationeries to the kids at school.
   f. The analyst needed more softwares for the new computer.

The carrier sentences for the all-important nouns contain relatively simple words. All target items were also examined for frequency, and lexical frequency was a factor in all statistical analyses. One limitation that the researchers acknowledge is that the target nouns in the acceptable sentences (14) and in the unacceptable sentences (15) were not the same. Since it is almost impossible to match mass and count nouns for frequency, cumulative frequency per condition may be added up. For example, the target items in (14) should have approximately the same cumulative frequency as those in (15).

This factorial design yielded 72 test sentences. They were mixed with 72 filler items of the same length and complexity, testing subject–verb agreement, for a total of 144 test items.

Depending on participant variables and with the addition of more fillers or distractors (see below), such a test may be considered too long. If test fatigue sets in, participants may start choosing responses at random. A solution could be to divide the items into lists so that participants see only part of the test items. Contemporary survey software can randomize items for each presentation so that researchers should only worry about how to split their test items. In the Tang et al. design, one possibility is to split the items into two within each condition. In other words, the top three items in (14) go into List 1 and the bottom three go into List 2 and so on. Alternatively, items in (14) and (15) can go into different lists. This decision ultimately depends on the research questions and design. Whatever the decision, lists should maintain an equal number of acceptable and unacceptable items as much as possible.

5.3.5 Fillers

As we saw in the extended example in the previous subsection, at least as many fillers as test items are needed in an AJT. In some psycholinguistic experiments, the ratio of test items to fillers is 1:3. Why do we need fillers? Their first function is to *distract* the participants from guessing the property under investigation. If participants figure out what is being tested, it is more likely that they would utilize some prescriptive or instructed rules or response strategies, which we want to avoid. Second, we may want to check the participants' accuracy on the fillers to see whether they have been paying attention. If L2 learners are accurate on fillers but less accurate on some test conditions, that is an indication of noteworthy difficulty. Furthermore, researchers may decide to use the fillers to test a completely different property, which would maximize their time and effort. Fillers can also be used to even out the overall balance of acceptable to unacceptable items in the whole of the test.

5.4 Extended example and summary

Acceptability judgment tasks remain a powerful tool in the GenSLA methodology arsenal. An AJT involves explicitly asking speakers of a language to "judge" or "evaluate" whether a particular string of words is a possible utterance in the language under investigation. If done right, they provide insights into a speaker's mental grammar that no other task can provide. As language is a mapping of form and meaning, test sentences in an AJT rely on a commonly held interpretation but interpretation is not what is being tested. While most of the time AJT sentences are presented in isolation, there are times when context is needed for better comprehension and easier processing. One such case is discussed in Case Study Box 5.2.

This chapter will help the novice applied linguist to understand some of the intricacies of this most important of GenSLA tasks. Carefully considering presentation and response types, as well as instructions, the factorial design, conditions with different lexicalizations, fillers, etc. will make for a successful and publishable design. It is a good idea to do power analysis before starting, to establish the sample size needed for the experiment. While

Case Study Box 5.2: Leal Mendez and Slabakova (2014)

In this box, we present a partial replication study of Tsimpli and Dimitrakopoulou (2007) by Leal Méndez and Slabakova (2014). In examples (12a–d), we offered a taste of the test items used by Tsimpli and Dimitrakopoulou (henceforth T&D). We focus on the AJT methodology here, not on the theoretical research questions. The T&D main task was a bimodal (aural and written), paced acceptability judgment task using a Likert scale with units ranging from −2 to +2. The variables investigated in the experimental design included subject versus object interrogatives, animate versus inanimate wh-words, d-linked versus non-d-linked wh-words and the presence or absence of complementizer *that*. Fifty-one sentences as in (12) were evaluated, consisting of 30 test items and 21 fillers. In calculating the results, the researchers conflated the +1 and +2 answers into an "accept" category, −1 and −2 into a "reject" category and disregarded zero answers. Intermediate learners were about 62% accurate in rejecting unacceptable resumptive pronouns, while advanced learners showed a mean of 74% on correct rejections; both groups were even more accurate in correct acceptance.

Leal Mendez and Slabakova (LM&S) argued that T&D's results may be misleadingly low, on methodological grounds. Furthermore, they divided their research participants into those individuals who liked resumptives in their native Spanish and those who did not accept resumptives, adding another variable to the research design. Next, all T&D's test materials were administered embedded under a context. According to LM&S, the original sentences were long and hard to understand without context. Therefore, the researchers added context to each test sentence, arguing that context facilitates comprehension and parsing. See an example in (i).

(i) Gabriel and Maria were chatting at the Java House. Maria said that Peter liked that new book *Going Rogue* so much that he memorized every word. Gabriel corrected her and said that *Going Wild* was the book Peter had read so carefully. To resolve the argument, Maria called Peter's best friend Vladimir and asked him:

Which book do you remember that Peter read (it) carefully?

Each context and question were delivered bi-modally through (a) written text on a computer screen and (b) audio recordings by a native speaker of

> English. Learners were given unlimited time to mark their judgments. A Likert scale with units between 1 (rejection) and 4 (acceptance) with a separate "I don't know" option was used.
>
> LM&S's results point to context increasing all learners' accuracy in evaluating the acceptability of long-distance wh-movement test items. Intermediate learners' accuracy ranged between 65% and 70%. In addition, it was established that advanced learners of English who liked resumptives in Spanish were on average 10% more likely to accept ungrammatical resumptives in English. In other words, some advanced learners were prone to transferring their (processing) tolerance to resumptives from their native language. However, the overall accuracy of advanced learners hovered around 90%. The variables of wh-word grammatical function (subject versus object), animacy, d-linking and presence of complementizer *that* did not have a significant influence on the judgments.

we do not discuss this analysis here, there are numerous online calculators that are quite accessible.[2] In the end, experimental results such as the ones we presented above, including their statistical treatment yielding effects of different sizes, exist to be interpreted by researchers. The results *interpretation* leads to theoretical claims and models of development. For example, the two studies we discussed in Box 5.2 come to different theoretical conclusions. T&D argue that their findings point to an impairment in adult L2 grammars, while LM&S conclude that their learners are successful in acquiring the new property of the L2 grammar. This choice may boil down to whether learners' judgments are compared with native speakers' judgments or whether learner grammar is considered an interlanguage system in its own right.

5.5 Discussion questions

1 Consider the test sentence *John always drinks his coffee black* as a part of an experiment checking knowledge of subject–verb agreement in the present tense. What is its unacceptable equivalent? Create six more lexicalizations (test sentences) for this condition. Would you include an adverb such as *always* in all of them? Why or why not?
2 Imagine that you wanted to examine knowledge of restrictive relative clauses in English in the interlanguage of Mandarin native speakers. Here is an example of a restrictive relative clause: *This is the girl (that/who) I will marry*. What conditions would you include in such an experiment and why?

3 Explain in your own words the point made in the conclusion: that researchers may disagree in the interpretation of similar results. What is the basis of such possible disagreement?

Notes

1 Several studies have directly compared the various judgment tasks. For example, Bader and Haüssler (2010) compared ME and YN tasks for several sentence types in German and found that both tasks detected differences between the conditions.
2 Free online sample size and power calculators can be found at https://sample-size.net/, among many other.

Further reading

Schütze, C. (1996). *The empirical base of linguistics: Grammaticality judgments and linguistic methodology*. Chicago: University of Chicago Press.

Ionin, T., & Zyzik, E. (2014). Judgment and interpretation tasks in second language research. *Annual Review of Applied Linguistics, 34*, 1–28. https://doi.org/10.1017/S0267190514000026

Ionin, T. (2021). Acceptability studies in L2 populations. In G. Goodall (Ed.), *The Cambridge handbook of experimental syntax* (pp. 373–393). https://doi.org/10.1017/9781108569620.015

6
INTERPRETATION TASKS

6.1 What are interpretation tasks?

Interpretation tasks lie at the heart of the GenSLA endeavor, since this framework is especially interested in the form–meaning connection and how forms (lexical items, functional morphemes, phrases and sentences) are interpreted in individual utterances and in discourse. For instance, do learners interpret the progressive tense in English (e.g., *Sheila is eating a sandwich*) as reflecting an action unfolding at the moment of speaking? Unlike many other second language acquisition research frameworks, however, GenSLA is also interested in learner interpretations of the "void": how do learners acquire and interpret meanings that are not expressed by an overtly pronounced or spelled form? For example, Mandarin and Italian, among many other languages, allow null pronouns in embedded clauses as in example (1), where *pro* stands for a silent morpheme (see Chapters 1 and 4). But how do we know who crosses the street, the old woman or the girl, when the embedded subject is not pronounced? And is there a difference in interpretation when the embedded subject is *lei* 'she'?

1 L'anziana signora saluta la ragazza quando lei/*pro* attraversa la strada
   the old woman greets the girl   when she/Ø crosses the street
   'The old woman greets the girl when she crosses the street.'
            (example 10b in Tsimpli, Sorace, Heycock and Filiaci 2004)

These are precisely the types of questions that we want to answer with interpretation tasks. To start with, let's take some obvious assumptions out

DOI: 10.4324/9781003160762-8

of the way. In interpretation tasks, the phrases or sentences being evaluated are always grammatical utterances, as in the examples above. What we want to find out is whether the utterances fit in a specific given context and whether one of a few possible interpretations is the correct one. In the case of ambiguous sentences as in (1), we may also seek to establish interpretation preferences: which of two interpretations is chosen more often. Potentially, we could approach the task in two ways: we can either provide a context and see if participants consider the test sentence to be a good description (or a good continuation) of the context or provide the test sentence and offer a few interpretations, forcing participants to choose among them. Truth-Value Judgment Tasks (TVJTs) and Acceptability Judgment in Context Tasks belong to the first category; Interpretation Choice and Picture Selection Tasks belong to the second category. In this chapter, we discuss their advantages and pitfalls.

6.2 The Truth-Value Judgment Task

The TVJT (Crain & McKee 1985; Gordon 1996; Crain & Thornton 1998) tests a speaker's ability to evaluate interpretations of test sentences in controlled contexts/scenarios. The participant must decide whether a test statement is True or False as a description of a particular situation. Crain and Thornton (2000) posit a number of essential requirements of this task so that it is methodologically rigorous and its results are dependable. One requirement is that the story renders an otherwise grammatical sentence unacceptable. Conservatively, only responses to stimuli expecting the answer False are considered to be truly informative of participants' underlying grammatical competence. Another requirement is the Condition of Plausible Dissent (Crain & Thornton 1998). This condition is satisfied if the grammatically inaccessible reading has been under consideration and is a genuine potential outcome of the story that almost comes to pass but, in the end, does not.[1] This requirement ensures that the decision in the TVJT is taken on the basis of grammar, rather than on the pragmatics of the story.

The TVJT is often modified when used in GenSLA. A story is supplied to establish a clear and unambiguous context. Sometimes the context can appear in the native language of the learners, if the research targets lower-level proficiency learners. A test sentence in the target language appears written below the story. Learners are asked to judge whether the test sentence is appropriate or fits (describes) the story well. Participants answer with Yes or No, True or False. In the case when a test sentence is ambiguous, the story supplies only one of its two available interpretations. In such a case, the same sentence appears under another story as well, supporting its second interpretation. Typically, stories and test sentences are squared in a 2 × 2 design, giving a quadruple of story–test sentence combinations, as illustrated below:

In the typical TVJT design, test sentences 1 and 2 are almost identical except for a crucial grammatical difference, as will be exemplified below from the experimental study reported in Slabakova (2003). The experiment investigates whether speakers of English know that a bare infinitive in a perceptual report sentence (e.g., *I saw him eat a cake*) must refer to a complete event, while the gerund (e.g., *I saw him eating a cake*) refers only to the process and need not refer to a complete event. Each story–sentence pairing is judged on its own in a different part of the test instrument, but we present them together next, for ease of observation.

2. Matt had an enormous appetite. He was one of those people who could eat a whole cake at one sitting. But these days he is much more careful what he eats. For example, yesterday he bought a chocolate and vanilla ice cream cake, but ate only half of it after dinner. I know, because I was there with him.

I observed Matt eat a cake.	True	**False**
I observed Matt eating a cake.	**True**	False

3. Alicia is a thin person, but she has an astounding capacity for eating big quantities of food. Once when I was at her house, she took a whole ice cream cake out of the freezer and ate it all. I almost got sick, just watching her.

I watched Alicia eat a cake.	**True**	False
I watched Alicia eating a cake.	**True**	False

In example (2), corresponding to Meaning 1 in Table 6.1, an unfinished event is presented (the cake in the story was half-eaten). Consequently, only the sentence with the gerund *eating* describes it correctly; the sentence with the bare infinitive *eat* should be rejected as False. In example (3), the story describes a complete event (Meaning 2), so both the test sentence

TABLE 6.1 Story–test sentence combinations in a TVJT

	Meaning 1	*Meaning 2*
Test sentence 1	*NOT available*	*Available*
Test sentence 2	*Available*	*Available*

with a bare infinitive and the one with a gerund are True. Note that all the test sentences are grammatical under some interpretation in the target language. As per Crain and Thornton's requirement, the False answers are the most informative because learners have to reject a possible interpretation of the test sentence, which just happens not to be True in this context. Furthermore, the test sentences differ only in one word, so that, if responses differ, lexical difficulties may be excluded. The TVJT's main advantage is that learners do not access metalinguistic knowledge that they may have acquired through language instruction, but rather engage in active comprehension and reveal their true linguistic competence.

Versions of this task can include context presented in pictures, as for instance in Gabriele (2009). The researcher examined the interpretation of several different aspectual tenses in two learning directions: learners of L2 Japanese and L2 English whose native language is English and Japanese, respectively. An example includes the progressive tense with an achievement verb as in (4):

4   The plane is arriving at the airport.

Achievement verbs present a change of state that is momentary. In English, the achievement verb *arrive* in (4) presents the action just before the state of arrival.

In Japanese, however, the imperfective marker *te-iru* combined with an achievement verb has a result interpretation, so the Japanese equivalent of (4) means that the plane has already arrived and is at the airport. A time-stamped sequence of two pictures accompanied by audio narration was shown for each trial; the test sentence appeared on the computer screen after the story had been presented. In the case of example (4), the complete-event story made it clear that the plane was already at the airport, while the incomplete-event story indicated that the plane was still in the air. The English sentence in (4) is unacceptable with the complete story, but acceptable with the incomplete story. For the Japanese equivalent of (4), the judgments are reversed.

What kind of answer choices are appropriate for a TVJT? As the name suggests, two categorical options are the logical choice. Dichotomous scales use Yes–No, True–False or Agree–Disagree responses. This is because, in logic, a proposition cannot be "somewhat true." However, some researchers have deviated from this choice. Instead of using True and False answers, Gabriele (2009) opted for a Likert scale with 5 option choices, from 1 standing for "I definitely cannot say this sentence in the context of the story" to 5, "I definitely can say this sentence in the context of the story." Likert scales are not common with TVJTs, because their answer options are

74 Methods typically used in GenSLA

not evenly spaced to represent equal intervals between neighboring data points as in an interval scale (see Chapter 5).

In summary, TVJTs are the instrument of choice for researchers who explore sentence interpretations in context. They have been widely used in GenSLA to investigate aspectual tense interpretations (Gabriele 2009; Montrul & Slabakova 2003), scope judgments (Grüter, Lieberman & Gualmini 2010) and anaphor binding (Finer & Broselow 1986). Case Study Box 6.1 presents yet another example of a TVJT as well as a comparison with an Acceptability Judgment Task (AJT) with context (see Section 6.3).

Case Study Box 6.1: Ionin, Montrul and Crivos (2013)

Research question: In English, bare plural nouns are interpreted as generic (e.g., *Tigers eat meat*), while for a specific reading, the definite article is used (e.g., *The tigers eat carrots*). In Spanish, on the other hand, definite plural nouns can be generic (e.g., *Los tigres comen carne*) but also have a specific reading. Can adult learners acquire the different morphological expressions of genericity and specificity in Spanish and English plural nouns? What is the greatest learning challenge?

Study 1

Task: TVJT, participants read short stories about two unusual representatives of various animal species: tigers who are vegetarian, birds who live in caves, zebras who have spots and so on. Each story was accompanied by a picture of the unusual animal. Participants then had to judge the target sentence as True or False in the context of the story and picture.

Sample test story: English study 1

Everyone knows that a zebra always has stripes. But not in our zoo! Our zoo has two zebras, and they are really unusual: they have spots instead of stripes! That's really strange.

a   Zebras have stripes.   TRUE
b   The zebras have spots.   TRUE
c   These zebras have stripes.   FALSE

Stimuli: 8 stories and test sentences as above, 8 fillers (Spanish options were slightly different)

Participants: 40 L1-Spanish learners of L2-English and 19 native English controls; 43 L1-English learners of L2-Spanish and 17 native Spanish controls

Study 2

Task: AJT, participants read a paragraph-long context followed by five different test sentences. They then had to evaluate the acceptability of each test sentence in the context of the preceding story, using a scale from 1 (unacceptable) to 4 (acceptable). The instructions specifically stated that two or more sentences could receive the same rating; that is, responses did not need to be ranked.
Sample test story: English study 2

It's my niece's birthday this Saturday—she is going to be three years old. I'm not sure what to get her. Maybe I'll just get her some toy, like a stuffed dog or bear. I can't go wrong with that. We all know that…

a Toy animals are good children's gifts.   1 2 3 4
b The toy animals are good children's gifts. 1 2 3 4

Stimuli: 20 stories each with 5 test sentences as the ones above, 20 fillers (Spanish options were slightly different)
Participants: 32 L1-Spanish learners of L2-English and 22 native English controls; 31 L1-English learners of L2-Spanish and 16 native Spanish controls
Results: Both L1 transfer as well as successful acquisition were attested. Ungrammatical forms (bare plurals in Spanish) were easily rejected. Learning the morphological expression of genericity in the L2 was more challenging. The differences between native Spanish speakers and L2 Spanish learners were a matter of preference rather than absolute judgment: Native speakers preferred the generic interpretation while lower-proficiency learners preferred the specific interpretation. Finally, learners were more accurate on the AJT than on the TVJT, perhaps because of its more explicit nature.

6.3 Acceptability judgment in context

AJT with context are quite similar to TVJTs but do not have to obey Crain and Thornton's (1998) strict requirements. The direction of interpretation is still the same: the context is established first and the test sentence is judged subsequently. The context could be presented either in a story or by pictures.

76 Methods typically used in GenSLA

Let us consider the task used in Marsden (2009), a study of scope interpretation. We will simplify the learning task here for the sake of highlighting the method. The English sentence in (5) is ambiguous:

5 Someone stroked every cat.

It could mean that there is one person, X, who stroked every cat Y (many Ys) involved in the discourse situation. Let us call this Meaning 1. It could also mean that for every cat Y in the discourse (many Ys), there is some person or other X who stroked it (many Xs). This would be Meaning 2. In Korean and Japanese, the neutral word order is Subject–Object–Verb (SOV), and it only allows the first interpretation, Meaning 1 (Figure 6.1). (The second interpretation, Meaning 2, is expressed by another word order.) Marsden investigated whether Korean-native and English-native learners of L2 Japanese could acquire the lack of the second interpretation with neutral SOV sentences. Note that English-native speakers allow that interpretation in their native language but have to pre-empt (unlearn) it in their L2 Japanese. Participants viewed a picture establishing the context for ten seconds on a projection screen. The test sentence was then presented in a written and aural mode. The researcher explains the motivation of her choice like this:

FIGURE 6.1 Picture representing Meaning 1 (one person stroking every cat), reproduced with permission from Marsden (2009).

Presenting the picture (that is to say, the interpretation) before the sentence was intended to reduce the possibility of participants determining their own interpretation of each sentence, then rejecting any picture sentence pairings—possible or not—that did not match their preconceived idea.

(Marsden 2009: 144–145)

If L2 Japanese learners had acquired the lack of the distributed meaning in SOV sentences, they would reject Meaning 2 given in the picture in Figure 6.2.

A different AJT methodology is provided by Ivanov (2012), a study of L2 Bulgarian that probed whether learners had acquired the pragmatic function of clitic-doubling (see also Slabakova, Kempchinsky & Rothman 2012, on clitics in L2 Spanish). The general context was provided in the native language of the learners, English, in order to secure better comprehension. The immediate context was a question establishing a Topic (for example, someone already mentioned in the question). Four answer options in Bulgarian appeared below the question and differed along two dimensions: Topic fronting and clitic-doubling. Note that in all other respects, the answer options are similar. Topics have to be clitic-doubled, in this case by *go* 'him', the third-person singular masculine clitic, no matter whether they are fronted as in (6a) and (6c) or not (6b) and (6d). Participants were instructed to rate each answer option separately, on a scale from 1 to 5, for its acceptability in the context of the question.

FIGURE 6.2 Picture representing Meaning 2 (every cat being stroked by a different person), represented with permission from Marsden (2009).

6 Q: Has anybody seen Ivan today?
   A: *Ivan go vidjah tazi sutrin.*   Acceptable
      Ivan him-cl saw-1sg this morning
      'I saw Ivan in the morning.'
   B: *Tazi sutrin go vidjah Ivan.*   Acceptable
   C: *Ivan vidjah tazi sutrin.*   Unacceptable
   D: *Tazi sutrin vidjah Ivan.*   Unacceptable

All four answer options are grammatical on their own, but since the object *Ivan* is already mentioned, hence Topic, the clitic-doubling is obligatory. When objects are not clitic-doubled, as in (6c) and (6d), they are not treated as Topics and the word order sounds confusing. Thus, this AJT truly tests acceptability in the discourse context, not grammaticality.

Let us consider the methodological choice here. Presenting all four target answer types side by side after each story and question cuts down on the length of the test, which is an advantage. At the same time, participants' attention is drawn to the target manipulation, since they can compare across the options given and focus on form. The latter is a potential disadvantage, especially if the grammatical phenomenon under investigation is explicitly taught. These considerations have to be carefully weighed in the design, keeping in mind that no design is absolutely perfect but some advantages are more important than others.

A final note on AJTs in context. The careful reader may remember that in Case Study Box 5.2, we exemplified one such task. How does that task differ from the ones discussed in this section? And why would we classify the latter as interpretation tasks? The careful reader would be correct in assuming that the difference is subtle. The context illustrated in Box 5.2 provides an explicit situation, in which the long and complex to process test sentence may be applied. Context is added to aid processing. Note, however, that the acceptability judgment does not depend on the context; it depends on the participant's grammar. The opposite is true in (6), where the introductory question mentioning a person's name creates a Topic context for the subsequent answers. In other words, without Topic context, the judgments of the test answers would have been quite different. Therefore, we can classify (6) as an interpretation task, evaluating how a test sentence fits a context.

6.4 Picture Matching Task

In the Picture Matching Task (PMT), learners interpret a target sentence based on word order or functional morphology, that is, grammatical information. The learner's task is to match the sentence to the correct picture.

Learners typically have to choose from two pictures representing two different interpretations of the target sentence (Montrul 2000). In some studies (Papadopoulou et al. 2011; Shimanskaya & Slabakova 2017), four pictures are presented to participants, two of which capture the crucial grammatical choice and the other two are distractors. Let us illustrate this task with an example from VanPatten and Cadierno (1993).

7 a. El señor la   sigue
      the man her follow
      'The man follows her.'
    b. La sigue   el señor
      her follow the man
      'The man follows her.'

As Spanish has some flexibility in subject placement, both sentences in (7a) and (7b) reflect exactly the same proposition, a man following a woman. However, English-native learners of Spanish often interpret (7b) to mean "She follows the man," since the feminine pronoun is in the subject position most frequent in English. In one task by VanPatten and Cadierno (1993), research participants were asked to match each sentence they heard with one of two pictures simultaneously presented on an overhead projector. The two pictures represented the same action, the difference between them being who the agent and the affected entity were. For example, in the case of (7b), participants had to choose between a picture of a woman following a man and a picture of a man following a woman. As the reader can appreciate, this design is almost diametrically opposed to the one in Marsden (2009), where the picture is presented before the target sentence. When choosing which design to use, researchers should carefully consider both the grammatical properties as well as the implicit or explicit nature of the linguistic knowledge. Including at least an equal number of distractors as target items is a way to mitigate against explicit, non-internalized information about the form.

It is interesting to compare the two interpretation tasks we discussed above to check which one, a TVJT or a PMT, better detects the interlanguage competence of the learners. White et al. (1997), investigating the interpretation of reflexives in French-English and Japanese-English interlanguage, did just that.

Consider the ambiguous sentence in (8).

8 Mary$_i$ showed Susan$_j$ a portrait of herself$_{i/j}$.

If we have to find out whether learners interpret *herself* to refer to Mary or to Susan, or possibly to either one, we can test their interpretation with a PMT. Participants would be offered a picture in which Mary is showing Susan a prominent portrait of Susan and a sentence underneath it like the one in (8) without the indexes. Participants have to indicate whether what is going on in the picture matches the sentence. If the learners allow Susan, the object of the sentence and the reflexive to co-refer, they will answer positively. The same sentence will appear under another picture (not side by side but at another location in the test), this time of Mary showing Susan a portrait of Mary, to check whether learners allow binding to the subject. It has been noticed (see White et al. 1997: 148 for discussion) that the PMT reflects, for the most part, the linguistic preferences of the learners. In the case of (8), for example, learners prefer to interpret the reflexive as co-referring with the subject and not the object. This does not mean that the other interpretation is missing from their grammar, but it does mean that experimental results capturing this preference actually underestimate the learners' competence.

To prove that, White et al. (1997) used both a PMT and a TVJT with the same learners. Recall that in the latter task, an explicit interpretation and a target sentence are evaluated on a True or False basis. Results showed that both native speakers and L2 learners were significantly more consistent in accepting a local object (Susan in (8)) as a reflexive antecedent in the TVJT, compared to the PMT. Since the two tasks are arguably tapping the same linguistic competence, it is clear that the TVJT better deals with licit but dispreferred interpretations of ambiguous sentences, disposing of preferences to a larger degree. However, when we are not dealing with interpretive preferences, the PMT is appropriate and very useful for its clarity (see the successful application of this task by Hirakawa 1999; Inagaki 2001; Montrul 2000; White et al. 1999).

6.5 Interpretation choice task

Just as in a PMT, sometimes researchers present learners with overt explicit meanings to choose from. This is only advisable when meaning choices are difficult to represent in pictures. This type of interpretation task has been used by Kanno (1997), Gürel (2006) and Slabakova (2005). After the target sentence, two (or more) interpretations are spelled out, as the example in (9) from Kanno (1997: 269) illustrates. In this case, the instructions made clear that participants were allowed to choose both (a) and (b) as possible answers, if this seemed appropriate. Note also that in the Japanese sentence, the embedded subject is null, a *pro*, and it refers to the main clause subject *dare* 'who'; in English null subjects are not acceptable in embedded clauses.

9 Dare$_i$-ga [*pro$_i$* kuruma-o katta to] itta no?
   who-NOM car-ACC bought that said Q
   'Who$_i$ said (he$_i$) bought a car?'
   a. the same person as *dare*
   b. another person

This task may be less effective than a TVJT and a PMT, because learners may find it more difficult to externalize how they interpret a particular structure. In a way, this task expects them to think about the meaning of the test sentence and then choose from a couple of provided interpretations, while the TVJT allows them to focus on the story context and then judge the test sentence in a more natural way, abstracting away from its grammatical form. However, Gürel (2006) used this task in conjunction with a TVJT to find out whether her learners allowed pronominal elements to be ambiguous, and her findings on the two tasks were similar, suggesting that her learners were able to overcome the problem mentioned above.

6.6 Sentence conjunction task

Another way of tapping interpretive judgments is through a sentence conjunction judgment task (SCT). In this task, the participants are asked to decide whether the two clauses in a complex sentence, or two sentences, go well together or not. In a sense, the first clause represents a context for the second clause. Take the sentences in (10) from Slabakova (2001) as an example.

10 a. Allison worked in a bakery and made cakes.
    b. Allison worked in a bakery and made a cake.

What is being evaluated is the felicity of combination of the first and the second clause. The two clauses in (10a) are a good fit because they represent two habitual activities, while the pairing in (10b) is less felicitous because a habitual and a one-time event are combined.

Duffield and Matsuo (2009) and Duffield, Matsuo and Roberts (2009) used this task to evaluate the interpretation of VP ellipsis. This is a construction in which a meaningful verbal phrase is substituted with an auxiliary verb, because it is mentioned before and should not be repeated. For instance, a sentence such as *Tom told us that Sally did* is perfectly grammatical, but not interpretable without preceding context, from where the content of the elided VP can be recovered. To test L2 English learners' sensitivity to the properties of VP ellipsis, Duffield and Matsuo (2009) presented participants with sentence pairs such as those in (11), where the first sentence provides the antecedent for the elided VP in the second sentence. Participants had to judge whether the second sentence was acceptable as a continuation of the first.

11 a. Someone took the wood out to the shed last night. Tom told us that Sally did.
 b. The wood was taken out to the shed last night. Tom told us that Sally did.

Under various testing conditions (timed judgments, scale versus categorical judgments, reaction times), (11b) with a passive antecedent for the elided VP was revealed to be less acceptable than (11a), hence it took longer to interpret.

In Duffield et al.'s study, the TVJT is not readily appropriate, as the elided VP is recoverable from any preceding context and the SCT is sufficient. However, the TVJT is superior to the SCT when considering aspectual meanings as in (10), because the former establishes the context in a clearer way. On the other hand, an advantage of the SCT is that it is shorter. In summary, the SCT should be used sparingly in learning situations that warrant it. It could also be used as part of a battery of interpretation tasks.

6.7 Conclusion

Interpretations and their mapping to morphological and syntactic forms are at the heart of GenSLA research; therefore, interpretation tasks are very important and have garnered a lot of methodological attention. Most interpretation tasks were introduced and used in child language acquisition first. However, these tasks have been modified for second language learners by introducing written or combined modes of presentation, a higher number of test items and more distractors. This is because adult learners have longer attention spans, and testing time is generally longer. When developing designs of their own, researchers have to consider carefully the two possible directions of interpretation: whether to present the meaning first (in TVJT and AJT) or the target item first (in picture matching, interpretation choice and sentence conjunction tasks). The choice is quite subtle and may come down to the researcher intuition. It is advisable to check the literature for the types of interpretation tasks used for a specific property, whether it is binding, scope, aspect, discourse, etc. In any event, using a healthy number of test items and distractors remains imperative.

6.8 Discussion questions

1 Consider the meaning of definite and indefinite articles in English. If you want to establish whether L2 learners of English interpret them correctly, what interpretation task would you use?
2 In continuation of the question above and considering also the tasks discussed in Chapter 5, which tasks are you going to use to establish whether learners use the articles correctly? Note that there may be overlap in tasks.
3 In Chapter 5, we mentioned that the results from an AJT can be interpreted differently, depending on the theoretical positions of the researchers. Do you think this is also true of interpretation tasks? Why or why not?

Note

1 This requirement is not often obeyed in GenSLA experimental studies, because it requires very long and detailed stories, which could be too difficult for L2 learners to understand. For one exception, though, see Slabakova, White and Brambati Guzzo (2017).

Further reading

Crain, S., & Thornton, R. (2000) *Investigations in universal grammar: A guide to experiments on the acquisition of syntax and semantics.* Cambridge: MIT Press.

Schmitt, C., & Miller K. (2010). Using comprehension methods in language acquisition research. In S. Unsworth, & E. Blom (Eds.), *Experimental methods in language acquisition research* (pp. 35–56). Amsterdam: John Benjamins.

Pinto, M., & Zuckerman, S. (2019). Coloring book: A new method for testing language comprehension. *Behavioral Research Methods,* 51(6), 2609–2628. https://doi.org/10.3758/s13428-018-1114-8

7
SPEECH TASKS

7.1 Phonetics and phonology

Perhaps it is appropriate to start off this chapter by reminding the reader what we are dealing with here. Linguists discuss phonetics and phonology separately, although they are closely related. The study of L2 speech has been informed by research in a number of areas, including phonological theory, but also acoustic and articulatory phonetics. Phonetics is the systematic study of human speech sounds, including their physiological production and acoustic qualities. It is commonly divided into production (articulatory), transmission (acoustic) and perception (auditory phonetics). On the other hand, phonology pays attention to how languages systematically organize their sounds. Phonology describes the system of contrastive relations among the speech sounds of a specific language, sounds that constitute fundamental components of that language just as morphemes, words and phrases do. In addition, phonology organizes segments into prosodic "chunks" for speech, such as syllables, metrical feet (or stress patterns) and intonation phrases. Linguists have long known that phonetics and phonology are intricately related. For example, much work in L2 speech research proceeds on the assumption that accurate perception must precede accurate production (Flege 1995), and the latter is not just an empty imitation of L2 sounds but is based on the interlanguage system of L2 sounds represented in the mind of the learner up to that point in development.

Let us take some real-life examples using linguistic terminology. It is well known that Spanish does not distinguish between /b/ and /v/, pronouncing both as a "bilabial approximant" (or fricative) in most contexts, except after a pause or a nasal consonant. In other words, the first sounds in *beber* 'drink' and *vivir* 'live' sound the same. Linguists would say that the first sounds of these words are in allophonic variation, such that voiced obstruents /b, d, g/ are realized as fricatives [β, ð, ɣ] intervocalically but as stops [b, d, g] elsewhere. Note that this is true even if the two sounds are distinguished in writing. Of course, /b/ and /v/ are contrastive in English, or they belong to different phonemes, since they distinguish minimal pairs, e.g., *ban* and *van*. In addition, phonemes may vary across languages with respect to their physical characteristics; for instance, /b/ in French and in English do not have the exact same acoustic properties. Nevertheless, they will be perceived as /b/ sounds in both languages. They are classified as allophones of the same phoneme, since their pronunciation is predictable from their position in the syllable.

In this chapter, we will be paying more attention to systematic, phonological knowledge as illustrated in the examples from the previous paragraph. However, just as in syntactic and morphological investigations, researchers cannot access knowledge straightforwardly, without assessing performance. Therefore, phonological contrasts are also implemented phonetically in both production and perception, and they must be studied through those two types of performance.

7.2 Research questions and models in second language phonology

There are some general research questions that the research in this field is attempting to address. These questions are too wide-ranging to be answered by one or even several experimental studies, but (the beginning of) an answer may emerge as a collective endeavor of many scholars. As in other branches of linguistics, the research questions largely depend on one's theoretical assumptions about how language acquisition proceeds. In the *functionalist* approach (e.g., Ellis & Wulff 2018), very broadly speaking, the L2/Ln language input *alone* drives acquisition. Learners learn from exemplars they encounter and, after a sufficient number of encounters, create associations between a form and its meaning in a given context. Within phonology, this type of learning entails that the phonemic inventory of the L2 (all the phonemic contrasts) has to be identified on the basis of perceiving contrastive phonetic environments and deducing which sounds in the language are contrastive.

The second broad approach to language acquisition, and the one adopted in this book, is the generative, or nativist, approach. Within the realm of phonology, this approach entails that learners, both children learning their native language and adults learning an additional language, come to the task equipped with some innate knowledge. The language faculty contains information about all the features that participate in potential phonemic contrasts (e.g., coronal place of articulation, approximant manner of articulation, vowel space), the possible shapes of syllables and the prosodic system (e.g., principles underlying stress assignment). This universal information aids L1 and L2 learners in the acquisition process by giving them an inventory of potentially relevant features for sound classification and principles of sound combination. In the Optimality Theory constraint-based framework (reference), the constraints or restrictions, with which we evaluate well-formedness and complexity are universal, but their ranking, or relative importance, may vary across languages.

The research concerns in phonology, and specifically in generative phonology, echo some of the concerns of the wider field. For example, scholars debate the influence of the native language, linguistic universals, that is, principles, as well as parameters that describe language variation in a constrained way (e.g., Archibald 1997, 1998). Crosslinguistic influence, or transfer, plays out in an interesting way in phonology. While most scholars recognize that L2 sounds are interpreted through the lens of native sounds, some models consider that influence to have a negative effect. For instance, the Speech Learning Model (SLM; Flege 1995), the Perceptual Assimilation Model (Best 1995) and the Native Language Magnet Theory (Kuhl & Iverson 1995) all describe ways in which the native language may interfere with the new sounds, modulo linguistic experience and other factors. The SLM and the Similarity Differential Rate Hypothesis (Major & Kim 1996) propose that sounds that are dissimilar in the L1 and the L2, while initially difficult, are acquired faster than similar sounds.

7.3 Global foreign accent

We start this section with the widely shared observation that speakers in a second or additional language have a "foreign accent," or they do not pronounce the L2/Ln sounds in the same way as the native speakers (NSs) do. This characteristic of learner speech can affect how well they are being understood by others (intelligibility). Logically speaking, this difference can be due to wrong articulation; that is, learners hear the foreign sounds very well, but they cannot pronounce them that well. Very few scholars give credence to this possibility. The more prevalent view is that learners do not entirely accurately hear or distinguish the L2/Ln phonological or prosodic properties, which would be a necessary prerequisite for acquiring them. Thus, perception is a fundamental obstacle in L2 phonological development, but some articulatory difficulties may persist as well.

What other variables influence global foreign accent? The single most robust finding in the literature is that accent correlates with age of acquisition (AoA).[1] The later the learner is exposed to the second language, the stronger accent they present, even at advanced, stages of acquisition (e.g., Abrahamsson & Hyltenstam 2009; Flege et al. 2006). This type of observation would be compatible with the Critical Period Hypothesis (Johnson & Newport 1989). However, not all scholars are convinced. Ellen Bialystock, for one, conceptualizes this question as whether AoA *causes* a foreign accent or is simply associated with it (Bialystok 1997, 2001).

Global foreign accent experiments typically involve ratings of a number of free-speech samples from groups of speakers. Phonetically untrained native judges listen to samples of interspersed learner and native speech; they are asked to rate the samples on how nativelike they consider them to be. The degree of nativelikeness is usually assessed on a Likert scale, which could have between 3 and 10 levels and frequently 5 or 6 (see Jesney 2004 for a review). The reader should notice that the reference point in evaluating foreign accent is the NS production. Since NS speech varies, a range of scores is established from the NS samples, and that range comprises the boundaries of nativelikeness. Some methodological concerns include how many NS samples to include in the rating task because that proportion has been found to skew results (Flege & Fletcher 1992). The more NS samples included, even up to 50%, the more the L2 learner speech stands out. The consensus is that 10% to 20% NS samples is optimal. The length of each sample also varies significantly among studies, with 10 to 20 seconds considered sufficient. Finally, the sample itself may include more formal speech such as participants reading word lists or casually elicited speech such as a story retelling or a description task. However, if free-speech samples are used in a rating task, other factors such as fluency and grammaticality of the language may intervene in the listeners' ratings.

A classical study in this literature, Munro and Derwing (1995) asked 18 English NSs to listen to excerpts of unrehearsed English speech produced by ten Mandarin NSs and two English NSs. The authors established that most judges displayed significant correlations between the accent ratings and the number of speech errors in the sample. In a later study, Derwing and Munro (1997) used 26 raters who listened to accented speech by Cantonese, Japanese, Polish and Spanish intermediate ESL students. The consistent conclusion was that accentedness, perceived comprehensibility and actual intelligibility were correlated, but the raters evaluated accent the harshest.

A more recent study, Hopp and Schmid (2013), compared the global accent in German of predominantly monolingual NSs, L1 attriters (people who no longer use their native language in a dominant fashion) and advanced L2 learners. The authors asked the German-native raters (n = 140) for a categorical judgment (native sample or not), but also for the raters' confidence in their judgment (on a scale of 1–3). While the results were complex, two findings can be highlighted. First, 37.5% of L2 learners (13 out of 40) fell within the range of monolingual controls, not a negligible percentage. Secondly, there was an overlap of 80% among learner and attriter ratings; in other words, 32 out of 40 learners fell within the range of the L1 attriters, bilingual individuals who had spoken German since birth. These results suggest that global foreign accent is not nearly as categorical as Critical Period proponents might predict. A sizable proportion of bilingual NSs were perceived as non-native, and a sizable proportion of L2 learners were evaluated as nativelike.

In summary, researchers seek to answer a number of different research questions by measuring foreign accents. An important issue is clarifying the relationship between intelligibility and accent at different levels of L2 oral ability; another goal is associating language experience with a foreign accent.

7.4 Speech production

While the global foreign accent is evaluated on the total impression of learners producing second language speech, research on production delves into specific segments, for example, stops, vowels, liquids and suprasegmental properties such as prosody. The literature on this topic is vast, and we cannot do justice here to all the diverse research questions investigated; for an excellent review, see Broselow and Kang (2014).

One research question that falls within the generative agenda is the interplay between native language transfer and linguistic universals in production. Lado's (1957) Contrastive Analysis Hypothesis is the starting point here, predicting that aspects of phonology similar between the L1 and the L2 will be easy to acquire. That turned out not to be the case, with studies attesting patterns of behavior not pertaining to either the L1 or the L2, prompting scholars to look at other explanations. One prominent approach was to look at *markedness* (Eckman 1977, 2008), the idea that some sounds are more basic and typologically more widespread, while others are more complex and rarer. One example of a markedness universal comes from the series of stop consonants: voiceless stops /p, t, k/ are found in more languages than the voiced series /b, d, g/; moreover, if a language does have voiced stops, it is bound to have voiceless ones as well, but not vice versa.

More recently, within Optimality Theory (OT; Prince & Smolensky 2004), markedness is encoded in a different way. In OT, there are two types of constraints. Faithfulness constraints require that the observed surface form (the output) match the underlying or lexical form (the input) in some particular way. Markedness constraints stipulate that less marked structures are favored. Both types of constraints are present in all languages, hence universal, but their ranking differs across languages. Furthermore, constraints may be active or inactive in a language, dialect or even idiolect. Exposure to

L2 data triggers reranking of constraints to better reflect the new grammar (e.g., Broselow 2004; Hancin-Bhatt 2000, 2008).

Production data often differs based on the research questions and on elicitation methods. As discussed above, if learners are asked to read word lists, they produce careful speech; if asked to answer a question or to describe something, they produce extemporaneous speech, which is less formal but also less controlled, in the sense that researchers might not encounter the features they seek to study. To control the production closely, researchers devise clever ways of elicitation. Take, for example, the method in Hancin-Bhatt (2000). Thai imposes greater restrictions on what segments can appear in the coda position of a syllable, compared to English. The researcher investigated whether Thai learners of English are capable of learning the greater or lesser restrictiveness, determined by the reranking of the constraints they needed to produce English-sanctioned codas. She asked Thai learners of English to produce nonce words with simple codas (e.g., *geet, fles, fum*) and complex codas (e.g., *nalt, farf, deerm*). The target words appeared in sentence pairs differing in acceptability; participants had to decide which was the correct sentence. In the examples below, sentence (2) contains a case violation.

1 Mary hopes they are ready to frulm today.
2 Mary hopes them are ready to frulm today.

Participants listened to the sentence pairs and were asked to repeat the sentence they thought was the grammatically correct one. Thus, the judgment task was actually intended to distract them from paying attention to the nonce words, whose production was the actual goal of the researcher. A similar task from Goad and White (2006) is exemplified in Case Study Box 7.1.

Case Study Box 7.1: Goad and White (2006)

Research question: Goad and White set out to test whether Chinese learners of English drop English functional morphology, for example, the *-ed* ending, due to lack of functional category representation in the morphosyntax or due to prosodic constraints on the pronunciation of verb endings. At issue is whether the native prosodic structure can be adapted to the new language.
Task: On a computer screen, the beginning of a sentence appeared, setting up a past or perfective context, as in (a) and (b), respectively.

   a. Last night after dinner

       – you show me photos of your daughter.
       – you showed me photos of your daughter.

> b. My parents can visit me today because
>   – I have cleaned my apartment.
>   – I clean my apartment.
>
> Participants had 12 seconds to choose and memorize the ending they considered appropriate to the context. Once they memorized their choice, they pressed a button to register their response. They then saw a blank screen and produced their choice aloud. Their uttered responses were recorded and transcribed by a trained NS.
>
> ***Stimuli selection:*** Based on earlier research and the goals of their experiment, Goad and White used all monosyllabic verbs as stimuli but selected short-stemmed (with two segments in the rhyme of the syllable, e.g., "wrap" [r.ap]) and long-stemmed shapes (which have three segments in the rhyme, e.g., "help" [h.elp]).
>
> ***Participants:*** Ten intermediate-level Mandarin-speaking learners of English and nine native English-speaking controls.
>
> ***Results:*** The results were reported as percent correct production of the inflection marker. Learners were highly accurate, unlike in a previous experiment (Goad & White 2004) where the task was picture description. The authors suggested that the forced choice task with production may have drawn the learners' attention to the inflection.

In summary, production tasks within a generative approach probe the learner's ability to build mental representations of phonological structure: segments, syllable structure and prosodic structure. Studies often address more general research questions such as whether L2 speakers are capable of creating new mental representations in the second language. Our old friends: age of acquisition, native language structure and language universals are at play again, as we have seen in other chapters of this book.

7.5 Speech perception

Phonetic perception involves the selection and integration of multiple acoustic parameters in order to recognize and categorize separate sounds as tokens of specific language phonemes. Developmental psychologists such as Janet Werker (see review in Werker & Tees 1999) have shown that infants are born with the ability to distinguish all phonetically relevant acoustic properties of speech sounds, even those sounds that do not belong to their native language. It is also experimentally established that children lose this ability somewhere toward the end of the first year of their life. For example, while Hindi- and English-learning six-month-old infants distinguished Hindi dental vs retroflex initial stop consonants, by 11–12 months of age, English-learning infants failed to discriminate the same contrast while Hindi-learning infants continued to perform well (Werker & Tees 1999). What happens when second and third and additional languages are being acquired after the first one?

Solving this puzzle depends on research methods addressing perception. When a researcher wants to establish how target language sounds are perceived, or heard, by a learner, there are two main tasks that they can use: an *identification* task or a *discrimination* task. An identification task gauges how well a learner can identify or classify L2 sounds. A discrimination task asks a slightly different question: can the learner distinguish between two members of an L2 contrast, say the /b/ and /v/ sounds in English? Remember, this can be a contrast that does not exist in the native language (e.g., Spanish), so it is not a given that a learner should hear that difference.

7.5.1 Identification tasks

In an identification task, research participants listen to some stimuli, which could be sounds or syllables or words or sentences, and they have to select a response on a piece of paper or on a computer screen. If the response choices are given in the learners' native language, the task involves matching, or mapping, what learners hear to the written choices. This matching is based on the similarity between the L1 and L2 sounds; therefore, the task is also known as a *perceptional assimilation task*. For example, this task was used in an experiment with Catalan-speaking learners of English by Cebrian, Mora and Aliaga-Garcia (2010). The researchers wanted to compare the perception of ten English vowels (/i ɪ ɛ æ ɑ ɜ ʌ ɒ ɔ u/) and two diphthongs (/eɪ/, /əʊ/) of British English, with seven monophthongs (/i e ɛ a ɔ o u/) and four diphthongs (/ai/, /ei/, /au/, /ou/) of Eastern Catalan. The vowels appeared always in the same environment: /b/-Vowel-/t/. As the context created some nonwords in both languages, the carrier sentences were of this shape: *Rima amb dit* 'It rhymes with ....' The stimuli were recorded by a number of NSs residing around London and Barcelona. After hearing the English stimuli, the learners had to label them according to the Catalan vowel categories and rate them for goodness of fit on a scale of 1 to 7. Such a rating task commonly accompanies identification and adds a matching and evaluation dimension: this native sound is an excellent exemplar/poor exemplar of the L2 sound. Some frameworks, such as the Perceptual Assimilation Model (Best 1995), ascribe formal status to "category-goodness" based on assimilation behavior and perceptual sensitivity.

Within the area of prosodic systems, including stress, pitch accent, tone and intonation, identification tasks aim to discover whether a different type of prosody registers on hearers. For example, Kijak (2009) investigated whether learners of L2 Polish from different language backgrounds are sensitive to stress. In Polish, lexical stress falls on the penultimate (last but one) syllable regardless of the number and quantity (heavy or light) of syllables. In her perception experiment, Kijak played research participants nonce words that obeyed phonotactic and stress rules of Polish. In other words, they could be words newly entered into the language. If participants heard *gadíma* with penultimate stress, their answer sheet gave them the following options to choose from (the accent mark identifies the stressed syllable)

3 a *gá.di.ma*   b *ga.dí.ma*   c *ga.di.má*

The study results (correct identification) demonstrated that the performance of the Polish L2 learners (see Figure 7.1) was heavily dependent on their native language, with French and Chinese learners having the most difficulty. Notice that the Polish NSs are themselves only 65% accurate. In addition, the effect of proficiency was much less straightforward.

There are several types of information linguists want to extract from this type of task. First, identification tasks can be used to ascertain the perceptual

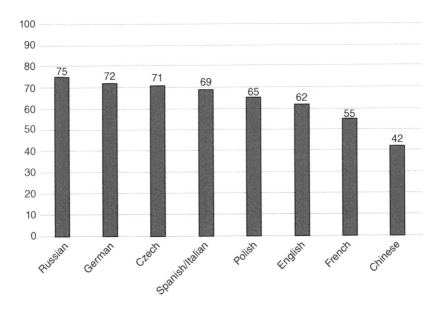

FIGURE 7.1 Percentage correct identification of Polish stress by different groups of speakers, modified from Kijak's 2009 figure 1, p. 139.

similarity of L1 and L2 sounds and prosodic structures, even for beginner learners. Second, and with more advanced learners, identification tasks can be useful in establishing whether the perception of the L2 sounds and structures varies as a function of learner experience with that language. The goodness-of-fit rating can also be used to predict how easy or how difficult it is going to be for the new sounds to be acquired (as argued, for example, by the Perceptual Assimilation Model, Best 1995; Best & Tyler 2007). The goodness-of-fit rating also reveals sensitivity to within-category differences in an identification task. If participants label two items with the same category, this choice might be interpreted as a failure to distinguish between the items. However, if they attribute different goodness-of-fit judgments to the items, then researchers can infer that listeners recognize differences between them.

In identification tasks, as in all other linguistic tasks, the response options available to the research participants should be carefully considered. A recent study, Benders, Escudero and Sjerps (2012), showed that perception is influenced by the response categories available to consider. The number of response options has implications for the statistical analysis of the data; for example, choosing between two options and among five options is not equally hard. It is also possible to provide an "other" choice, so that the participant does not feel forced to choose between options unless that is a specific feature of the research design.

7.5.2 Discrimination tasks

Another way to gauge perception is through a discrimination task. In this task, learners are not asked to identify but to compare two or more sounds presented on a single trial. The task is intuitive in the sense that participants do not need to explicitly know or name the nature of the similarities or differences of the stimuli. A simple version is called the AX task. Sounds from the target language appear in carrier syllables, words or sentences, and the participant is asked whether the two stimuli sound the same, AA, or different, AB. Let us consider how this task was applied in Brown (1998). The author wanted to establish whether Japanese and Chinese-native learners of English perceived the /l/-/r/ contrast, deemed to be difficult for Japanese speakers. The participants heard a minimal pair of natural English monosyllabic words such as *rip* and *lip*, spoken by a NS. The sounds under investigation appeared in three different syllable positions: in the onset (*lake* and *rake*), in a complex onset (*flute* and *fruit*) and in coda position (*pail* and *pair*), six pairs for each position. Word pairs without the /l/-/r/ contrast (*light* and *night*) (n = 7) were included as a means of checking that poor performance on the task was not due to difficulty with the task itself, as well as to distract from the main contrast. More importantly, identical pair foils also appeared (*lice* and *lice*, *rock* and *rock*) (n = 17).

Participants have to perceive there to be a genuine judgment necessary, with some pairs *light* and *night* clearly different and others such as *night* and *night* clearly the same.

Those participants who answer Different all the time are exposed as not paying attention to the task. If participants respond correctly to the foil items, they show they are making judgments based on fine acoustic cues. This task can be made more taxing if it is "speeded"; that is, reactions of less than 500 ms are encouraged and longer decision times are cut off. Another interesting manipulation is of the inter-stimulus interval (ISI), effectively the duration of the pause between the A item and the X item. When the ISI is quite short (250 msec), discrimination is easier and listeners have access to fine acoustic detail; with long ISIs (1,500 msec) listeners must depend on phonologically encoded representations to render a judgment.

The AX discrimination task we discussed in the previous paragraph is considered to be the least taxing to the memory of the participants. As the listener has to retain an auditory memory of the first word (A) to compare to the second (X), stimulus variation, or uncertainty, makes the experimental task harder (Strange & Shafer 2008). Even in this optimally simple task, researchers have attested response bias (more false Same answers than false Different answers), as it is hard to know what each participant considers to be a relevant difference to discriminate between sounds. Response bias in this case refers to individual differences in performance that are not based on the acoustic characteristics of the investigated sounds.[2]

To minimize response bias, research has introduced more complex three-way discrimination. The following designs have been used: ABX, AXB, Oddball and Oddity. In an ABX task, A and B are tokens of different phonetic categories and X is the same as A or B; after listening to all three stimuli (retaining auditory traces of them), the listener specifies whether X = A or X = B. In the AXB variation of this task, again A and B are tokens of different phonetic categories, and X is the comparison stimulus. Let us take an example from a study on L2 Arabic, Shehata (2018). In the perception experiment of this study, 20 monosyllabic Consonant-Vowel-Consonant Arabic nonwords were used as stimuli. The tokens comprised ten minimal pairs contrasting the target Arabic phonemes (i.e., /t-t̪/, /d-d̪/, /θ-ð/, /ð-ð̪/, /s-s̪/, /h-ħ/, /k-q/, /ʔ-ʕ/, /χ-ɣ/ and /ħ-ʕ/) in onset position (e.g., /daːk-d̪aːk/). As the stimuli were not real words, the tokens were quite uniform and no lexical access was involved. Participants heard three nonwords (A, X and B) and decided whether the second (X) was more similar to the first (A) or the third (B). Four test items were generated for each of the ten contrasts, as exemplified below in (4).

4 AAB /taːk/, /taːk/, /ṭaːk/
  ABB /taːk/, /ṭaːk/, /ṭaːk/
  BAA /ṭaːk/, /taːk/, /taːk/
  BBA /ṭaːk/, /ṭaːk/, /taːk/

This design structure resulted in 40 contrasts altogether, each presented four times in blocks. Test items were randomized per block. Responses were registered by pressing a computer key. Note that this task is cognitively more demanding than the AX task, as it has increased memory load as well as high stimulus uncertainty.

The Oddball task, also known as a Category Change task, takes a leaf from the playbook of infant speech perception. Experimental tasks with babies allow the infant to hear a stream of syllables and respond by either looking at a visual stimulus or sucking on a pacifier. When the acoustic stream changes in some detectable way, babies produce a reaction, for example, intensified sucking on the pacifier (Eimas, Siqueland, Jusczyk, & Vigorito 1971). This is how researchers know that the baby distinguishes the two sounds in their carrier syllable. The Oddball task uses the same effect, with modifications for adults. L2 learners are exposed to sounds of one category, the background one. Interspersed with the baseline sounds are sounds from another, change category. Participants are asked to signal when they perceive the change. From the point of view of memory load and stimulus uncertainty, this task is similar to the AX perception task. Versions of this design are now being used in brain imaging tasks where continuous stimulus presentation is important, e.g., fMRI.

Finally, in an Oddity task, participants hear three stimuli in a row and are asked to choose which of the three is different, or alternately, that they are all the same. Daidone (2020) used an Oddity task as one of a battery of tasks to make sure that her research participants discriminate between the sounds before she could probe their lexical representation. If the participants heard [nerra-nera-nerra], they were expected to indicate that the second stimulus was different. Control and filler items representing other contrasts were also included. The Oddity task is considered a cognitively more demanding task in comparison with other perception tasks such as AX or ABX (Strange & Shafer 2008) and therefore less likely to result in ceiling effects for the easier contrasts. Another advantage is that the chance level is lower in an Oddity task (25%) compared to an AX or ABX task (50%). Daidone and Darcy (2021) used a response schema with three differently colored robots representing different answers and an X picture standing for "The sounds are the same."

How do researchers report the responses in perception tasks? Accuracy is one metric, but d' (d-prime) is considered to be a superior metric. D' is a measure of an individual's ability to detect signals; more specifically, a measure of sensitivity or discriminability that factors in response bias by including relative proportions of "hits," "misses" and "false alarms" in the equation (for instance, a tendency to answer Different).

7.5.3 How to create stimuli

The type of stimuli used in speech research can be broadly categorized as falling in either the natural or the synthetic type, although hybrid stimuli do exist as well. Naturally produced stimuli are recorded from the natural speech production of a talker and as such they represent most closely sounds "in the wild," without any control of features or parameters. Such stimuli are used in global accent research, for example, where speech samples are further evaluated by native listeners. In addition, some discrimination and identification tasks rely on stimuli produced by NSs. Such speech samples should be recorded in a sound-attenuated room using the best recording equipment that is available.

Computer-synthesized, or synthetic, stimuli are constructed from scratch to test various perceptual or production research questions. A widely used software application for synthesizing is Praat (created by Paul Boersma and David Weenink, link). Synthetic stimuli are used when tight control of temporal or spectral parameters of the stimuli is needed, such as when investigating whether vowel duration and formant frequencies affect L2 learners differently from natives (Flege et al. 1997). A concern with such stimuli is their ecological validity. They sound quite different from the natural speech L2 learners are exposed to and so may not be able to represent natural categories.

When creating stimuli for perception studies, a variable that researchers keep in mind is the number of speakers recording the natural stimuli. The choice of single-talker or multiple-talker designs generally depends on whether researchers want to tap abstract categorical representations and side-step consistent acoustic cues present in the speech of a single-talker or whether they want to assess what listeners are capable of, even with the added complexities introduced with multiple talkers. Higher variability due to recording different speakers is likely to be reflected in lower learner accuracy, since learners will have to abstract away from more acoustic parameters, as compared to one speaker. This is because recorded speakers might vary in age, education and gender; as a consequence, their speech will be acoustically diverse. This issue can be mitigated by creating stimulus blocks where speaker variation is kept to a minimum. However, all stimuli within a block and all blocks should be randomized across individual participants, to avoid presentation order effects.

7.6 Linguistic universals in phonology

As we discussed at the outset of this chapter, generative L2 phonology argues that not all acquisition is completely dependent on information learners get from the input signal. A role for language universals is also postulated. In Case Study Box 7.2, we summarize a study by Özçelik and Sprouse (2017), which addresses an innate locality constraint that is exemplified in non-canonical vowel harmony in L2 Turkish. At issue is whether learners can take advantage of a universal constraint that is not supported by classroom instruction and for which evidence in the input is quite rare.

Case Study Box 7.2: Özçelik and Sprouse (2017)

Background: Looking at vowel harmony in L2 Turkish, Özçelik and Sprouse test a constraint on non-canonical vowel harmony. Vowels in Turkish suffixes are specified for the feature [±high] only. They receive their full specification in harmony with the root vowel. Non-canonical vowel harmony involves borrowed and newly coined words where the typical process is disrupted, and the lateral segment /l/ is pre-specified as clear [l] or dark [ɫ]. An innate locality constraint then ascertains that /l/can trigger vowel harmony on its own.

Research question: The authors set out to investigate the role of Universal Grammar and, more specifically, the role of this innate phonological principle, in non-native acquisition. The constraint is not taught and is underrepresented in the input.

Task: Participants were presented with uninflected Turkish nouns or pseudo-nouns. They were asked to choose the correct variant of the nominal suffix from among four or two options, depending on whether the suffix contained a [+high] vowel (four allomorphs) (half of the items) or a [−high] vowel (two allomorphs) (the other half of the items).

Stimuli selection: The stimuli tested every logically possible combination of stem vowel + suffix vowel. There were 16 stimuli in each of 16 conditions (e.g., i–i, o–u, ö–ü), of which 8 were experimental (words that ended in /l/) and 8 were fillers ending in other consonants.

Presentation mode: All uninflected nouns or pseudo-nouns were presented auditorily. Half of the stimuli (both experimental and filler words) were presented auditorily only, and participants had to choose the correct suffix from among choices presented on a computer screen. The other half of the stimuli were presented both auditorily and visually; for these items, participants were instructed to also read the stimuli, in addition to listening to them, before choosing the correct option.

Participants: 34 English-native learners of Turkish and a comparison group of 14 native Turkish speakers.

Results: The results were reported as proportion of participants' correct suffix choices, as a dependent variable. The independent variables were mode of presentation (whether the stimuli were presented only auditorily or orthographically as well) and level of proficiency. All learner groups, irrespective of their level of proficiency, performed more accurately in the "auditory only" condition, suggesting an effect of orthography in the acquisition process. Learners had largely acquired the knowledge that the lateral /l/ can be a harmony trigger in Turkish, knowledge that could not have come from instruction, input or L1 transfer.

7.7 Conclusion

As you will have appreciated in this chapter, research tasks investigating phonology, the system of mental representations of sounds and prosody in the mind of learners, are quite different from those tasks that probe syntax or semantics. Nevertheless, common research variables include native language influence and linguistic universals. However, there is also a crucial difference between L2 acquisition of sounds and morphosyntax: the interplay between phonetics (mastery of articulatory routines) and phonology (acquiring features and representations). Phonetics has no counterpart in morphosyntax, in the sense that learners do not perceive phrases and sentences based on some surface form, distinct from a deeper representation. As pointed out cogently by Broselow and Kang (2014), the problem of separating phonological from phonetic explanations in L2 acquisition is far from trivial (see also Archibald 2009). It appears that there are distinct acquisition tasks facing the learner: representations, constraints and operations like harmony or assimilation being phonological; articulatory settings and acoustic correlates being phonetic. Acquisition at each level could well be distinct, if not independent.

7.8 Discussion questions

1 Consider the research design from Goad and White (2006) presented in Case Study Box 7.1. If the learners in this study, Chinese NSs, were joined by Dutch NSs, would you expect different results? What other information would you need to know to answer the question?

2 What stimuli would you use to test knowledge of English interdental fricatives [θ] and [ð] in the interlanguage of German NSs?
3 Explain in your own words how you understand the points made in the conclusion: (a) that the interplay of phonetics and phonology complicates the interpretation of results obtained from different tasks; and (b) that there is no counterpart of phonetics in morphosyntax. You may disagree with claim (b) and indeed find a parallel between phonetics and some functional morphology acquisition processes. This is an open question where arguments for and against a certain position will help you to understand the fundamentals of acquisition processes.

Notes

1 For some authors, AoA stands for "age of arrival," since they consider full immersion in the language to be crucial for immigrant populations (Johnson & Newport 1989).
2 Experiments also vary in whether "same" trials contain the identical audio file repeated twice, in which case there is no physical difference whatsoever between the items and "false alarms" reflect response bias, and two separate recordings of the same item, in which case false alarms may reflect judgments based on acoustic cues not relevant to the contrast.

Further reading

Broselow, E., & Kang, Y. (2014). Second language phonology and speech. In J. Herschensohn & M. Young-Scholten (Eds.), *The Cambridge handbook of second language acquisition* (pp. 529–553). Cambridge: Cambridge University Press.

Colantoni, L., Steele, J., & Escudero, P. (1915). *Second language speech: theory and practice*. Cambridge: Cambridge University Press.

Strange, W., & Shafer, V. L. (2008) Speech perception in second language learners: The re-education of selective perception. In J. G. Hansen Edwards & M. L. Zampini (Eds.), *Phonology and second language acquisition* (pp. 153-191). Amsterdam: John Benjamins.

8
LATENCY-BASED MEASURES

8.1 Latency-based measures

In this chapter, we give an overview of methods that have been used to investigate sentence processing and produce response latencies, or reaction times, since these behavioral indices are some of the most frequently used in psychological and psycholinguistic studies. Response latency refers to the length of time between administering a stimulus to a research participant and the participant's response to that stimulus. Although there are notable exceptions—for example, research using eye-tracking equipment that can cost tens of thousands of dollars—latency-based methods have been enduringly popular because they allow for reaction times to be economically and reliably recorded with equipment that is widely available: a personal computer outfitted with the appropriate software. While none of the methods discussed here were specifically developed to investigate L2/Ln acquisition, there is wide agreement that these can elucidate parts of the acquisition process in ways that offline methodologies cannot, which is partly why these methods have enjoyed a growing currency within L2 research (Marsden et al. 2018).

Many behavioral tasks fall under the rubric of latency-based methods, but here we limit ourselves to three methods that have been frequently used in GenSLA research to study sentence processing: Self-paced reading, self-paced listening, and cross-modal priming. However, many of the principles that we discuss in the chapter are pertinent to research that records latencies in general, since many of these methods share common assumptions about what reaction times can index and how these can be

DOI: 10.4324/9781003160762-10

used to answer research questions about sentence processing specifically, and about language acquisition in general. Although a great variety of research questions regarding language acquisition can be addressed with these methodologies, many studies have focused on the processing of sentences.

Apart from word decoding—mapping the aural or written input to a language user's stored lexical representations—*sentence processing* broadly entails recognizing syntactic structures so that these can be integrated in real time, allowing speakers to construct meaning. Historically, the study of sentence processing has had a strong emphasis on methodology because, as Nicol et al. (2006) aptly note, the study of sentence comprehension is *inferential*, meaning that researchers must find non-direct ways to tap into mental, implicit processes. As we will see in this chapter, latency-based measures offer many such opportunities, although task characteristics should be carefully weighed, since these affect the data we derive from these measures. In the words of Nicol and colleagues, language researchers must thus "attempt to maximally reflect underlying sentence processing details while minimizing effects introduced by the task" (Nicol et al. 2006: 216).

Because sentence comprehension is typically accomplished in an incremental fashion and inside a few hundred milliseconds, models of language processing must account for the speed with which language users seamlessly and incrementally integrate morphosyntactic, semantic, pragmatic, prosodic, and contextual information to interpret language strings (Leal & Shea 2018). Presently, although most researchers of sentence processing agree that all these information types are at play during comprehension, there are differences in terms of the proposed *timing* of their availability during processing.

For instance, a debated issue in this context has been the importance and timing of syntactic information in sentence processing. While some proposals place syntax in a privileged position (e.g., Frazier's *Construal* account; see Frazier & Clifton 1996), others propose no such special consideration for the accessibility and use of syntactic information, such that syntactic, contextual, semantic, and probabilistic information should all affect parsing in parallel, from the earliest stages of sentence processing (e.g., such as in *Constraint Satisfaction* models; see MacDonald et al. 1994, Spivey & Tanenhaus 1998; Tanenhaus & Trueswell 1995; a.o). Within L2/Ln acquisition studies, only a few have focused on testing these competing hypotheses, however. An example of such an investigation was conducted by Jegerski (2012), who focused on the processing of subject–object ambiguities using a self-paced reading task and found support for Frazier's Construal account.

Moving beyond the potential centrality of syntactic information, Juffs and Rodríguez (2014) have noted that L2/Ln research on sentence processing has been based largely on formal grammar descriptions of one variety or another, particularly those proposed by generative linguists first under the Principles and Parameters framework (Chomsky & Lasnik 1993) and, more recently, under the tenets of the Minimalist Program (Chomsky 1995). This situation should not be surprising, since formal theories have been particularly adept at describing and explaining the system of L2/Ln abstract knowledge, paying special attention to the way this knowledge is represented in the minds of learners. Research in this vein has historically given heed to a handful of constructions and phenomena, most notably (verbal) argument structure, long-distance dependencies, relative clauses and relative clause attachment, and noun phrases and agreement. Overall, as summarized by Hopp (2022), we find that research in L2 processing has shown that learners process sentences in the same way as L1 speakers do, except learners "tend to make *attenuated* use of grammatical information and prediction" (p. 243; our emphasis).

Although during the past two decades, latency-based methods have become increasingly common in GenSLA research, these are hardly new tools. Studies using methods such as self-paced reading date to the mid-70s for L1 research on reading mechanisms and even earlier for eye-tracking, although only in the 1980s was the technology common and convenient enough to use video-based eye-trackers (Singh & Singh 2012). Yet for all their popularity among psycholinguists studying L1 comprehension, these tools were not used in L2 research until decades later, as we will see momentarily.

Before delving into more detail regarding the methods, we should talk about some advantages that these bring about. Minimally, latency-based methods offer researchers two clear advantages: (a) they can be used to investigate language incrementally, as it unfolds, and (b) these methods are thought to tap into more implicit processes. Studying language incrementally became a focus for psycholinguists because a clear takeaway of early research in L1 processing using self-paced reading is that sentence processing transpires in an incremental, word-by-word fashion (Just & Carpenter 1980). This finding led researchers to utilize online methods, which measure comprehension while language is being processed, rather than offline methods because the latter could only offer insight into responses once the language had already been processed (van Gompel 2013).

In terms of the implicit/explicit debate, Jegerski (2014: 28) notes that within L2 studies, latency-based methods such as self-paced reading are typically understood as a "more direct or more implicit measure of grammar than offline judgments" because such methods impose time constraints that restrict participants from turning to explicit grammar rules that might (or not) be internalized.

Finally, we should mention that latency-based methods have been instrumental in testing GenSLA hypotheses such as the Interface Hypothesis (IH) (Sorace 2011) or the Shallow Structure Hypothesis (SSH) (Clahsen & Felser 2006), which predict that L1–L2 processing differences will be most evident with such methodologies.

8.2 Latency-based methods and L2 and GenSLA studies

The use of latency-based methods has a long tradition in GenSLA studies. In fact, the first investigation using self-paced reading in L2 was a GenSLA study on subject and object long-distance extraction that aimed to determine the specific regions of processing difficulty depending on the site of the extraction of a *wh*-word (Juffs & Harrington 1995).

Moreover, Rothman and Slabakova (2018: 431) propose that the notion of Universal Grammar itself can logically be derived from the idea that processing and grammatical representations are closely and complexly linked. Historical connections aside, however, GenSLA studies have also used recent findings from psycholinguistics to address existing claims about L2 acquisition and development, as well as to propose new explanations of the nature of L2 linguistic competence. As an example of a proposed explanation, let's take the SSH (Clahsen & Felser 2006), which proposes that sentence processing in L1 and L2 are qualitatively different. While L1 processing is purported to make use of "complete" underlying representations, L2 processing may use incomplete representations, which may "prevent learners from successfully establishing syntactic dependencies on-line" (Clahsen & Felser 2006: 21). In a similar vein, the IH suggests L2 speakers may have difficulty incorporating information from external modules such as discourse into their computation (Sorace 2011). Because the SSH and IH propose that these differences may arise during online processing, the hypothesis has spurred increased interest in studying L2 (online) processing (Keating & Jegerski 2015).

Many studies have shown that a learner's first language can influence their L2/Ln processing, in terms of transfer of both processing strategies and the grammatical knowledge used to process language. Yet there are additional ways, perhaps idiosyncratic to the processing of languages beyond the first, in which L1–L2 processing may be different. Hopp (2022) notes at least three such ways. The first is that the L2 cognitive architecture may itself be "noisier" (Hopp 2022: 236), which may cause processing to proceed more slowly and be more effortful and prone to error. This is not surprising because L2 speakers may face challenges deploying and integrating grammatical information in real time, since they likely operate under limited working memory and other cognitive resources (e.g., Dekydtspotter &

Renaud 2014). The second way is that L2/Ln learners might place different weights for a given processing constraint or may rely on processing heuristics that are incomplete or less detailed. Finally, there is the possibility that maturational constraints, typically associated with the Critical Period, might place certain restrictions on the grammatical processing system such that L2 learners may rely, instead, on explicit knowledge while processing. While extant research has yet to disentangle the factors behind L1–L2 differences, it does indicate that learners are less efficient at predicting upcoming linguistic elements, although this may very well indicate differences in how useful certain cues are in L2 processing (see Hopp 2022).

In this brief opening section, we have merely scratched the surface of current sentence processing in GenSLA, since we have not touched upon many topics of relevance, including the importance of individual factors such as differences in working memory, lexical knowledge, or morphological knowledge (e.g., Hopp 2013; Slabakova 2019).

In what follows, we will briefly summarize the three methods that are the focus of this chapter: self-paced reading, eye-tracking, and cross-modal priming.

8.3 Self-paced reading

Like other psycholinguistic methods focusing on measuring online comprehension, self-paced reading allows researchers to measure the time that it takes a participant to read/process a given segment of text (in milliseconds). These can be single words or "segments" (phrases, or parts of phrases, as selected by the researcher). The name of the method comes from the fact that the experiment allows for participants themselves to determine how long a particular segment appears on a computer screen, since participants are required to press a button so that the next segment of text appears. The choice of segment vs. word is typically related to the research question, the L1/L2 combination under study (e.g., whether the languages are agglutinative or not, but should also consider readability and other issues related to ecological validity). As Stowe and Kaan (2006) note, care should be taken so that each condition or version of an item is comparable. Furthermore, the choice of segment length should be influenced by factors such as a word's length, log-frequency, or its plausibility in context.[1] What is crucial to note is that these segments, across all the conditions in the study, should be comparable in as many of these dimensions as possible.

Self-paced reading is a flexible tool because it allows for different options when presenting the text on a computer screen, although some presentations have clear drawbacks. One of the most frequently used modes of presentation in L2 studies is the *non-cumulative* presentation, whereby segments are presented such that only one segment at a time can be read, while the rest of the sentence is masked (typically with hyphens). In *cumulative* presentations, the text that appears on the screen stays unmasked, allowing participants to potentially re-read segments. A downside of this presentation option is that the researchers cannot exactly determine whether participants are reading or re-reading, and unlike what eye-tracking allows researchers to uncover, we do not know which word is being read among those available. Early adopters of the method, such as Just et al. (1982), used several presentation modes to determine their comparability with normal reading and noted that, in the cumulative presentation, some participants developed undesirable strategies such as pushing response buttons to read several segments at once, rather than reading them individually (thus rendering individual latencies meaningless). Thus, it appears that the non-cumulative presentation mode has some advantages.

In terms of alignment, most self-paced reading studies present the text in a *linear* fashion either from left to right or from right to left, depending on the language, mimicking normal reading (e.g., English would be presented left to right, Hebrew right to left). Researchers may also choose *centered* displays, where segments appear in a non-cumulative fashion at the center of the screen. Just et al. (1982), however, also showed that left-aligned, non-cumulative presentations more closely resembled normal reading (when compared with gaze durations using eye-tracking). Finally, self-paced reading tasks can also include a moving or non-moving discourse context (i.e., text that precedes the experimental sentence), which is especially pertinent for studies that focus on the processing of information-structure categories such as Topic or Focus (Leal, in print). Figure 8.1 shows a non-cumulative, left-aligned self-paced reading trial from Leal and Hoot (2022). This study is described in Case Study Box 8.1.

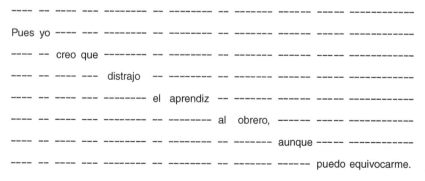

FIGURE 8.1 Self-paced reading trial modified from Leal and Hoot (2022).

Most self-paced reading tasks include a secondary behavioral task. These tasks typically consist of a (Yes/No) comprehension question, although some studies can include acceptability judgment tasks with discrete choices (e.g., grammatical, ungrammatical) or with Likert-scale choices. Because the software used to code these types of experiments is increasingly flexible, other secondary tasks could be devised and implemented. Care should be taken with the design of these tasks, however, since the type of task could potentially affect participants' behavior in experimental trials (see, e.g., Leeser et al. 2011, for discussion). Although some researchers have made use of the behavioral data from these secondary tasks, they can also function as distractors to help mask the primary purpose of the experiment (Jegerski 2014). In terms of their timing, secondary tasks can appear after every trial or following a certain number of trials, typically in a randomized fashion. Finally, some researchers use these secondary tasks as a measure of attention, discarding either trials or participants when these questions are missed. Although some researchers choose to discard experimental trials where the comprehension question was answered incorrectly, this might not always be the appropriate choice, since Tokowicz and MacWhinney (2005) have shown that participants' accuracy and grammatical sensitivity might not be closely linked.

8.2.1 Data that is elicited with the method

The main data from self-paced reading tasks, in raw form, are the reaction times per word/segment for each item. It is crucial to note, however, that these reaction times can only be understood *in comparison* to other segments, which is why the design of self-paced reading tasks should be highly controlled such that every condition in the study should vary only in the dimensions that are to be measured.[2]

As we saw in Chapters 2 and 4, (quasi-)experiments include "conditions" or versions of a single item (lexicalization), so that researchers can infer a relationship of the type *cause-and-effect*, if and when significant differences between conditions are registered. In self-paced reading, researchers typically select a "control" condition against which other conditions will be compared. This is because the interpretation of self-paced reading tasks, like many latency-based methods, relies on the assumption that longer reading times (when compared to a control condition) index processing difficulties or syntactic reanalysis. This crucial comparison is illustrated in Case Study Box 8.1.

Case Study Box 8.1: Leal and Hoot (2022)

Research question: Leal and Hoot tested whether L1 English learners of L2 Spanish showed evidence of processing (discourse) contextual restrictions in real time, which is predicted to be difficult by the IH (Sorace 2011). Leal and Hoot focused on two infrequent, V-initial sentences in Spanish (VSO vs. VOS) in contexts biasing for either subject or object focus. According to syntactic descriptions, the focused constituent (the answer to the question) should be the last element in the answer. Consequently, VOS sentences are felicitous under subject focus context (when the subject is roughly "new," non-presupposed, non-retrievable information), while VSO is felicitous under object focus. Thus, the felicitous conditions (VOS under subject focus and VSO under object focus contexts) constituted the control condition. At issue is whether learners can integrate syntactic and information-structure information in real time, unlike what the IH predicts for late sequential, highly advanced bilinguals (Sorace 2011).

Task (only the self-paced reading task is reported here): non-cumulative, left-aligned self-paced reading task with a preceding discourse context. 2 × 2 factorial design with *Word Order* (VSO/VOS) and *Focus* (subject/object) as factors. The critical region (segments 3–5) was preceded by two segments (1–2) and followed by two more (6–7) (Table 8.1).

TABLE 8.1 Self-paced reading task design with predictions for RTs, Leal and Hoot (2022), critical region

	Subject focus context *Who distracted the worker?*	Object focus context *Whom did the apprentice distract?*
VSO	Distrajo el aprendiz al obrero # (slower)	Distrajo el aprendiz al obrero ✓ (faster)
VOS	Distrajo al obrero el aprendiz ✓ (faster)	Distrajo al obrero el aprendiz # (slower)

Distrajo el aprendiz al obrero
 distracted the apprentice$_{NOM}$ to-the worker$_{ACC}$
 "The apprentice distracted the worker."

Stimuli selection: Because the canonical order in Spanish (SVO) fits almost any information-structure situation, only V-initial orders were used to create the factorial design. The study included 32 experimental items

> (8 per condition) in a Latin Square design. Noun phrases were controlled for syllable length, animacy, specificity, syntactic category, and reversibility in context.
> **Participants:** 76 L1 English-L2 Spanish speakers (late sequential bilinguals) and 42 monolingual L1 Spanish controls.
> **Results:** In the critical region, a test of fixed effects revealed a significant Focus*Order interaction. Follow-up Bonferroni-corrected post hoc pairwise comparisons conducted revealed that VOS was read significantly faster in subject focus contexts and VSO was read significantly faster in object focus contexts, compared to the opposite context. Because no group differences were attested (either as main effects or as interactions), the authors concluded that the processing of information focus in Spanish did not pose insurmountable difficulties when processing syntax-discourse constraints in real time.

Before we explore how stimuli are created, we should briefly note a peculiarity about reaction times. Because there is a limit on how fast we can react to a stimulus (e.g., there is a threshold on how fast we can decode/interpret word strings), reaction times tend to be positively skewed. In other words, when we plot reaction times, we will find that the distribution will be longer on the right side of the graph than on the left, which effectively means that our data will not be normally distributed. Since normality assumptions underlie most inferential statistics, many researchers use log transformations to analyze their data.[3]

8.2.2 How to create stimuli?

Stimuli must be carefully constructed in self-paced reading tasks because means are calculated per condition, collapsing across items. Because reaction times in these tasks are sensitive to word length and log frequency, items are typically controlled for length (e.g., number of syllables), frequency, and other relevant factors, depending on the aims of the study (e.g., syntactic category, syntactic function, animacy, plausibility, gender). Since the results of self-paced reading tasks are typically presented as line graphs where each word/segment and condition are graphed, researchers typically construct items that are identical except for what is called the *region of interest* or the *critical region*, which is where we expect to see differences by condition. In addition, researchers typically analyze what is called the *spillover* region, i.e., the region directly following the critical one, which is analyzed for any delayed effects (an outcome typically found in L2/Ln studies).

In addition, as noted by Just et al. (1982), non-cumulative self-paced reading tasks (when compared to eye-tracking with text) are disproportionately sensitive to factors such as word novelty and first mention of the topic. Furthermore, they show elevated sentence *wrap-up effects*, since the last word/segment in the experimental presentation typically evinces much higher latencies than expected. Thus, researchers usually avoid placing critical segments at the end of sentences. Similarly, researchers typically avoid placing critical regions at the *outset* of the sentence, to avoid any potential issues with involuntary responses. The choice of methodology must consider these characteristics.

In self-paced reading tasks, stimuli are typically presented in a Latin Square design, which is generally viewed as an efficient, although incomplete, design because it allows researchers to optimize the amount of information they can derive from a study by minimizing the number of experimental units needed (Grant 1948; Kutner et al. 2005). Following the visual presentation of Stowe and Kaan (2006), let us imagine that we have an experiment where we have four conditions: a, b, c, and d. Because each condition in self-paced reading tasks is typically identical to the others except for the critical region, we must ensure that participants are not exposed to all four conditions, which would be repetitive at best and confusing at worst.

To use a Latin Square, we would construct four lists (I, II, III, IV), where each list contains every item (lexicalization), but in one condition per item (that is, one version of the item). If we cross an identical number of lists with an identical number of conditions, we have a Latin Square (4 conditions × 4 lists), which will accomplish our task. In Figure 8.2, imagine an experiment with four conditions (a, b, c, and d), with eight items (1–8), which we have arranged into four lists (I, II, III, IV).

Now, we would want for each list to have a comparable number of participants, so we would ensure that we have 30 participants per list (30 participants per list x 4 lists = 120 total participants). We have to gather data from at least 120 participants.

List I	List II	List III	List IV
1a	1b	1c	1d
2b	2c	2d	2a
3c	3d	3a	3b
4d	4a	4b	4c
5a	5b	5c	5d
6b	6c	6d	6a
7c	7d	7a	7b
8d	8a	8b	8c

FIGURE 8.2 A Latin Square presentation of a study with four conditions and eight total items/lexicalizations.

We should note several things at this point: first, each list includes every item, such that every list has the numbers 1–8, which represent each lexicalization. Further, we should note that Figure 8.2 is a simplified version of an experiment because although we don't have a fixed guideline for how many items we need, Keating and Jegerski (2015) have recommended including 8–12 items per condition. Mardsen et al. (2018), however, note that few studies in their database actually met this threshold (15 of the 44 studies analyzed), which led them to underscore the need for more standardized practices. Following our example above, because we have four conditions, we would need a minimum of 32 items (8 items per condition × 4 conditions).

If we present each version of an item to our participants, they would see 128 experimental stimuli, without counting the necessary fillers. If we present our participants with only *one* version of each item, as in the Latin Square design, the number of experimental items to which a participant would be exposed to would drop down to 32 (one per lexicalization). Thus, it is easy to see why Latin Square designs are often used in these situations, when each participant can only receive one treatment (in this case, one condition of our experiment). Additionally, there is the non-trivial issue that we would not want to expose a single participant to four versions of each item because of the strong priming effects that this exposure would bring about. Such a practice could completely negate the purpose of the experiment, since the effects of the manipulation would not be able to be differentiated from the priming/practice effects.

In the next section, we will review a methodology that, while similar in its aims to the self-paced reading task, does not require participants to be literate in the target language.

8.3 Self-paced listening

Although the procedural details differ, self-paced reading and self-paced listening tasks both assume that the time spent either reading or listening to words/segments indexes processing difficulties arising from integrating segments into the ongoing syntactic and semantic structure. As the name suggests, the crucial difference between these methodologies is that self-paced listening involves auditory stimuli instead of written text. A clear advantage of the method lies exactly in this difference, since it does not require the participants to be literate in the target language. Thus, in principle, this method is preferable when focusing on populations such as children.

The authors of the first study utilizing self-paced listening dubbed the method the *auditory window technique* and showed that speakers displayed sensitivity to lexical frequency and syntactic complexity when processing sentences in real time (Ferreira et al. 1996). Although this result mirrored extant findings from self-paced reading and eye-tracking, the authors noted that "providing a profile of processing load across a sentence" (Ferreira et al. 1996: 325) was not something available auditory tasks at the time could accomplish.

The task, as conceived by Ferreira and colleagues, allows participants to listen to words or segments of a sentence by pressing a button in a self-paced manner, such that participants have control over the timing of when the next segment will be played. As in self-paced reading, the dependent variable is the latency between button presses, which the software records in milliseconds. Self-paced listening and self-paced reading have many commonalities, including the presentation of stimuli and the need for careful controls in the design of the experiments. Another similarity is that the effects can appear in a delayed fashion, such that spillover regions must also be analyzed for lingering processing effects. An important difference involves the fact that, unlike in non-cumulative self-paced reading tasks, the listener has no indication of the length of the upcoming word string. For this reason, Marinis (2013) has likened self-paced listening tasks to self-paced reading tasks with centered, non-cumulative presentations. (We will explore this type of presentation in more detail when we describe Event-Related Potentials in Chapter 10).

Unlike self-paced reading, however, self-paced listening has not been used as extensively in L2 research, although there are notable exceptions. One significant innovation made to self-paced listening tasks in L2 research was conceived by Marinis (2007), who followed up a self-paced listening task with a picture verification task. This task is described in Case Study Box 8.2.

Case Study Box 8.2: Marinis (2007)

Research question: Marinis tested whether simultaneous bilingual children over-rely on lexical-semantic cues during online auditory processing as the SSH predicts for adult learners (Clahsen & Felser 2006). Previous research showed that the processing of passive sentences is slower than actives for L1 adults (e.g., Townsend & Bever 2001) and that comprehension was also higher for active sentences (e.g., Ferreira 2003). Marinis aimed to test the processing of passive sentences in L2 children, since no online evidence existed at the time.

Task: Self-paced listening task with a picture verification task. After receiving instructions, the children were exposed to a picture which remained on the computer screen for 2,500 ms. Then they listened to sentences in a segment-by-segment self-paced fashion, pressing the button as quickly as possible. The end of a sentence was indicated by a beep, which was played after the last segment. At the end of the sentence, children were asked to determine (offline, without time pressure) whether the sentence they had just heard matched the picture they were shown at the outset.

Stimuli selection: Design was a 2 × 2 with Voice (Active/Passive) and Picture Match (Match/Mismatch) as factors. Experimental items included reversible sentences that were either active or full passives (including the preposition "by"). Both event participants (Agent and Theme) were animals. Ten monosyllabic verbs were repeated four times. The study included 40 experimental items (10 per condition) plus 20 fillers and 10 practice items in a Latin Square design. The pictures shown could either correspond (match) the events described in the sentence or not (mismatch). (Table 8.2).

Table 8.2 Self-paced listening task design (critical regions) from Marinis (2007), where the picture showed a zebra kissing a camel

	Active	Passive
Match*	the zebra / was kissing / the camel	the camel / was kissed / by the zebra
Mismatch	the camel / was kissing / the zebra	the zebra / was kissed / by the camel

Participants: 28 L1 Turkish-L2 English children (age range: 6;10 to 8;8) who spoke Turkish as a minority language (at home) and 42 monolingual L1 English controls (age range: 6;9 to 8;9). Both groups resided and were tested in the U.K.
Results: For the (offline) verification task, inferential statistics showed an interaction between Group and Voice Type (Active/Passive), showing that L1 children were more accurate in judging passive sentences. Tests also showed a Group × Match interaction, with follow-up comparisons showing that L2 children were less accurate in the mismatch conditions overall. For the online task, Marinis reported the outcomes of Segment 4 (*was kissed/was kissing*) and segment 5 (*the camel/by the camel*). The analysis on Segment 4 (critical region 1) showed a main effect of Match (longer reaction times (RTs) in the mismatch condition) and Group (longer times overall for L2 children), but no interactions. Latencies on Segment 5 only showed a main effect of Group (again, longer RTs overall for L2 children) and Voice (passive sentences were longer because of the preposition "by"). This lack of qualitative differences in the online results obtained, even though L2 children scored substantially lower in the grammar (2.5 SDs) and vocabulary tasks (2.0 SDs). Overall, results showed that both groups of children used morphological cues (*-ing/ed*) to process active and passive sentences, as well as to assign thematic roles, showing that the children did not rely on lexical-semantic cues during processing (although it did negatively affect their accuracy during interpretation).

8.3.2 How to create stimuli?

In most respects, creating stimuli for self-paced tasks, be it for reading or listening, entails tightly controlling experimental sentences so that factors that are extraneous to the experimental design (e.g., frequency or phonological weight) do not constitute mediating factors. There are, however, some important differences that must be considered.

An important matter when developing stimuli for self-paced listening involves the inclusion and manipulation of prosodic or suprasegmental information (speech information that extends beyond a single segment/phoneme). This is important because speakers tend to make use of syntactic and prosodic information to mark phrase boundaries. Early research using *click displacement* techniques found that participants use phrase boundary information to process sentences such that clicks that occur after or before a phrase boundary are (falsely) perceived as happening at phrase boundaries (e.g., Garrett et al. 1966). Furthermore, there is research showing that prosodic information can have an influence on the interpretation of globally ambiguous sentences.[4] Carlson et al. (2001, Experiment 3) found clear evidence that the size of a pause could affect how globally ambiguous sentences are interpreted, such that the phrase *after Tim visited* in the sentence *Sally learned that Pat telephoned after Tim visited* would be interpreted as modifying *telephoned* when there was a longer pause between *Pat* and *telephoned*. Alternatively, the phrase *after Tim visited* would be interpreted as modifying *learned* if there was a longer pause after *telephoned*.

Because the choice of including or manipulating prosodic information is closely related to the aims of the research, there is no one-size-fits-all recommendation available. Although self-paced listening experiments are typically presented in a segment-by-segment fashion, rather than in a word-by-word fashion, since the latter sounds unnatural (Papadopoulou et al. 2013), researchers have choices. Experimental sentences can be presented with flat prosody, with experimentally manipulated prosody, or with natural prosodic contours. These choices can be manipulated with computer software used to develop auditory stimuli (e.g., Praat, downloadable at https://www.fon.hum.uva.nl/praat/).

8.4 Cross-modal priming (with sentences)

By now, we are quite familiar with many of the advantages that latency-based methods can offer language researchers. Chief among them is that (a) these methods are thought to tap into more implicit processes, (b) they don't *require* metalinguistic responses, and (c) these methodologies allow us to investigate sentence processing incrementally, as it unfolds. In this section, we will explore the methodological technique known as cross-modal priming, which offers many of these benefits.

Let's start by exploring the phenomenon known as *priming*, which gives the method its name. Priming describes a cognitive phenomenon whereby exposure to a given stimulus (or *prime*) can either *facilitate* or *interfere* with subsequent production or processing of a second stimulus (the *target*). Because priming is thought to constitute an implicit process, taking place outside of the conscious awareness of the participants, researchers such as Trofimovich and McDonough (2011: 4) place priming as "part of a larger system of [...] implicit memory" that involves "cognitive operations or procedures which are learned [...] through repeated use." Roberts (2014) notes that facilitation of a target is typically understood in terms of activation, such that the level of activation of the target is higher after the processing of the prime.

Primes can be of different types according to their relationship to the target, with identical primes (cases where the prime and the target are the same) producing the strongest effects (Forster et al. 2003). When processing visual stimuli, it has been shown that (visual) targets show evidence of facilitation when following a visually or semantically related prime. Linguistic primes are categorized according to the relationship between the prime and the target, such that we speak about semantic priming, syntactic priming, or auditory priming (Trofimovich & McDonough 2011). *Semantic priming*, as the name suggests, arises when the prime and the target are semantically linked, as is the case for (near) synonyms (e.g., fair /v/ just), antonyms (e.g., fair /v/ unfair), hyponyms (e.g., flower /v/ rose), or categorically related words (e.g., dog /v/ cat), among others. *Syntactic priming*, on the other hand, describes cases where a similar syntactic structure shows evidence of higher activation after encountering similar syntactic primes. Finally, auditory priming describes the phenomenon whereby language processing of a word (or group of words) is processed more quickly and accurately when it has been encountered before.

What is special about cross-modal priming, as opposed to other priming methods (e.g., rapid serial visual presentation), is that cross-modal priming is a two-fold task, often involving both visual and auditory stimuli. In a typical cross-modal priming task, participants are exposed to stimuli presented auditorily (usually a sentence). At a specific point during the presentation of the stimuli, participants are exposed to a target, which could be in the form of text (e.g., a word) or a picture. When participants encounter the target, they are instructed to engage in a binary forced-choice task. If the target is a word, participants could be asked to engage in a lexical decision task, which prompts them to determine whether the target is a (real) word or not. Alternatively, participants can be prompted to engage in a semantic categorization task, whereby they must determine whether the target (which could be a word or a picture) has a certain semantic feature (e.g., whether the target is [+human] or [+animate]). Because researchers control where the probe appears, they can compare activation levels (i.e., faster or slower latencies) at different points of the sentence, which serve as reference points.

As can be gleaned from the foregoing, the choice of presentation of the target is particularly important and, in the case of studies focusing on the processing of syntactic structures, often theoretically motivated. As an example, let's take the processing of long-distance dependencies. Previous research with L1 speakers has shown that the processing of such dependencies relies on *traces* or *gaps*, which are theoretically predicted to be located at specific points in the structure. To illustrate the concept of traces, let's take the following sentence pairs (from Gibson & Warren 2004: 60–61), where traces are indicated thus ($<t_i>$):

1 The manager who$_i$ the consultant claimed $<t_i>$ that the new proposal had pleased $<t_i>$ will hire five workers tomorrow.
2 The manager who$_i$ the consultant's claim about the new proposal had pleased $<t_i>$ will hire five workers tomorrow.

We can see that (1) and (2) differ in particular ways. At a superficial level, we see that while (1) includes two traces (an *intermediate* trace located before the subordinate clause headed by the complementizer *that* and a second trace after the verb *had pleased*), (2) only includes one trace, again after the verb *had pleased* (thus, no intermediate traces are present). Although the placement of traces is theoretically motivated (e.g., Chomsky 1986a), Gibson and Warren (2004) showed evidence from a self-paced reading task that demonstrated the facilitatory effects of traces in sentence processing. Namely, the processing of the verb compound *had pleased* was read faster when there was an intermediate trace, as in (1), compared to the processing of *had pleased* in (2), where the long-distance dependency is particularly long, without the presence of an intermediate trace.

At this point, we might wonder: what is the explicit connection between traces and priming? Since the intermediate trace is predicted to reactivate the referent (in the case of (1), the referent would be *the manager*), this trace can function as a prime to process a later (visual or textual) target. To see how this situation was addressed in previous research, let's review the details of a study by Felser and Roberts (2007), which is summarized in Case Study Box 8.3.

Case Study Box 8.3: Felser and Roberts (2007)

Research question: Felser and Roberts sought to determine whether L2 learners processed (theoretically posited) traces in L2 English (L1 Greek) as L1 English speakers do. They tested the SSH (Clahsen & Felser 2006), which proposes that learners over-rely on lexical-semantic information instead of computing detailed syntactic relations in real time, when these represent long-distance dependencies (such as *wh*-movement). In this case, the SSH predicts that although learners might be able to associate a fronted constituent with the corresponding lexical head, processing of long-distance dependencies will not be aided by structurally defined gaps (p. 12). In other words, the researchers sought evidence of reactivation (facilitatory) effects at trace positions when processing fronted indirect objects in L2 English.

Task (participants also completed a reading-span task to measure working memory): Cross-modal priming task. Participants were asked to sit in front of a computer monitor and listen to experimental sentences. When pictures (primes) appeared on the screen, participants were asked to engage in a forced-choice task, deciding whether the prime was alive or not. The software recorded accuracy and reaction times (Table 8.3).

TABLE 8.3 Felser and Robert's (2007) cross-modal priming task design

	Prime type: Identical	*Prime type: Unrelated*
Fred chased the **squirrel** to which the nice monkey explained …		
Gap position	… the game's difficult rules [**SQUIRREL**] in the class last Wednesday.	… the game's difficult rules [**TOOTHBRUSH**] in the class last Wednesday.
Pre-gap position	… the game's [**SQUIRREL**] difficult rules in the class last Wednesday.	… the game's [**TOOTHBRUSH**] difficult rules in the class last Wednesday.

Stimuli selection: The task constituted a 2 × 2 design crossing Prime Type (Identical/Unrelated) and Gap position (Gap/Pre-gap). 20 experimental items (5 per condition) were presented in a Latin Square along with 60 fillers. Targets were visual stimuli (pictures of animals (identical prime) or inanimate objects (unrelated prime)). Nouns were controlled for syllable length and (lemma) frequency.

Participants: 24 L1 Greek-L2 English learners, 54 adult L1 English speakers, and 44 monolingual L1 English children (mean age: 6.25; range: 5–7). All groups resided and were tested in the U.K. (L1 data was previously reported on in Roberts et al. 2007).

Results: L2 learners were very accurate (98%) in their selection (alive/not alive), as were L1 English adults (94%) and children (97%). This data served as an exclusion criterion since RTs were only analyzed for those trials with correct responses. Reaction times over 2,000 ms were also excluded (1.2% of the data). Finally, participants whose RTs were beyond 2SDs from the mean were removed (5.9% of the data). Results showed that although L2 learners were indeed faster with identical primes, their reaction times at gap and pre-gap sites did not differ (thus, there was no evidence of facilitation at structural gap positions). Further examination showed no contribution of working memory (measured by a reading-span task). Previous research (Roberts et al. 2007), which served as comparison, showed that high-span L1 adult and child speakers did evince faster RTs in identical targets at the gap position (and slower at the pre-gap/control position). Low-span L1 adult and child speakers did not show evidence of facilitation for identical targets, although their performance differed.

8.5 Summary

In this chapter, we discussed three latency-based methods that have been frequently used in GenSLA studies: Self-paced reading, self-paced listening, and cross-modal priming. In so doing, we also reviewed the advantages of latency-based methods, as these pertain to the investigation of L2 sentence processing. The usefulness of these methods is particularly critical for GenSLA studies since researchers believe that online processing can shed light on how L2 learners represent and store linguistic knowledge in their mind/brain (Slabakova 2008). Furthermore, we have seen how latency-based methods can be used to test hypotheses of L2 acquisition that postulate difficulties with online processing (e.g., the SSH: Clahsen & Felser 2006; the IH: Sorace 2011).

8.6 Discussion questions

1 Although we have discussed some advantages of latency-based methods, we should note that these methods are used in tandem with other methods, in what is known as method triangulation (see Hoot et al. 2020 for

discussion). What do you surmise are some possible benefits of using latency-based methods in triangulation with other (online or offline) methods?
2 Since cross-modal priming and self-paced listening do not require highly literate L2 learners, these are methods that could potentially be used with less-studied populations, including children and naturalistic learners who are not literate in the target language. Why are these advantages important for the field? What do we leave out when most of the data we analyze comes from highly literate classroom learners?
3 Come up with a research question that could be better answered using data from any of these three methods (rather than with online methods). Explain your choice.

Notes

1 Briefly, a word's log frequency indicates how often the word appears in a corpus. Log frequency is generally calculated by taking the logarithm of the number of times the word appears in the corpus, and then dividing it by the total number of words in the corpus. To give an example: if a word appears 100 times in a corpus of 10,000 words, its log frequency would be 2.0.
2 If the task includes a secondary task, the software might also provide the reaction times for the secondary task and the behavioral responses associated with it.
3 The logarithm of a given number is the power to which a base number is raised to equal that number. For instance, the logarithm of 100 to the base 10 is 2, since $10^2 = 100$. These transformations, which can be easily performed with statistical packages such as R, are used to make data more normal (read more "symmetrical"), which facilitates interpretation.
4 An example of such a sentence is: *The bus driver angered the rider with a mean look* (Carlson, Clifton, & Frazier 2001). This sentence is syntactically ambiguous because the prepositional phrase *with a mean look* could be interpreted as having high attachment (*the bus driver* had a *mean look*) or low attachment (*the rider* had *a mean look*).

Further reading

Hopp, H. (2022). Second Language Sentence Processing. *Annual Review of Linguistics, 8*, 235–256.
Juffs, A., & Rodríguez, G. A. (2014). *Second language sentence processing*. New York; London: Routledge.

9
EYE-TRACKING

9.1 Introduction

It shouldn't be surprising that the human eyes (more specifically, eye movements) have been often dubbed a "window into cognition." Think about any task you perform during the normal course of your day: each task potentially involves shifting your *gaze* (and, thus, we assume, your *attention*) to the endeavor at hand. Knowing where and when your eyes move can provide rich information about a variety of cognitive processes. This relationship (between your eye and your mind/brain), which is typically known as the eye–mind hypothesis or the eye–mind link,[1] is why researchers track eye movements. Evidence that mind and attention are tightly bound together comes from early studies such as those conducted by Hoffman and Subramaniam (1995), which show that participants are more accurate when detecting targets that match where the eyes land. These experiments also show that participants are generally unable to attend to targets that do not align with where the eyes move.

Within psycholinguistic research, eye movements have been one of the most widely used measures because, like self-paced methods, the methodology provides an implicit measure of language processing. Unlike self-paced methods, however, eye-tracking is a more sensitive and naturalistic measure (that is, it is a more ecologically valid measure), which can record data without interrupting ordinary language-related tasks such as listening to a stream of words. Using eye-tracking as a comprehension index is also very desirable as a methodology because participants are not asked to engage in metalinguistic tasks of varying explicitness, such as judging stimuli. This

DOI: 10.4324/9781003160762-11

feature is particularly helpful with certain populations, including participants with special needs or with limited literacy skills such as recent adult immigrants or children (see Trueswell et al. (1999) for the suitability of the method with children). This is important in L2 studies because these populations are typically underrepresented in psycholinguistic research (see, e.g., Rocha-Hidalgo & Barr 2022).

While we will not go into much detail regarding equipment choices for eye-tracking research, we should mention that, in addition to considerations such as cost, mobility (of the equipment and the participants), and training needs, study features like the population under investigation should influence researchers' set-up choices. Eye-tracking experiments can be conducted with different equipment, from commercial video cameras to professional equipment that can be mounted on a tower, a desk, or even the participant's head. Early on, many eye-tracking experiments with children used video cameras that were commercially available and affordable. These cameras were often hidden so that the children could act naturally, without having a (visible) recording device directly in front of them. The data was then manually extracted and coded—a time-consuming procedure with higher potential for coding errors.

Most present-day eye-tracking experiments, however, use commercially available (video-based) eye-trackers, which analyze the recorded images of the eyes as these are illuminated by a light source, typically an infrared light. Infrared light is used because it emits wavelengths that the eye can reflect, but that humans cannot perceive (i.e., it does not distract the participants) (Bojko 2013). In addition to the light-emitting source, eye-trackers are equipped with a video camera that is sensitive to infrared light so that it can record information such as the reflection of the light from the *retina* (the tissue at the back of the eye) and the *cornea* (the transparent part of the eye that covers the pupil and allows light to reach the retina). Using the information from the reflected light, the eye-tracking software can determine (x, y) coordinates on the screen to locate the participants' gaze location relative to the interest areas (Duchowski 2017). As we will see later, eye-trackers can also measure other eye characteristics, such as the size of the *pupil* (the black-appearing round opening at the center of the *iris*, which is the colored tissue that distinguishes our eye color), although these measures have not been widely explored in L2 acquisition research.

Within eye-tracking research, there is an important methodological divide that determines, in large measure, how the data is treated and analyzed, as well as the types of research questions that investigators can address. On the one hand, eye-tracking can be used to conduct *Reading Studies*, which investigate how participants engage with text, either in print or on a screen. On the other hand, the last 30 years have seen an increase in the number of

Visual World Paradigm studies, also known as *looking-while-listening* studies. In these studies, participants are typically presented with a visual scene while they listen to auditory stimuli or instructions. Additionally, participants can be asked to perform a task (e.g., clicking on a stimulus). This secondary task might yield data of its own (e.g., accuracy of choices), but its presence might influence eye movements. Dussias et al. (2014), for instance, note that studies requiring this type of task, which they call *action-based* studies, tend to yield cleaner data and to require fewer trials per participant. As we will see momentarily, the measures that researchers analyze from Reading Studies can vary widely. In Visual World studies, however, the main focus is on (fixation) proportions—the amount of time (in proportion) that a participant's gaze spent on a given stimuli or location.

9.2 Data collected by eye-tracking

Before we delve into the data that is elicited with this method, we must understand the nature of eye movements. Most people are surprised to learn that eye movements do not represent fluid, unbroken gestures. Instead, our eyes move in what are called saccades: short movements that are ballistic—movements to a target that are not typically influenced by feedback because of their short duration (Optican & Pretegiani 2017). Researchers gathering eye-tracking data typically distinguish between eye movements of two types: *fixations* (movement pauses, where eyes are positioned at a given region) and *saccades* (ballistic movements between fixations). To date, L2 studies have only analyzed fixations because these are the moments where readers can obtain information to decode text or a visual scene.

Earlier, we mentioned the difference between Reading Studies (eye-tracking with text) and Visual World studies (eye-tracking while listening). Since the measures that are drawn from each study are different, we will address each in turn after presenting the basics of the methodology.

Figure 9.1, an image created by the American Academy of Ophthalmology, depicts clearly how our eyes do not smoothly move over a string of words. Instead, reading is made up of saccades and fixations that move both forward (see the movement between "2" and "3") and backward (see the movement between "5" and "6," which represents a regression), although the latter are less frequent in (proficient) adult readers.

In addition to showing the fragmented, stepwise nature of eye movements during reading, Figure 9.1 shows important notions such as first fixations and regressions, while noting the interest area (marked in yellow). We will describe these measures in more detail below.

As you can tell from examining Figure 9.1, *regressions* are saccades that correspond to backward movement. For instance, number "6" in the figure represents a regression, since the reader returned to the verb *attacked* after reading the object *windmill*. In general, regressions are believed to index either processing difficulties or lower proficiency or literacy levels, although this can vary depending on whether the text is static (e.g., fixed words or images on a screen or a piece of paper) or dynamic (e.g., self-paced subtitles or moving pictures) (Kruger & Steyn 2014). Importantly, regressions can also represent corrections of oculomotor control, which are not related to language comprehension processes. Basically, these represent rectifications when overshooting a planned saccade. Distinctions between regression types (i.e., oculomotor error vs. processing difficulty) can have repercussions for the design and analysis of eye-tracking data because these two types of regressions rely on different processes (Eskenazi & Folk 2017). Thus, researchers must take these distinctions into account when designing stimuli.

As represented in Figure 9.1, the pink dots of various sizes represent fixations—moments where the eyes rest on a word or visual cue. Normally, fixations are substantially longer than saccades, although they may have varied durations. Typical fixations during reading last between 200 and 250 ms, although they can vary depending on the type of (reading) task, whether reading out loud or silently (Rayner 2009). In Figure 9.1, we can see variation between the duration of each fixation (duration is represented by the *size* of the pink dots), such that we can tell that the fixation in a (functional) short word such as *the* (see number "1" in Figure 9.1) is much smaller in duration than the fixation on the lexical verb *attacked* when it was first read (see number "3" in Figure 9.1).

At this point, you will probably have noticed something interesting: there is no fixation (pink dot) either on the second definite determiner (*the*), preceding the noun *windmill*, or on the possessive determiner (*his*), which

FIGURE 9.1 Example of eye movements while reading the phrase *The knight attacked the windmill on his donkey* (reproduced with permission).

appears before the noun *donkey*. When there is no fixation time on a particular word, we say that the word was *skipped*. But how can we derive meaning from a word that was literally skipped? To understand how this happens, we must be aware of how our eyes work.

When we move our eyes, we move a part of the macula called the *fovea* (centralis), which represents two degrees (2°) of our central visual field (~.35 mm in diameter). The fovea is packed with photosensors and thus is the region with the highest-resolution vision (Rehman et al. 2022), which is essential for reading. The region surrounding the fovea is called the *parafoveal* region. While we can still perceive stimuli that fall in the parafoveal region, perception comes at a cost: acuity is lower the farther we are from the fovea. That is why as soon as we detect a stimulus that requires examination, our eyes will trigger movement so that the area of interest falls under the foveal region (Schotter et al. 2012), typically around three times every second (Tatler et al. 2014). Beyond the parafoveal region, we speak of the peripheral region, in which we perceive stimuli with even less visual acuity. Figure 9.2, from Schotter et al. (2012), depicts the sentence *The quick brown fox jumped over the lazy dog*, showing the foveal, parafoveal, and peripheral regions.

So how does this relate to the words that we skip? Even if our gaze is not directly fixated on a word (note how the foveal region in Figure 9.2 is mostly taken by the noun *fox*), we can still perceive it—especially if the word is short (Drieghe et al. 2004), frequent (Drieghe et al. 2005), or predictable in the context (Altarriba et al. 1996). Yet our capacity for perception is not symmetrical, as Figure 9.2 might suggest. Not all the letters in the parafoveal region will be perceived equally by all readers—language has a lot to do with this asymmetry. Readers can extract information from the so-called *perceptual span*, which in English extends from 3 to 4 letters to

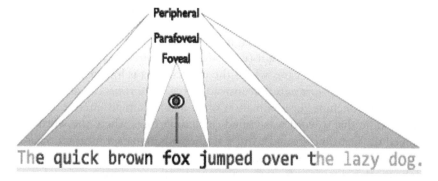

FIGURE 9.2   Example of foveal, parafoveal, and peripheral regions from Schotter et al. (2012). Replicated with permission.

the left of the fixation point to 14–15 letters to the right of fixation (Rayner et al. 1980).[2] This is because English is read left-to-right, and the upcoming information is to the right of the fixation point. As you may expect, readers of languages that are read right-to-left, such as Hebrew, have the opposite asymmetry, with more letters perceived on the left than to the right (Pollatsek et al. 1981).

We have seen that, for L2 research, investigators are mostly interested in fixations. Yet if you examine Figure 9.1, you might ask yourself: which fixations should we analyze and how should we analyze them? Undoubtedly, the answer will depend on the research question that your study is after, but what is especially exciting about eye-tracking as a methodology is that we can answer more (and more varied) questions because we can analyze different measures. In Figure 9.1, we see that the researchers have highlighted the word *windmill* as the *interest area* (also known as region of interest). Note, however, that our interest area contains three distinct pink dots, which, moreover, do not happen subsequently. When we count the number of fixations, we are looking at *fixation counts*, which document the number of fixations in an interest area. Furthermore, fixation counts can be distinguished by whether these happened during a single pass or not. In Figure 9.1, we see that numbers "4" and "5" are *consecutive* fixation counts because they happened in the same pass. We can also count the number of passes that a reader did over a region of text: In this case, we see that *windmill* was visited twice, so we can set the *visit count* at two. (As we will see momentarily, counts make little sense for Visual World studies, so we focus on fixation proportions instead, since we are interested in the proportion of time that participants spent on a given region or image.)

While the choice of which measure to analyze responds to the purpose of a particular study, each measure offers different types of information. L2 researchers are often interested in the fixation duration of the first time that the reader visits an interest area, called the *first fixation duration* ("4" in Figure 9.1). First fixation is distinct from *gaze duration*, which is the result of adding up all the fixations in an interest area comprised of a single word until the eye withdraws from it (e.g., adding the duration times of "4" and "5" in Figure 9.1). In cases where the interest area is longer than a single word, we speak of *first pass time* instead. *Second pass times* can also be analyzed, which include the summation of all fixations in an interest area the second time that a word was visited (including cases where the word was skipped the first time around). In L2 studies, an important measure regarding second pass times is *regression-path duration*, which represents the sum of the fixation durations from the moment that the eyes visit a region during the second pass reading until the eyes continue in the direction of reading (right for English, left for Hebrew). Finally, *total time* refers to the summation of all durations in an interest area (e.g., adding the duration times of "4," "5," and "7" in Figure 9.1).

Godfroid (2019), which constitutes the most comprehensive methodological handbook and eye-tracking literature synthesis to date for L2 and bilingualism research, tallied the types of measures used in eye-tracking studies in 16 journals focusing on language learning and second language acquisition (SLA). In her tally, she found that what she characterized as the "big four durational measures" accounted for 84% of the measures used in the studies she analyzed. These measures were total time (33% of all studies), gaze duration (24%), first fixation (17%), and regression-path duration (13%). The rest of the studies (16%) used eight other measures, including rereading time and second pass time. Although the measures mentioned so far are the ones used in L2 studies, there are several more that can be used, including saccade amplitude, skipping probability, or refixation probability. As we have noted, this flexibility constitutes a clear advantage of eye-tracking over other methodologies because of the richness of the data we obtain. However, this embarrassment of riches can have a downside.

By now you will have noticed that many of these measures are not exactly unique but interrelated. Further, two (or more) measures might specify the same latency magnitude in some cases. For instance, if we had chosen *knight* instead of *windmill* as our interest area (Figure 9.1), the first fixation duration would be equal to the gaze duration. While measures are more easily distinguishable because they constitute either *early* vs. *late* measures (in terms of their effects on processing), researchers such as Kliegl and Laubrock (2017) have noted that reporting the results of interrelated measures can lead to fallacious—yet statistically significant—effects. To avoid such adverse consequences, many researchers are turning to open science practices such as study pre-registration and registered reports, which require researchers to document not only their instruments but also the analytical tools and measures they use. These options can reduce publication bias while also decreasing the chances of spurious effects, in part because they undergo a process of peer review *prior* to data collection that reviews the explicit plans for analysis. For a thorough discussion of the benefits of such practices, see Marsden and Morgan-Short (2023).

9.3 Eye-tracking in the Visual World

Early psycholinguistic research discovered a remarkable link between eye movements and linguistic processes (e.g., Tanenhaus et al. 1995, 2000), which Holmqvist et al. (2011) identify as the Time-locking Hypothesis. This hypothesis came about when researchers noted the exceptional speed with which eyes could fixate on stimuli based on linguistic cues (around 220 ms).

The speed of this is exceptional when we consider that simply launching a saccade takes around 200 ms, a comparison that provides evidence of a tight link between linguistic processing and eye movements. Thus, broadly, the hypothesis proposes that eye movements are time-locked to linguistic and cognitive processes. One of the most significant implications of this hypothesis is what we can learn about linguistic processing over time: when we plot the proportion of eye movements over time, we can infer the development (the time-course) of the linguistic and cognitive processes associated with the task (Holmqvist et al 2011: 199). Visual World studies capitalize on this link because the most important measures derived from them are proportions of fixations over time.

9.3.1 Representative studies

Visual World studies have been used to study a wide variety of language-related processes and structures. One such process is lexical activation, which has been the focus of research with monolingual and bilingual populations. An early example of such research is the work by Allopenna et al. (1998), which we will use to exemplify a typical Visual World study. Allopenna and colleagues were interested in researching the lexical activation of words when these were in competition with others that either shared an onset (part of a cohort, e.g., *beaker* /v/ *beetle*), rhymed (e.g., *beaker* /v/ *speaker*), or constituted unrelated competitors (e.g., *beaker* /v/ *carriage*). Participants were presented with pictures of the four objects (*beaker*, *beetle*, *speaker*, and *carriage*) on a computer screen while they listened to a directive which asked them to click on the object (and then drag it with the mouse). One such directive was "Pick up the beaker." Taking into consideration that launching a saccade takes approximately 200 ms, the authors predicted that, after that time, participants would direct their gaze at the potential objects that would compete. The prediction was that *beaker* would complete with *beetle* at first, but once the coda (*ker*) appeared, competition with *beetle* should drop. The results of the study (Experiment 1) indeed showed the effects of the cohort word (*beetle*) and, later, of the rhyming word (*speaker*). Importantly for our purposes, these results echoed computer simulations, showing evidence that the time-course of eye movements (the proportion of fixations) matched existing models of lexical activation.

In bilingualism research, Visual World studies have also been used to investigate whether L2 learners can anticipate (or predict) upcoming linguistic material like L1 speakers do. In Case Study Box 9.1, we have presented the details of an eye-tracking study conducted by Hopp and Lemmerth (2018), which focused on whether learners could predict the gender of an upcoming segment using lexical and syntactic cues.

Case Study Box 9.1: Hopp and Lemmerth (2018)

Research question: Hopp and Lemmerth (2018) investigated adult L2 learners of German (L1 Russian) to determine whether they could use gender cues predictably (that is, whether they could anticipate the gender of an upcoming segment). Lexical congruency was investigated because, although Russian and German both have a tripartite gender-class distinction (masculine, feminine, and neuter), nouns typically differ in terms of their gender assignment in both languages. Syntactic congruency was investigated because prior evidence shows that the placement of gender markings can affect processing (e.g., Tokowicz & MacWhinney 2005), and Russian and German differ regarding the placement of gender marking (i.e., postnominal suffixes in Russian, prenominal determiners in German). Given the wealth of evidence showing that proficiency plays a role during online processing, the authors also investigated the effects of L2 proficiency on processing.

Task (only the eye-tracking task is reported here): The authors used eye-tracking within the Visual World Paradigm. Participants' gaze was directed at a fixation cross. Then, participants heard experimental stimuli after a sound signal while their eye movements were recorded. The design was 2 × 2 × 2, with *Condition* (article/adjective), *Congruency* (congruent/incongruent), and *Type* (different gender/same gender) as factors, counterbalanced in the stimuli.

Stimuli selection: German stimuli were embedded in a question that included gender marking either in the *determiner* (Wo ist **der/die/das** gelbe [noun]? "Where is the $_{MASC/FEM/NEUTER}$ yellow (noun)?") or the *adjective* (Wo ist ein **kleiner/s** gelber [noun]? "Where is a small $_{MASC/NEUTER}$ yellow (noun)?"). Pictures included 100 experimental nouns and 145 fillers (pretested). All objects were colored (red, green, yellow, & blue).

Participants: 24 L1 Russian adult learners of L2 German and 15 German native speakers (NSs) of German. Participants completed two different proficiency measures focusing on lexical and grammatical knowledge (Goethe Institut placement test and LexTALE-gr), which the authors used to compute a composite score.

Results: L2 learners, overall, showed evidence of exploiting gender information to predict the gender of the upcoming noun (although at lower levels than L1 speakers), but *only* in the adjective condition (as a group). Proficiency and Congruency also modulated fixation proportion times, such that advanced learners could, like L1 speakers, use the information from both the genders and the determiners predictively.

128 Methods typically used in GenSLA

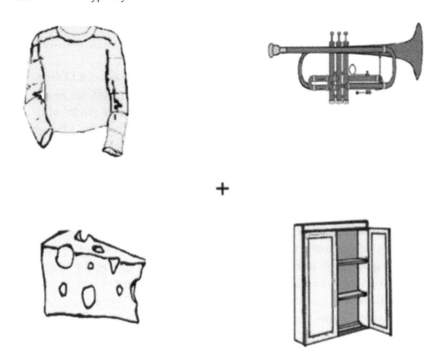

FIGURE 9.3 Sample display (determiner + same condition) (yellow objects have the same gender; green object is a distractor and a different gender). Reproduced with permission.

As you can see in Figure 9.3 within Case Study Box 9.1, the researchers presented four stimuli neatly arranged in four quadrants, which is a rather typical setup for Visual World studies, but not the only one. Kamide et al. (2003), for instance, used a more naturalistic Visual World setup when studying (verb) subcategorization differences (intransitive vs. transitive verbs).

9.3.2 How to create stimuli?

As in the case of the latency-based methods we discussed in the previous chapter, stimuli must be carefully constructed since means are collapsed by condition (across items). In the case of Visual World studies, researchers manipulate both visual input (images on the screen) and auditory input (recorded sentences that play while participants scan the screen); both inputs have different requirements and best practices.

Because what is measured in Visual World studies is (listening) comprehension, researchers must avoid any aspect of the Visual World that would draw attention to itself *independently* of the (auditory) linguistic signal. Thus, researchers control aspects of the images shown, such as size, color, style, location, ease of identifiability, or any other aspects that could bring about unexpected or unplanned visual salience to any image. For this reason, many researchers using the Visual World conduct norming studies to determine whether participants can indeed associate the visual stimuli with the intended referents as to avoid confounding factors related to defects or peculiarities in the visual stimuli.[3] Alternatively, they can use databases already including normed images, many of which are publicly available (see, for example, Godfroid 2019; Souza et al. 2020). Godfroid (2019) further notes that researchers should attempt to rotate images such that reference/experimental items in one trial might be fillers/distractors in others. If researchers are using quadrants (such as the research in Case Study Box 9.1), she also recommends rotating the pictures so that no one picture always appears in a given (x, y) coordinate. Finally, she urges researchers to consider other aspects of the visual presentation, such as whether participants can preview the visual materials or whether a fixation cross should appear at the outset of trials.

A final practice echoes the discussions we touched upon in Chapter 8. Because of the type of experimental design used in these types of measures, we can only obtain results that speak to differences as *compared* to a control condition. Thus, researchers ensure that the only differences among trials are those manipulated by the experimenter. If the researcher is interested in differences related to the acoustic signal (the recording played), the images should stay constant. (If, conversely, the researcher would be hypothetically interested in differences related to changes in the visual display, the auditory signal should remain constant among conditions). This consideration is of extreme importance because any effects related to differences between items could potentially constitute a mediating factor that could not be accounted for in the analysis.

As with the visual stimuli, researchers must ensure clarity in their materials, which for audio materials involve myriad considerations regarding the speaker (e.g., the speed with which they talk, their native dialect (and accent)), the materials themselves (e.g., the frequency of lexical items, suitability in context, use of regional language), or the audio setup (e.g., signal clarity, volume). A special concern involves the presence of suprasegmental information in the audio stimuli (e.g., prosody), since languages convey a great variety of information through these means (e.g., the information structure of a given phrase or clause). All audio materials should typically be recorded during the same session to avoid trivial differences that might cue participants to notice patterns that are not related to the experimental manipulation (e.g., background noise or a speaker being hoarse).

Having said all this, however, stimuli are typically further processed to ensure evenness in terms of amplitude (volume) or to filter background noise (e.g., noise from the air conditioning of the room).

9.4 Eye-tracking with text (Reading Studies)

Because we have so far discussed the Visual World and Reading paradigms as different "flavors" of eye-tracking, one could get the impression that both methods share more commonalities than not. However, this impression would not be exactly accurate, as will soon be evident, because these methodology strands are distinct in ways that affect the types of research questions that can be answered, the main units of analysis, or even the constructs measured, to name just a few crucial differences. In fact, Boland (2004: 51) believes that Visual World and Reading paradigms are so distinct that using the eye-tracking label for both "is almost a misnomer." Bolan's logic, summarized below, is that these paradigms gauge essentially different constructs.

Visual World studies measure (listening) *comprehension* by measuring the proportion of fixations (or the speed of such fixations) on objects that are referenced in the (audio) linguistic signal. Often, the goal is to draw (indirect) inferences about the participants' linguistic representations based on these proportions. Reading Studies, on the other hand, can provide highly accurate temporal measures of *processing difficulties* in a more direct way because these can be gauged at the precise region predicted to provoke them. In fact, evidence from Reading Studies (using both eye-tracking and self-paced reading) have shown clear findings linking reading times to factors such as word length, frequency, or predictability in context.

By now we know that there are a great number of measures that can be used in Reading Studies, including gaze duration, first fixation, total time, or regression-pass duration. At the present time, however, there is no broad consensus on how these measures are linked to distinct cognitive processes, although broad assumptions can be inferred (i.e., longer reading times indicate processing difficulties of one sort or another)—a state of affairs that can complicate (or limit) the interpretations we can draw from the data. A further complicating factor is also one of the most appealing aspects of Reading Studies: the fact that there exist multiple measures that can be drawn from the same data set. Boland (2004) reminds us, however, that these measures are not truly independent because these units of measure are all computed from two basic eye-movement measures: fixation duration and directionality (forward vs. regression). For this reason, she argues that there is much to be learned from studies that show divergent results among the different measures analyzed.

Godfroid's (2019) overview of eye-tracking studies in bilingualism research found that Reading Studies have been more common than Visual World studies (k = 52 and k = 32, respectively). Further, she notes that Reading Studies fell under five different strands: studies focusing on (a) grammar, (b) the bilingual lexicon, (c) instructed SLA, (d) subtitles, and (e) assessment. Within the studies focusing on grammar, Godfroid found a further quadripartite division according to the paradigm used. To wit, *anomaly* paradigms (also referred to as *violation* paradigms) focus on reading sentences that include ungrammaticalities or infelicities with the purpose of determining whether learners display sensitivities to such violations. *Ambiguity* resolution paradigms are predicated on sentences including (global) syntactic ambiguities. *Dependency* paradigms measure the processing of sentences that include long-distance dependencies, since these are of theoretical importance to hypotheses such as the Shallow Structure Hypothesis (Clahsen & Felser 2006). Finally, she identified studies that included no anomalies or other such manipulations, which she characterizes as studies using a *non-violation* paradigm.

In what follows, we provide an overview of a reading study focusing on grammar and using the ambiguity paradigm. Case Study Box 9.2 shows this research, which was conducted by Roberts et al. (2008).

Case Study Box 9.2: Roberts, Gullberg, and Indefrey (2008)

Research question: Roberts and colleagues investigated online pronoun resolution in L2 Dutch, a non-null-subject language. By including learners of two typologically different languages, the authors could determine whether the L1 influenced real-time pronoun resolution. Speakers of null-subject languages (Turkish, in this case) were expected to show influences from their L1, in which overt pronouns have distinct functions (e.g., contrast, topic shift) since null pronouns are possible. Because speakers of non-null-subject languages (here, German) were not expected to experience L1 interference, the authors did not predict differences between this subgroup and NSs.

Task: Eye-tracking with text, followed by an Acceptability Judgment task and a Comprehension Questionnaire (not reported here). Participants were asked to read stimuli including three sentences appearing on different lines: a context, the target sentence, and an additional sentence (such as *It's a quiet day*). The measures of interest were 5: first fixation, first pass, second pass, total time, and proportion of regressions (Table 9.1).

TABLE 9.1 Experimental design in Roberts et al. (2008)

(Translated) context and potential antecedent	Experimental item	Expected resolution
"*The workers* are in the office." PLURAL NP	Terwijl Peter aan het werk is, eet *hij* een boterham. "While Peter is working, *he* is eating a sandwich."	Local resolution (he = Peter)
"*The workers* are in the office." PLURAL NP	Terwijl Peter aan het werk is, eten *zij* een boterham. "While Peter is working, *they* are eating a sandwich."	Disjoint resolution (They = the workers)
"*Peter and Hans* are in the office." TWO NPs	Terwijl Peter aan het werk is, eet *hij* een boterham. "While Peter is working, *he* is eating a sandwich."	Optional resolution (he = Paul or Hans)

Stimuli selection: 24 experimental items were presented (along with 32 fillers) in a Latin Square including three conditions, which differed in terms of the expected pronoun resolution: local, disjoint, or optional. Local and Optional resolutions were expected to be easier for L1 speakers. After each sentence, participants were asked a Y/N question.

Participants: 30 adult learners of L2 Dutch, divided by L1 (14 Turkish learners and 16 German learners), along with 30 adult native Dutch speakers. Participants completed a proficiency test to ensure Turkish and German speakers were matched for proficiency.

Results: First-pass measures (first fixation, first pass) yielded a main effect on the group, since learners read more slowly than NSs. Later measures (second pass, total time, and proportion of regressions) showed similar results across both L2 groups, showing no evidence of L1 influence. Later measures indicated interactions between group*(resolution) type. Both learner groups spent more time in the Optional resolution condition, while L1 Dutch speakers' reading times were the lowest in this condition.

9.4.1 How to create stimuli?

If you are familiar with the creation of stimuli for tasks such as self-paced reading, some of the directives on how to create stimuli might sound very familiar. This shouldn't be surprising because many of the findings in the reading literature have resulted from researcher outcomes from both methods, which, by and large, have yielded similar findings (Mitchell 2004). Thus, just as with self-paced reading, researchers should pay close attention to the stimuli in terms of length (or phonological weight in syllables), frequency, predictability in context, etc.

In Chapter 8, which focused on latency-based measures, we discussed that researchers typically avoid placing critical regions either at the outset or at the end of sentences, for different reasons. Placing material at the end of sentences is typically avoided to bypass the so-called sentence *wrap-up* effects. While the cognitive processes involved in sentence wrap-up are not completely understood, there is an indication that this process entails a substantial cognitive workload—especially for older adults (Payne & Stine-Morrow 2012). Avoiding critical material at the outset is also recommended for eye-tracking to avoid the area being skipped over, since readers tend to skip words at the beginning of sentences.

The size of the area of interest also matters, since it has been shown, using different methodologies, that short words get skipped often (e.g., Hollenstein et al. 2018). Defining an area of interest on a word with a single letter (e.g., the article "a") might yield a skipping rate that could complicate the analysis. However, that particular article might be skipped for independent reasons. As mentioned earlier, frequency also must be considered, since frequently used words get skipped more frequently (e.g., Brysbaert et al. 2005). Another factor to take into consideration is that word predictability (independently of length) can also affect skipping rates (e.g., Drieghe et al. 2004). Because these factors are thought to operate independently, a highly predictable short and frequent word might be *particularly* likely to be skipped. Since functional elements (articles, clitics, auxiliaries) tend to be short, frequent, and (depending on the context) highly predictable, researchers should take special precautions when preparing materials focusing on such functional items. For additional practical solutions to these problems, see Godfroid (2019), who suggests using margins and double spacing between lines and after periods to decrease the changes of a region being skipped.

Spacing between letters (which varies by font type) is important because of the effects of *crowding* (Pelli et al. 2004), meaning that the perception of a letter is more difficult when surrounded by other letters. This issue is typically addressed by using monospace fonts (fonts in which all letters take up the same amount of visual space, such as Courier or Roboto). Monospaced fonts have additional advantages. Since every letter has a fixed width, researchers can calculate the number of letters that participants can perceive in a fixation (the *visual angle*). Using monospaced fonts, however, is not the only option. There exists research showing that font width does not affect reading times (e.g., Minakata & Beier 2021), since readers quickly adapt to font styles and, as noted by Walker (2021), monospaced fonts are representative of a typical print reading experience. This brief discussion, however, does indicate that the choice of font type is not a trivial one.

Because our aim is not to provide an exhaustive methodological guide to the preparation of materials, we do not cover every potential issue extensively. However, we hope that this brief introduction will be helpful when considering eye-tracking with text as a methodology.

9.5 Summary

In this chapter, we have discussed the two main experimental paradigms that can be used in eye-tracking research, which determines where participants look as well as other characteristics of eye movements to study (the time-course of) linguistic processing. The main two paradigms (Reading Studies vs. Visual World studies) differ in their methodological procedures and also in the types of research questions that can be addressed with them. We also reviewed a great variety of eye-movement measures, including first fixations, regressions, first and second pass, or total time, which derive from two basic measures: fixation duration and directionality (forward, regression). Finally, we surveyed sample studies from both Visual World and Reading Studies, while reviewing some of the most important aspects of stimuli design.

9.6 Discussion questions

1 How do the methodologies of Reading Studies and the Visual World Paradigm in eye-tracking research provide distinct insights into language processing, particularly in SLA?
2 In what ways can eye-tracking data challenge existing theories in psycholinguistics and bilingual language processing? Think of the hypotheses we have discussed so far or others that you may be aware of.
3 Discuss the implications of the eye–mind hypothesis in eye-tracking research. How does this concept help in understanding the cognitive processes underlying language comprehension?
4 Considering the methodological complexities of eye-tracking research, what are some additional key factors to consider when designing an eye-tracking study in the context of language acquisition and bilingualism?

Notes

1 For a discussion on potential neurological limitations regarding the eye–mind link, see Reichle and Reingold (2013).

2 When talking about scanning a visual scene, we speak of a *field of view*, or *region of effective vision*, instead of a perceptual span (Rayner & Castelhano 2007).
3 For more information regarding the importance of norming procedures when using visual stimuli, see Souza et al. (2020).

Further reading

Godfroid, A. (2019). *Eye tracking in second language acquisition and bilingualism: A research synthesis and methodological guide.* New York: Routledge.

10
EVENT-RELATED POTENTIALS

10.1 Introduction

In his book *The Language Instinct*, cognitive psychologist Stephen Pinker said, somewhat facetiously, that humans "have no right to be as good at sentence understanding as they are. Not only can they solve a viciously complex task, but they solve it *fast*" (Pinker 1994: 194). Joking aside, however, Pinker is right to be astounded: we have seen that sentence comprehension is a singularly complex process that transpires at such velocity that we measure it in milliseconds. This processing speed explains, at least in part, why language researchers need methods that can measure how language is comprehended in real time and why these methods have grown in popularity in the last three decades. In the previous two chapters, we reviewed methodologies that have high to very high temporal resolution. These methods measure reaction or fixation times to linguistic stimuli, and they have been used to advance our understanding of how humans can comprehend their first and second languages in such a speedy and accurate manner. In this chapter, we will survey a method that can also have high temporal resolution and that can (non-invasively) record activity in our brains: Event-Related Potentials (ERPs).

10.2 Event-related potentials

10.2.1 Data that is elicited with the method

In a nutshell, the methodology known as ERPs produces measures of electric activity from the brain via electrodes (thin metal disks with wiring that connect back to an amplifier and, eventually, to a computer) that are placed

DOI: 10.4324/9781003160762-12

on a participant's scalp. These recordings are possible because the specialized cells in the brain called neurons have electrical properties (Bradley & Keil 2012). The recording of electrical activity in the brain is done via an electroencephalogram (EEG), which can capture the electrical activity of (thousands to millions) of neurons by tracking changes in voltage, called *electrical potentials*. Because this neural activity (i.e., changes in voltage) is always happening in our brains—regardless of whether we are awake or asleep—EEG signals are continuous measures of these voltage changes (i.e., they record unbroken, sustained brain activity). As with other psycholinguistic methods, one advantage is that the methodology taps into more implicit processes, such that participants do not have to produce language or make (metalinguistic) judgments about stimuli. For this reason, ERP is a relatively friendly methodology to use with children. This is especially useful when researchers are interested in studying language in children who are too young to produce language or make judgments about stimuli. Rispens and Krikhaar (2010) note that studies have used babies that are just 48 hours old.

As we mentioned, one of the main advantages of these continuous EEG signals is that their temporal resolution is extremely high (EEGs can sample these voltages every millisecond), which can be useful to determine the timing of cognitive processes such as real-time sentence processing, as we will see later. The problem is that these continuous EEG signals, in their raw forms, are composite measures that are too complex to be useful to researchers of language or cognition. This is the case because EEG signals reflect brain activity *in general*, without distinction of the different neural processes associated with specific cognitive or linguistic events. So, what is a (neuro)linguist interested in recording the correlates to linguistic events to do? Enter ERPs, which are designed to do exactly that. ERPs are created by processing EEGs to extract brain responses that are time-locked to an event (e.g., the presentation of a visual or auditory stimulus). What this means, in more practical terms, is that when participants are exposed to a given stimulus, this stimulus is marked with a code that tags it as an "event." This code indicates, in the EEG signal, when the stimulus was presented to the participant. In any given experiment, many events can be coded, not only the (onset of) stimuli that are presented to participants. If a participant is asked to produce a response, for instance, the onset of this response is also marked in the EEG signal. Indeed, one of the many advantages of using ERPs is the variety of events that can be coded (and thus tied to the EEG signal). The EEG signal is then processed to extract the electrical potentials (the changes in voltage) associated with each event (hence the name: Event-Related Potential).

We can see how, by tying the electrical responses of the brain to a specific stimulus, researchers can investigate temporal information about a wide array of cognitive and linguistic phenomena. To this end, researchers use epochs, a term that denotes a specific time window in the EEG signal that is time-locked to a coded event. Importantly, these methodological innovations have allowed researchers using ERPs to investigate what Bornkessel-Schlesewsky et al. (2016) called the "time course of sentence processing"—a notion that has held an important place in linguistic-cognitive theories of sentence processing as well as in theories that aim to determine how information from different sources is integrated/processed.[1]

As in the case of reading or fixation times, the ERPs associated with an event during each trial are averaged. Before averaging across trials, however, EEG data must be preprocessed so that artifacts that are not the focus of the study (e.g., voltages associated with eye blinks, monitored by special electrodes) can be filtered or rejected. These processes require a great deal of expertise, as there are many parameters associated with filtering procedures, the detection of artifacts, and the correction of the baseline to "maximize the signal-to-noise ratio" (Morgan-Short & Tanner 2013), procedures which will not be discussed here. Beyond data processing, we can note that the average of epochs is done point-by-point such that graphs depicting ERPs display the voltage fluctuations associated with the event over time. Typically, the averages of individual participants are averaged to create a "grand average." Averaging over trials is crucial because EEG recordings represent composite measures of all brain activity. By averaging over many trials, the brain activity that is not related to the event in question should be "washed out," leaving the activity associated with the stable event (Osterhout 2023). Bradley and Keil (2012) note that averaging is important not only because the EEG signal is "noisy" but also because the magnitude of EEG voltage fluctuations can be on a scale of hundreds of volts, while the changes associated with events are typically "on the scale of several microvolts" (one microvolt is a millionth part of a volt) (Bradley & Keil 2012: 79).

When taking part in an ERP experiment, participants must be prepared for an EEG recording, which can be a somewhat time-consuming procedure. Figure 10.1 (from Osterhout et al. 1997) illustrates a participant with a cap that is connected to an amplifier. Amplifying the signal is necessary because the electrical activity produced by neurons is relatively weak, especially since it is further dimmed when the signal travels through the skull, the scalp, and other tissues. Once a participant is fitted with a cap, a conductive gel is inserted into a small opening at each electrode. By filling the gap between the electrode and the scalp, the gel improves the connectivity between them, which effectively reduces the so-called electrical impedance (resistance to the flow of the electrical current). Reducing this resistance is important because impedance is negatively related to the strength of the EEG signal (higher impedance means a weaker EEG signal).

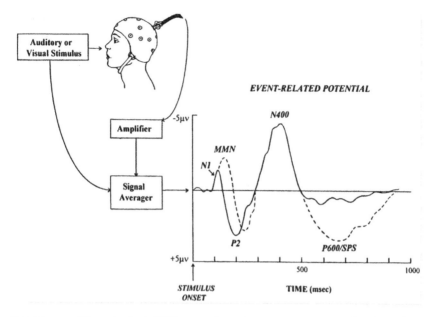

FIGURE 10.1 Hypothetical ERP waveform in response to a stimulus (from Osterhout et al. 1997).

Once outfitted with their cap, participants typically sit in a sound-attenuated booth in front of a computer screen, where they are asked to read or listen to linguistic stimuli. Because of the noisiness of the ERP signal, the number of items needed per condition tends to be several orders of magnitude higher than for methodologies such as self-paced reading. It is not uncommon to have 40–60 items per condition, for instance, where self-paced reading studies can have 8–10 items per condition. Because ocular movements (saccades, blinks) are considered undesirable artifacts, written stimuli are typically presented at the center of the screen, one word at a time in a technique known as rapid serial presentation (Steinhauer 2014).

Figure 10.1 depicts a hypothetical ERP waveform in response to an auditory or visual stimulus, which can have multiple "peaks." ERPs, being representations of electrical potentials, have negative and positive deflections. On the y-axis, we have the electrical potentials, which are measured in microvolts (µV). Note that, following electrophysiology conventions, negative tends to be plotted upward, while positive is usually plotted downward (while common, this convention is not ironclad, however, and can vary depending on the field or the researcher's preference). On the x-axis, we have time over milliseconds. Typically, a vertical line marks the onset of the relevant stimulus, as shown in Figure 10.1. Although this particular figure does not include a depiction of the waveform *before* the onset of the stimulus, typical language-related ERP studies include such a waveform for the purposes of comparison.

As shown in Figure 10.1, waveforms can have multiple different peaks, which can be positive or negative. A number of these peaks have been linked to particular cognitive processes such that particular combinations of the potential's magnitude (positive or negative) and the timing (or latency) of its peak are known ERP components. As we will see in some detail, components are generally categorized regarding several dimensions: polarity (negative or positive), latency (in milliseconds), amplitude (in microvolts), and localization (scalp topography) (Rispens & Krikhaar 2010). One such component, illustrated in Figure 10.1, is the N400, which is one of the most well-known ERP components in linguistic research. This component is characterized by a negative deflection in the ERP waveform that occurs approximately 400 milliseconds after the onset of the visual or auditory stimulus (hence the name). Before revealing why this component is so famous and how it has been interpreted and explained, however, a cautionary note is needed.

Conceptually, researchers such as Luck (2005) have argued that latency, polarity, and distribution are epiphenomenal or "superficial features" that can be used to classify a component but do not "capture its essence" (p. 66). While Luck acknowledges that these dimensions can be helpful in classifying components, he advocates for researchers to think more conceptually about components. To provide a more "operational" definition, Luck (2005) modifies Donchin et al.'s (1978) definition to define ERP components as:

> a set of voltage changes that are consistent with a single neural generator site and that systematically vary in amplitude across conditions, time, individuals, and so forth. That is, an ERP component is a source of systematic and reliable variability in an ERP data set.
>
> *(Luck 2005: 68)*

Furthermore, researchers such as Politzer-Ahles (2020) have urged language researchers not to associate ERP components with distinct linguistic modules, such as syntax, morphology, or pragmatics, because these brain responses are not "uniquely attributed" to a given one (Politzer-Ahles 2020: 12). Hence, we cannot associate these components as a straightforward measure of the processing of a given linguistic structure. To illustrate this point, Politzer-Ahles uses the following analogy to explain why a given index, such as the N400, cannot be taken to directly index a particular structure, such as a scalar implicature.

> We could think of the brain responses in such experiments as being like a high-tech thermometer. A person who is sick might show a higher reading on a thermometer than a person who is not sick. But this happens because the sickness causes the person's body temperature to rise and that temperature in turn affects the thermometer. A person observing the thermometer reading is not directly observing the illness; rather, they are only observing a downstream consequence of it. In the same way, a person observing N400 effects in an experiment is observing downstream consequences of a pragmatic computation, rather than observing the computation itself.
>
> *(Politzer-Ahles 2020: 12)*

Empirical evidence that the N400 does not index a particular linguistic module or structure is extensive. Morgan-Short and Tanner (2013) have noted that efforts to classify these components, which do not constitute language-specific effects, as categorical identifiers of either semantic anomaly or syntactic ungrammaticality have failed, with a number of counterexamples available in the literature. Some early studies attempting to tease out violations of different types (semantic, morphological, or syntactic; e.g., Friederici et al. 1993) have indeed identified different components for each, but can find it difficult to disentangle from potentially mediating effects (e.g., prosody). Morgan-Short and Tanner (2013) further point out that some researchers have attempted to recast such interpretations, suggesting instead that components such as the N400 and the P600, which we will review below, are reflective of more general processes, like memory-based or combinatorial processes. Osterhout et al. (2012), for instance, suggest viewing language processing functions within a framework of "streams of processing," in which information (e.g., visual information) gets separated at the level of the cortex. These streams are assumed to be independent yet to interact with others. If this proposal is on the right track, Osterhout and colleagues suggest that the ultimate goal would be to "identify the neural circuits that mediate these processing streams [...] to link the neurobiological evidence with a psycholinguistic theory of language processing" (Osterhout et al. 2012: 357). With these cautionary notes in mind, let's review some of the most important language-related ERP components and how they have been interpreted, at least historically, starting with the N400 effect.

In linguistic research, the N400 effect has been generally taken to be associated with the processing of meaning or semantic information, especially in response to a semantic anomaly or incongruity. This effect was first identified by Kutas and Hillyard (1980), who found evidence of the N400 effect when participants read sentences such as *He took a sip from* ... when the word replacing the ellipsis was unexpected, thus representing either moderate incongruity (*...a waterfall*) or strong incongruity (*...a transmitter*). Most interestingly, Kutas and Hillyard found that the magnitude of the amplitude of the N400 component was positively related to the type of incongruity. In other words, the effect was smaller in cases of moderate incongruity (*He took a sip from a waterfall*), where the word was unexpected yet technically possible, and larger in cases of strong incongruity (*He took a sip from a transmitter*), where the last word would have been completely inconsistent or unexpected, given the preceding context.

At this point, we should briefly touch upon a difference in terminology. At the outset of the chapter, we talked about an ERP component, which we defined as a negative deflection in the waveform around the 400-millisecond mark after the onset of the presentation of the stimulus. This component tends to be present when participants process any meaningful (linguistic) stimulus (Morgan-Short & Tanner 2013: 132). When we discussed the landmark study by Kutas and Hillyard (1980), however, we mentioned an ERP effect. At this point, you might be wondering what the difference between an N400 component and an N400 effect consists of, exactly. As is the case with methodologies such as self-paced reading, discussed in Chapter 8, we understand the magnitude of the effect of ungrammaticality or infelicity only in reference to a control condition. Thus, N400 effects refer to the magnitude changes in amplitude between specific conditions, which typically reflect different language stimuli or contexts. Thus, it is often the case that the important measure is the effect (that is, the difference between the experimental and control conditions) and not the component (the latency of the waveform's peak) that is of interest to language researchers.

An early review of the conditions eliciting the N400 effect in linguistic studies (Kutas & Van Petten 1998: 144) noted what is now well known about the N400, which is that it is an "extremely robust component" that has been elicited with semantic anomalies, be it with visual or auditory presentations, across multiple languages. Furthermore, it has been noted for being a "remarkably stable" effect in terms of its latency, since the timing across experiments and languages appears to be consistent (Rommers & Federmeier 2018: 249). A more recent review of 30 years of research on the component (Kutas & Federmeier 2011) further reported that the N400 has been found to be modulated by factors such as a word's frequency, concreteness, or semantic relatedness. Importantly, findings also show that this effect appears when participants process not only the meaning of individual words but also pragmatic anomalies (see van Berkum 2009 for review). Miller and Rothman (2020) caution researchers to take into consideration methodological design issues when interpreting effects such as the N400. Since the N400 can be modulated by the lexico-semantic relationship of words, often measured by the frequency with which these lexical elements occur or its Latent Semantic Analysis (LSA) value, it is important to distinguish whether the main effects are attenuated (or exacerbated) by LSA values.[2] Overall, however, the N400 effect is still largely thought to reflect the ease or difficulty of accessing and integrating semantic and pragmatic information during language processing.

The second most well-known ERP component in linguistic research is known as the P600. As you may now have guessed, the P600 component signals a positive deflection in the ERP waveform that is typically visible around 600 milliseconds after the onset of the stimulus, as illustrated in Figure 10.1. Unlike the N400 effect, however, the P600 tends to last longer and to not be as stable in terms of the latency of its peak. In fact, this component does not always have a single clearly identifiable peak, since the magnitude of the amplitude (and latency) of the P600 has been found to vary depending on the nature of the anomaly and the task demands of the experimental paradigm (Rommers & Federmeier 2018).

Early on, the P600 effect was elicited when participants were exposed to ungrammaticalities or other syntactic violations, such as subcategorization violations. Osterhout and Holcomb (1993), for example, evoked the component using sentences that have been found to induce garden path effects such as *The broker persuaded the investor to sell the stock* vs. *The broker persuaded to sell the stock was sent to jail*. Note that in the second sentence, readers typically show difficulty because they (mistakenly) interpret the verb "persuaded" as being the main verb of the clause, leading them to reanalyze the sentence when they encounter the prepositional phrase "to sell the stock." Friederici et al. (1996) also elicited P600 components with violations of syntactic category in L1 German speakers (e.g., *Das Metall wurde veredelt von dem Goldschmied* ... 'The metal was refined by the goldsmith ...' vs. * *Das Metall wurde zur veredelt von dem Goldschmied* ... 'The metal was for refined by the goldsmith ...'). Other conditions that have been associated with the effect include morphosyntactic violations of agreement (e.g., White et al. 2012) or tense morphology. Although the P600 effect has typically been associated with syntactic reanalysis, Kaan et al. (2000) have suggested that the P600 component is not only associated with reanalysis but indexes a more generalized difficulty with syntactic integration processes.

Although, as we have seen, the difference between the N400 and P600 components has blurred somewhat in more recent studies, early evidence that the N400 and P600 effects are distinct came from studies like Friederici et al. (1993), which investigated whether the processing of semantic, morphological, or syntactic information evinced distinct patterns in terms of the temporal and topographical characteristics of the evoked potentials. Friederici et al. (1993) had participants read sentences in their L1 (German), comparing an auxiliary verb in four different conditions: no anomalies (e.g., *Der Finder wurde belohnt*, 'The finder was rewarded'), semantic anomalies containing a selectional restriction violation (e.g., *Die Wolke wurde begraben*, 'The cloud was buried'), morphosyntactic violations (e.g., *Das Parkett wurde bohnere*, 'The parquet [wood flooring] was polish'), or syntactic violations (e.g., *Der Freund wurde im besucht*, 'The friend was in the visited'). While the semantic anomaly condition evoked an N400 effect, the morphosyntactic violation elicited an early negativity followed by a late positivity.

These results notwithstanding, we have learned that many researchers of the neurobiology of language who have studied the incremental nature of sentence processing emphasize that the field has not reached a "truly neurobiologically grounded perspective" just yet (Bornkessel-Schlesewsky et al. 2016: 615). However, as we mentioned earlier, one of the insights emerging from this research is that ERP components such as the N400 and the P600 are not specifically linked to any particular linguistic or cognitive operations. As a result, Bornkessel-Schlesewsky et al. (2016) note that an increasing number of researchers are adopting more "general mechanistic interpretations" of these components and thus avoid emphasizing the distinction between them. They also highlight that a second important insight that emerges from the research is the importance of predictive (top-down) processes, which they note is compatible with assumptions of "hierarchically organized neural architecture" (p. 615), which is particularly interesting to consider in the light of recent trends in bilingualism research (see, e.g., Kaan 2014).

Up until this point, we have talked about the temporal acuity of the ERP technique, but we have not talked much about information regarding (scalp) topography. This is because, although ERPs offer good temporal resolution, there are important limitations when researchers attempt to obtain spatial information. As Luck (2005) notes, if we have evidence of voltage distribution from the scalp, researchers cannot pinpoint, with full certainty, where the effect was generated. Nevertheless, Morgan-Short and Tanner (2013) note that topographical information can be useful since, when it is coupled with information about the conditions giving rise to the effects, it can help determine whether effects that share certain characteristics, such as the N400 and the Left Anterior Negativity, are indeed distinct effects, potentially linked to different components. In addition, methodologies such as magnetoencephalography (MEG) can be used for this purpose, since this methodology retains the temporal acuity of EEGs, but can also identify source location with much more precision (Rommers & Federmeier 2018).

Within GenSLA studies, most investigations focusing on sentence processing have tested hypotheses that make predictions based on theoretically principled distinctions. For instance, the Interpretability Hypothesis (Tsimpli & Dimitrakopoulou 2007; Tsimpli & Mastropavlou 2007) is based on the theoretical distinction between *interpretable* features—features with semantic content that play a part in the interpretation of a sentence—and *uninterpretable* features—formal features that are relevant only for the syntactic derivation.[3] To exemplify, Tsimpli and Mastropavlou note that interpretable features include [definiteness], φ-features on nouns (person, number, gender), or [*wh*] features in interrogatives, while φ-features on verbs and adjectives and case (e.g., accusative, dative) are uninterpretable. Based on this distinction, the Interpretability Hypothesis predicts that learners whose L1 does not instantiate a given uninterpretable feature will not be able to acquire it in their L2. Interpretable features, on the other hand, should pose no insurmountable difficulty. Crucially, because the Interpretability Hypothesis proposes that learners can use compensatory strategies when uninterpretable features are not properly analyzed, online methodologies can be elucidating since these can measure processing in real time. Case Study Box 10.1 presents an exemplary ERP study that tests the Interpretability Hypothesis and examines the processing of gender and number in L2 Spanish (Gabriele et al. 2021).

Case Study Box 10.1: Gabriele et al. (2021)

Research question: Gabriele et al. studied the processing of number and gender agreement in L2 Spanish by English native speakers. This comparison is particularly interesting because, while the L1 (English) displays number agreement, the gender agreement is unique to the L2 (Spanish). The authors test the Interpretability Hypothesis, which proposes that uninterpretable features that are not instantiated in the L1 (such as those involved in number and gender agreement) will pose insurmountable challenges to L2 learners. The authors also tested whether the sensitivity to grammatical violations (expected to be indexed by P600 effects) was related to performance in an Acceptability Judgment Task and an oral production task. Finally, they tested whether individual-level abilities (verbal and nonverbal) could predict performance across the three experimental tasks (ERPs, GJT, production).
Task: ERPs focusing on agreement, an oral production task, was administered. ERPs were obtained multiple times to examine development longitudinally (three times for beginning learners; at two months, six months, and eight months of continued Spanish instruction; intermediate learners were tested two times, at two months and six months of continued Spanish

TABLE 10.1 Experimental design (for ERP experiment) in Gabriele et al. (2021)

	Subject–Verb (number agreement)	Noun–Adjective (number and gender agreement)
Gram.	El obispo católico medita… *The catholic bishop meditates…*	El laboratorio es modern… *The lab is modern (SG)…*
Ungram. (number)	*El obispo católico meditan… *The catholic bishop meditate …*	*El laboratorio es modernos… *The lab is modern (PL)…*
Ungram. (gender)		*El laboratorio es moderna… *The lab is modern (FEM)…*

instruction). Participants also completed a battery of individual-level measures (including measures of Working Memory) (Table 10.1).

Stimuli selection: ERPs testing gender and number agreement under three agreement environments: Subject–Verb number agreement, Noun–Adjective number agreement and Noun–Adjective gender agreement. For the Subject–Verb agreement condition (which tested number agreement), 80 sentence pairs were constructed; for the Noun–Adjective conditions (which tested both number and gender agreement), stimuli consisted of 120 sentence triplets. Both conditions (along with 40 grammatical fillers) were presented in a Latin square (40 sentences per condition). Only third-person singular subjects/nouns were used. Nouns and adjectives were all canonical (i.e., not exceptions). After each sentence, participants were asked to rate the grammaticality of each stimulus.

Participants: Adult learners of L2 Spanish divided by language experience: beginning-level learners (100-level classes; n = 23) and intermediate-level learners (200-level classes; n = 29). L2 data was compared against L1 data from an analogous study (Bond et al. 2011).

Results: Both the beginning and intermediate L2 groups evinced P600 effects for number violations (in both Subject–Verb and Noun–Adjective conditions). P600 effects for gender, however, were only significant for the intermediate L2 group. Performance in the oral production task (for Subject–Verb agreement and Noun–Adjective agreement) was related to larger P600 effects in the ERP experiment. Finally, Working Memory was the only significant predictor for Noun–Adjective (number) violations; the relationship with Noun–Adjective (gender) violations was marginal but trending in the right direction.

10.3 Conclusion

As we have seen, ERPs is a methodology that offers undeniable advantages to researchers in terms of the temporal definition that can be obtained. It affords researchers the opportunity to investigate the time course of language processing, providing them with neurophysiological information regarding language processing at several levels (words, segments, sentences, or even longer discourse), while doing so non-invasively. They should be attempted only after substantial training in a neurolinguistic laboratory, since ERP correct implementation involves a lot of technical requirements.

10.4 Discussion questions

1 Although many of the studies that we have described in this and other chapters include more than one experiment, we have not talked in much detail about method triangulation (the use of multiple methods to answer a research question; see Hoot et al. 2020 for a discussion regarding triangulation types). What advantages do you believe that triangulation can offer, specifically when it comes to ERP research? What kinds of research questions do you believe *require* the use of method triangulation?
2 We have seen that the EEG technique can be used with a variety of populations since the stimuli can be auditory or visual (text or images) or even include video clips. However, an important caveat is the technique does restrict certain stimuli or presentations that generate eye-movement artifacts (saccades, blinks, etc.). How do you think that researchers can address these constraints? Can you think of research that cannot be conducted with this method because of these restrictions?

Notes

1 An important issue that Bornkessel-Schlesewsky et al. (2016) raise is that these "information sources" are typically thought of in terms of units that are relevant to linguistics subdomains (e.g., phonology, syntax, or semantics). However, they note that "the utility of such concepts for the neurobiology of language is considerably less clear" (p. 607). The reader is referred to their chapter for more information regarding this view.
2 Latent semantic analysis (LSA) is a technique in natural language processing; more specifically, in distributional semantics. It analyzes relationships between a set of documents and the words they contain. LSA assumes that words that are close in meaning will occur in similar pieces of text (that is, have similar distribution).
3 This hypothesis was the theoretical foundation of the studies reviewed in Box 5.2, although we did not emphasize the theory there. However, the theoretical distinction is crucial in the studies testing the Interpretability Hypothesis.

Further reading

Morgan-Short, K. (2014). Electrophysiological approaches to understanding second language acquisition: A field reaching its potential. *Annual Review of Applied Linguistics, 34*, 15–36. https://doi.org/10.1017/S026719051400004X

Steinhauer, K. (2014). Event-related potentials (ERPs) in second language research: A brief Introduction to the technique, a selected review, and an invitation to reconsider Critical Periods in L2. *Applied Linguistics, 35*(4), 393–417. https://doi.org/10.1093/applin/amu028

11
PRODUCTION TASKS

11.1 Introduction

This chapter presents oral and written production elicitation tasks used to investigate a specific research question in a single study. There are also large collections of speech samples, known as learner corpora, which are shared among researchers and can be used to suit varied theoretical agendas.[1] Different production tasks have been employed, ranging from free narratives and interviews to very controlled tasks designed according to a set of variables. In this latter type of task, participants are prompted to produce structures from one word to whole sentences in length.

This chapter shows that production data, much like acceptability tasks, can be very useful in investigating grammatical competence as well as implicit knowledge. Oral and written data can also reveal when a particular structure starts to be produced, whether target forms are used appropriately in different contexts and how the meaning of those forms develops.

Production tasks are quite versatile and can be easily adapted to suit different research questions. They are often combined with interpretation/introspective tasks to elicit different types of evidence on the use of one single structure. Some of the main theoretical debates in GenSLA research have been elucidated by studies using production data, in particular samples of spontaneous speech from bilingual children and adult learners. For example, Lardiere (1998a) used oral production data from an adult Chinese immigrant learner of English called Patty to show that although she does not always produce the morphological expression of past tense in English

DOI: 10.4324/9781003160762-13

(i.e., the *-ed* ending of verbs), her near-native grammar has the full syntactic representation of the functional category of Tense.

Production tasks can elicit either oral or written data. Which one is more appropriate depends on several factors, including the research question and the overall goal of the study. Some studies (e.g., Sanz 1997; Perpiñán 2013) have found that participants show better results in written tasks, partly because speaking in real time utilizes more computational resources and puts more pressure on the participants. Different oral tasks have been found to yield different results as well (see Domínguez 2019). For instance, Domínguez and Arche (2022) examined oral data from English learners of Spanish which completed three oral tasks (a paired discussion task, an interview with a researcher and a picture-based narrative). The examination of the use of null and overt subjects showed that these tasks vary in their success in eliciting the target forms for all participants (native Spanish speakers as well as learners). Careful consideration of the type of production task to be used is necessary when including oral elicitation tasks in the design of a study.

11.2   Open-ended, naturalistic production tasks

These tasks involve very little researcher manipulation and are relatively straightforward to design. The goal is to elicit oral or written productions which are as natural as possible, often to investigate what speakers can produce at that specific time or whether the use of a particular form changes over a set period. These tasks can be valuable when the goal is to produce a wider range of structures and forms. Another advantage of using open-ended tasks is that they allow researchers to observe innovations and new forms emerging in the data.

Longitudinal studies investigating spontaneous speech are common in both monolingual and bilingual child language studies, including those investigating L2 child acquisition. The children are often audio-recorded while engaged in daily activities at set intervals (i.e., every two weeks, every month, every three months, etc.) and recording can take place for months or even years. These data are suitable for gaining insights into when a particular form emerges and whether it is used consistently or not (what is known as "optional or variable use"). Often, studies combine production data, especially if naturalistic, with acceptability data which are obtained through experimentally controlled tasks and target speakers' intuitions. Spontaneous productions can be analyzed both quantitatively and qualitatively.

Studies which investigate oral production in older children and adults often employ the interview technique between a bilingual speaker and an investigator to stimulate free conversation. The interview can be semi-structured if the investigator uses a set of predetermined questions to guide the conversation. The interview elicits open-ended answers and typical questions often require the participants to describe their everyday lives, their families or some past experiences. If the investigator is interested in eliciting specific structures, (e.g., verbs in the past tense), it is important to include questions that would prompt participants to use the past tense in their answers (e.g., asking about their last holiday, some activities they liked doing as a child and what they did last weekend).

Whether a spontaneous production task (which elicits open-ended answers) is appropriate to answer a particular research question depends on the target structure being investigated. These tasks can be valuable in eliciting structures which are produced frequently such as articles, verbal endings, canonical word order, null subjects or gender marking. However, they may not be completely appropriate to investigate less frequent structures such as *wh*-questions, negation or non-canonical word orders. For the latter structures, controlled elicitation tasks (e.g., picture-based narratives or elicited imitations) may be more suitable. These are reviewed in Section 11.5.

Many studies examining the use of uninflected verbal forms (termed "root infinitives") in child and adult L2 acquisition have used spontaneous oral data to settle an important debate in GenSLA: namely, whether missing inflectional forms are due to lack of syntactic knowledge or some problem with accessing surface morphology (specifically, mapping the syntactic structures onto the appropriate surface forms). Studies which support a mapping problem have used oral naturalistic speech to conclude that when L2 children and adults use L2 verbs in the infinitive (e.g., *Lucas eat cake*), these uninflected forms cannot be taken as evidence that the speakers lack the appropriate functional category (i.e., Tense and Agreement). Such findings provide evidence for the Missing Surface Inflection Hypothesis (Prévost & White 2000) and the Missing Inflection Hypothesis (Haznedar & Schwartz 1997). These studies investigated speech productions of research participants from a variety of backgrounds, including Russian children learning English (Ionin & Wexler 2002); a group of adult L2 learners of French and German (Prévost & White 2000); one adult Chinese speaker of English (Lardiere 1998a, 1998b); one Turkish child learning English (Haznedar & Schwartz 1997) and one adult Turkish learner of German from Klein and Perdue's (1992) ESF oral corpus (Schwartz & Sprouse 1996). Key evidence obtained by oral data revealed that the uninflected forms gradually disappear, the incorrect use of null subjects seems to be an independent phenomenon and, when tense/agreement morphology is produced, it is almost always correct.[2]

11.3 Coding and analysis

Oral data, especially if it is part of a large dataset, needs to be transcribed and coded. The transcription can apply to a selection of the data or the whole set and it can be as detailed as needed depending on the research questions. How the data are coded can vary as well. Many studies have made use of "obligatory contexts" to determine when target forms should be supplied (see details in Pica 1983). The researcher first needs to identify all the places where the target form is required in the standard variety of the target language. For instance, in the English sentence *I am cooking dinner*, there is one obligatory context for the use of the progressive verbal marker *-ing*. Any inaccurate uses of *-ing* would be picked up by this method, for instance, if participants produced *I am cook* instead. The use of obligatory contexts allows researchers to determine how accurately L2 speakers use target forms and how much of the underlying grammar they have acquired.

However, the obligatory context method has been criticized because it does not consider that functional morphology may be used by speakers in contexts where it is not needed in Standard English (e.g., the plural in *one more movies*) (Pica 1983). This is an important objection since interlanguage grammars are known for variable use of forms as well as overgeneralizations. Researchers should also take these cases into account when analyzing production data, including when coding.

Coding the transcribed/written data can be done in various ways according to the specific research question. Some studies use a coding method in which the numbers 0, 1 and 2 are given to each morpheme as in (1) (Pica 1983).

1   2 = morpheme supplied and it is correct (e.g., *I am cooking*)
    1 = morpheme supplied but it is incorrect (e.g., *I am cooked*)
    0 = no morpheme supplied (e.g., *I am cook*)

Other studies prefer a simpler binary coding system using just "1" for correct uses and "0" for all incorrect uses. This was the case in a study by Albirini and Benmamoun (2014), which investigated L2 transfer effects on four grammatical areas of Arabic (adjectives, plural nouns, the analytic genitive and restrictive relative clauses) by eliciting oral data through three different elicitation tasks. In one of these tasks, Egyptian and Palestinian heritage speakers in the USA were audio recorded when talking about themselves and their families.

Other studies prefer to present the results as averages and means of use to show the number of times that a target form is used (or not) in an obligatory context. Let's say there are 50 obligatory contexts for the use of the English definite article and an L2 speaker has only produced it in 25 contexts. That means that the article has been correctly supplied 50% of the time by this speaker. Reporting of percentages is useful as it allows for easy comparison and analysis between more than one learner. However, this way of presenting the results does not reveal much about whether the forms are used appropriately in the correct contexts.

To examine appropriate use, further analyses are needed for each obligatory use of the form. For instance, Ionin, Ko and Wexler (2004) carried out a study to investigate the use of English definite and indefinite articles by Korean and Russian learners, languages without articles. Their analysis was based on the basic assumption that definiteness and specificity determine the use of articles in languages with two articles, such as English which has a [+definite] article (i.e., *the*) and a [−definite] article (i.e., *a*). Both articles can be used in specific and non-specific contexts. The authors collected data from two tasks, including a written production task, administered to L1 Russian speakers and L1 Korean speakers learning English. The production task was intended to elicit the production of articles in a relatively natural setting. Learners were presented with five prompts and were invited to answer with three to five sentences in an open-ended format, as they were free to write what they wanted. It was important for the research team to get a very good sense of what contexts were unambiguously definite and indefinite. To achieve this, a group of native English speakers (coders) saw all the contexts in which an article was used but with a blank space replacing the form produced, so they did not have access to the actual productions. The coders were asked to determine which of the contexts were definite and which contexts were indefinite according to their judgment as native speakers.

Many other studies have analyzed the use of forms across semantic and/or pragmatic contexts to obtain a better insight into how much learners know about the appropriate use of the target form. For instance, Domínguez (2013) analyzed over 17 hours of learner recordings from English learners of Spanish at three proficiency levels (beginner, intermediate and advanced). The recordings were elicited through a semi-structured interview and were part of the SPLLOC database (www.splloc.soton.ac.uk).[3] The researcher investigated the use of null and overt subjects in obligatory contexts as well as whether each form had been used appropriately. An analysis of whether a null or an overt pronoun was supplied in each possible context of use was carried out. This allowed for a more accurate and detailed investigation of the use of both forms in the interlanguage of the learners. This type of more detailed analysis focusing on the distribution of forms can be easily adapted to suit a wide range of target forms.

11.4 Semi-controlled elicited narratives

Using prompts to elicit oral and written productions can be quite helpful when investigating forms that are frequently used (see e.g., Ionin et al. 2004 in the previous section). Some tasks include asking participants to write a mini-essay on a particular topic, describe a picture or a series of pictures or finish a story after the beginning has been provided to them. Other prompts for eliciting narratives could include a series of pictures without words or a clip from a silent film. Such prompts ensure that participants can produce free responses without the constraints that usually apply to highly manipulated tasks such as acceptability tasks or some of the oral/written elicitation tasks reviewed in Section 11.5 in this chapter. They are also preferred when researchers are interested in examining samples that resemble what speakers would produce in naturalistic speech.

Participants are often given the chance to examine the pictures available to them, or watch a video clip, before the actual task commences. If the participants are bilingual, they could be asked to do the task in both languages. A vocabulary list can be prepared beforehand to help learners with words they may not know, especially if they are beginners.

In this type of task, very little interaction between the participants and the researcher is needed as, once the task is explained, they are left to complete the task on their own. As in the case of longer oral productions, oral narratives are audio-recorded and later transcribed to facilitate data analysis. Although these tasks are not as free as open-ended tasks (i.e., interviews), one advantage is that they prompt participants to produce a narrative with a (semi)-fixed structure which facilitates comparisons across participant groups.

11.4.1 Picture-based elicitation

In this task, participants are asked to tell a story based on a series of pictures which are used as prompts. This is a very common method of elicitation of oral narratives as the pictures are easy to prepare, the task is easy to administer, and the pictures/story can suit a wide range of proficiencies. Because there are no words presented to the participants, their production fully relies on their knowledge of the target language.

Once participants are ready to start the task, the investigator provides clear instructions, for example, "Now I would like you to tell me the story using your own words." The task ends after the participants finish telling the story. In some cases, a short interview based on the story may follow. This can provide the researcher with extra naturalistic data that can complement the data already obtained through the story retelling.

One of the most widely used picture-based narrative elicitation tasks is the Frog Story (Berman & Slobin 1994), based on the book *Frog, Where*

Are You? written by Mercer Mayer (1969). The story has a basic narrative structure using 24 pictures and shows events that are easy to understand, so it is well-suited to collect data from children. This task has been used for investigating multiple morphosyntactic structures and can suit an array of research agendas.

Several studies have employed the "Nati y Pancho" story developed by the SPLLOC project (www.splloc.soton.ac.uk) to investigate the acquisition of past tense forms in Spanish. The task was adapted from the storybook *Missing* by Jonathan Langley ©Frances Lincoln (2000) which depicts the story of Natalia who looks for her cat after he goes missing. To ensure that past tense forms were used, the team included the following prompt on the first page of the picture story: *Todas las mañanas eran iguales* 'Every morning was the same'. The task has been used by researchers interested in eliciting oral productions which contain past tense forms by L2 learners and heritage speakers in an array of languages (see Arche & Domínguez 2024).

The level of engagement between the investigator and the participant can vary across tasks. For instance, Bayram (2013) investigated the acquisition of passive structures (e.g., *The exam is being taken by the students*) in Turkish by a group of heritage speakers in Germany. Since this is an infrequent structure in naturalistic speech, Bayram developed a picture-based description task to force participants to use it. A series of pictures depicting an action was used to engage participants in conversation. Some of the pictures used are shown in Figure 11.1:

Bayram (2013: 120) describes a common interaction which can arise using this method as follows:

2 Researcher: What do you see in the first picture?
   Participant: There is a small fish and a big fish.
   Researcher: What is happening in the second picture?
   Participant: The big fish sees the small fish.
   Researcher: What is happening to the small fish in the third picture?
   Participant: The small fish **is being chased** by the big fish.
   Researcher: What is happening to the small fish in the fourth picture?
   Participant: The small fish **is being eaten** by the big fish.

This elicitation method can facilitate obtaining useful data on the target form as well as comparisons across experimental groups.

Researchers are free to choose whatever story or pictures they find suitable for the purpose of their own research. Using the Frog Story, or other widely used tasks, is convenient if comparisons across populations and across studies are necessary.

FIGURE 11.1 Pictures used in the elicitation task in Bayram (2013).

11.4.2 Silent film elicitation

As with picture-based narratives, the goal is to encourage participants to construct a narrative based on a visual prompt. When a silent film is used, the task can become a recalling exercise since participants typically tell the story based on a clip which they have just watched, but which is no longer available to them. This contrasts with story-retelling tasks which use pictures as prompts, as participants can still see the pictures when performing the task. To avoid this, researchers can ask participants to watch the video twice, asking them to retell the story as they watch the video the second time (see Zyzik 2008). For some researchers, film-based retell tasks are preferred over pictured-based ones, as using a set of pictures is regarded as too artificial when the goal is to elicit spontaneous speech.

One silent film which has been widely used in second language acquisition research is "Modern Times" by Charles Chaplin (1936) and in particular the "Alone and Hungry" segment, which is around eight minutes long and depicts a sequence of actions which are easy to recall and narrate. The task can be used to elicit both oral and written narratives and participants are allowed to watch the clip just once or multiple times. The researcher often leaves the participant alone watching the film and then asks them to describe what they saw (to make the retelling part of the task more realistic).

As Bardovi-Harlig (2000: 201) explains, film-retell tasks can be useful to "elicit comparable language samples across learners while maintaining learner control over the construction of the narratives." However, she also notes some disadvantages, such as the fact that the number of tokens produced can vary across participants, making comparisons less straightforward. It may also be the case that not all contexts in which the target form is used are represented in the clip. This is why studies which have used story retells often also combine them with experimental tasks manipulated to include all the contexts which are relevant to the study (see Domínguez 2019).

11.5   Controlled production tasks

In this type of task, participants are prompted to elicit short answers which reveal in a straightforward manner whether the target form is part of the speaker's grammar. Unlike open-ended tasks, which aim to elicit semi-naturalistic productions, controlled tasks are manipulated so participants are forced to use the target form in relevant contexts. The investigator constructs these tasks based on variables, just like in comprehension tasks, and the use of distracters is common as well. One advantage is that the task ensures elicitation of the target structure, which can be an issue with open-ended tasks. Researchers often use a binary coding system for the answers: they give 1 if the answer is correct and 0 if incorrect.

There are many types of controlled production tasks (e.g., picture/video description task, cloze test, sentence-completion task and forced imitation task) which can be used to elicit oral or written data on a wide range of grammatical structures (e.g., gender marking, articles, aspectual distinctions, focus and prepositions). In all these tasks, the participants are given a prompt (a picture, a short contextual text, a video clip, etc.) and are asked to complete a sentence or choose a word which makes sense in that context. The following subsections present some of these tasks in more detail.

11.5.1   *Cloze test*

Gap-filling or fill-in-the-blank tasks are also known as "cloze tests." This type of task is widely used to measure speakers' proficiency in a second language (Tremblay 2011) by presenting a text in the target language which has every fifth (or sixth, seventh, etc.) word deleted. Participants provide the missing word based on what they can understand from the textual and linguistic cues available.

A recent study by Judy et al. (2023) employed a cloze task based on the story of Goldilocks and the Three Bears (also used by Rothman 2008) to investigate the effects of explicit instruction on the acquisition of Spanish aspectual distinctions. The test included 55 gaps targeting past tense verbs in either preterit (perfective aspect) or imperfect (imperfective aspect). Each gap showed participants the choice between the two possible forms, only one being appropriate in that context. Example (3) shows a structure with the target responses in bold. Each bracket includes a verb showing both preterit and imperfective morphology:

3   Como ya (fue$_{pret}$/**era**$_{imp}$) mediodía, los osos (**se sentaron**$_{pret}$/se sentaban$_{imp}$) a comer.
    'As it was already midday, the bears sat down to eat.'

In this type of elicitation task, participants are forced to make a choice between the two available forms. Since this can be too metalinguistic (it clearly draws attention to the form to be used and not the meaning of the sentence), some researchers prefer to use prompts like pictures to elicit the target words. For instance, to examine the acquisition of reflexive pronouns in Spanish by L2 speakers and heritage speakers, García-Tejada et al. (2023) used an oral elicited production task which included a pair of pictures showing a scene. An introductory text in Spanish explained the context behind each set of pictures, as shown in (4) and in Figure 11.2:

4   Rosita and her mom are happily walking home. Suddenly, Rosita sees a dog, starts crying and her mom says:

FIGURE 11.2   Prompt: "My little daughter, why _____ (to scare)" from García-Tejada, Cuza and Lustres Alonso (2023).

Each set of pictures was followed by an incomplete sentence as in Figure 11.2. The participants had to fill the gap in each sentence with the correct form of the verb supplied in brackets based on the context and the action depicted in the pictures. In this example, the expected answer is "Why are you getting scared" which in Spanish requires a reflexive pronoun (*¿Por qué te asustas?*). If participants were influenced by English, they may prefer to use *Why are you scared?* instead, which does not require a reflexive pronoun in Spanish (*¿Por qué estás asustada?*). The researcher read the context and the prompt in front of the participants using a rising intonation. As is typical in this type of task, the oral responses were audio recorded and later analyzed for accuracy (suppliance of the clitic was coded as 1 and absence of the clitic was coded as 0).

11.5.2 Contextualized elicitation tasks targeting sentences

In this design, participants see a context followed by a question prompting them to produce a sentence which includes the target structure. The context is key in providing the necessary cues to answer the question appropriately. The context and prompt question can be provided orally as in a study by Cuza and Frank (2015) which used a sentence-completion task to investigate the acquisition of double complementizer questions in Spanish. The task was administered to a group of advanced L2 learners of Spanish and a group of Spanish heritage speakers and targeted sentences as in (5):

5 a Ramón le dijo a Celina que dónde cenó anoche.
    'Ramon asked Celina where she ate dinner last night.'
  b Rosa me preguntó (que) cuándo íbamos a salir.
    'Rosa asked me when we were going to go out.'

The participants were asked to complete a sentence based on the information provided in a short context, a preamble, as suggested by a prompt:

6 Preamble: Rosa le contó a Juan adónde fue de compras y Juan le dijo: ¿Cuándo fuiste?
    'Rose told John where she went shopping, and John asked her: When did you go?'
    Prompt: *Juan le dijo a Rosa …* 'John asked Rose …'
    Target: *que cuándo fue de compras* 'when she went shopping'
    Non-Target: *Ø cuándo fue de compras* 'when she went shopping'

In this type of task, the context can be quite short, often just a sentence as in a study by Grüter et al. (2014). These authors used a written story continuation task adapted from Rohde et al. (2006) to examine the acquisition of

160 Methods typically used in GenSLA

aspect by Japanese- and Korean-speaking learners of English. The minimal information available to the learners consisted of one full sentence describing an action. The participants had to complete a second sentence which only included a pronoun which could refer to any of the two people involved in the action. Example (7) shows that the learners saw two pairs of sentences with only one difference, whether the verb was perfective or imperfective:

7 a Emily brought a drink to Melissa. (She) _____ [perfective]
  b Emily was bringing a drink to Melissa. (She) _____ [imperfective]

In a different study, Tuniyan (2018) investigated the acquisition of definiteness and its expression through articles by Chinese and Russian learners of English who are native speakers of languages with no articles. The participants completed a written sentence-completion task. They were given the start of a story and were asked to continue each story by constructing sentences using the words in parentheses as shown in example (8). They could add any words they thought were needed. The words in parenthesis did not include articles and the participants were not given any explicit instructions about using articles.

8 Context sentence: It was Penny's birthday last week, and her best friend gave her a necklace.
    Sentence to complete: (she be very happy) (she wear necklace straight away)
    Possible target answer: "She was very happy, so she wore **the** necklace straight away."

In this context, the participants are expected to produce the definite article if this form is a part of their grammar. This task included contexts in which the target form (articles in this study) is required, providing useful insights on the acquisition of this form by L2 speakers.

11.5.3 Picture/video elicitation tasks

Participants are asked to describe what they see in a series of pictures or video clips by means of short questions. The task aims to elicit short answers which are expected to include the target form(s). The task can be used to investigate a wide range of grammatical structures as well. For instance, Montrul et al. (2013) investigated knowledge of gender agreement and its interaction with diminutive formation. Diminutives in Spanish are nouns which denote small size and carry a suffix (e.g., *-ito, -ita*), which agrees in gender features with determiners and adjectives, as in example (9):

9 El cochecito viejo
   the$_{masc}$ car$_{DIM-masc}$ old$_{masc}$
   'The little old car'

In this study, Spanish heritage speakers and L2 learners completed an oral elicitation task based on a series of pictures which prompted participants to use diminutives in their productions. The participants heard a recording of a native speaker asking a question about the picture, typically the location of an object in the format "What is there on top/under, to the left/ to the right of an object?" The participants had to answer the question naming the appropriate images and were explicitly told to use the diminutive form when appropriate (i.e., when they had to answer about the smaller image). The participants were asked to use sentences with an indefinite determiner, a noun and an adjective of color, since all of these need to agree in gender.

Using video clips, rather than pictures, Leal et al. (2018) developed a similar task, a speeded oral production task, to investigate focus and word order variation. The task elicited short sentences with a subject, a verb and a direct object. The participants saw a short silent video clip which was followed by a question about what happened in that clip. Participants answered the question with a short sentence as if they were providing information for someone who had not watched the video. Although participants could answer freely, they were biased toward producing the expected answer. Trying to elicit structures with different word orders is not easy, as the task needs to cover all the appropriate contexts for each word order. This video-based elicitation task was more natural than previous research which had used written prompts (typically a context).

Case Study Box 11.1: Espírito Santo et al. (2023)

Research question: Relative clauses exist in both European Portuguese (EP) and Chinese, but they vary with respect to whether they allow resumption and wh-movement (e.g., *This is the debate$_i$ that the politician mentioned __/it$_i$ yesterday*). EP shows overt wh-movement through two strategies, pied-piping or movement with the deletion of the preposition. In Chinese, on the other hand, there is no conclusive evidence that wh-movement exists in prepositional relative clauses, but a resumptive pronoun is required in this structure. *Can adult Chinese learners acquire movement properties in different relativization strategies in Portuguese? Specifically, can they use resumptive relative clauses and the appropriate pied-pipping strategies?*

Task: Oral elicitation task. Participants saw a scenario (two pairs of pictures) on a computer screen and some information describing each image. This information was also read to the participants by a researcher. The second picture showed a selection of the previous image followed by a question which they had to answer as quickly as possible.[4] For instance, participants saw a picture of a woman who dreamed of a watch. The second picture showed a picture of just the watch followed by a question which prompted them to elicit the target sentence "This is the watch…. Of which Ana dreamt."

Stimuli: 34 items, for a total of 68 scenarios (16 relative clause items and 18 non-relative clause items). The scenarios were randomly assigned to List A or List B, the only difference being the order in which items appeared. Half of the participants completed List A first and half completed List B first.

Participants: 72 L1-Chinese learners of L2-EP (38 Mandarin speakers and 18 Cantonese speakers) and 30 native controls. 36 intermediate and 36 advanced learners.

Results: Unexpectedly, Chinese speakers did not transfer their full native grammar since they did not resort to a non movement account resolved with resumptive pronouns, the strategy used in Chinese. This could be because they were intermediate and advanced learners with enough knowledge and experience to help them resolve any L1 transfer issues. The participants showed evidence of having acquired the properties of wh-movement, as they consistently produced relative clauses with pied-piping and did not produce resumptive pronouns, the option available in their L1.

Finally, Perpiñán et al. (2020) used a map as a visual prompt in an oral elicitation task. The target structure was a sentence with a copula (*ser/estar* 'to be') in Spanish and a prepositional phrase. The participants saw a map of a city in a Spanish-speaking country which included pictures of notable buildings (e.g., cinema, hospital, theatre, hotel, church, disco, university, restaurant and stadium). The participants had to locate four objects and four events on the map using the target structure.

This section has shown that a wide range of formats can be used in controlled production tasks. Careful consideration of the target structures and contexts in which they should/should not appear is necessary. These tasks can be used for eliciting insights into grammatical competence for a wide range of properties.

11.6 Elicited imitation

The benefits of elicited imitation (EI) or repetition tasks have been widely discussed by authors from various theoretical backgrounds (e.g., Bley-Vroman & Chaudron 1994; Rebuschat & Mackay 2013; Perpiñán 2013).[5] In this oral elicitation task, participants are asked to repeat a word or words which they hear aurally. There needs to be a controlled pause between the input sentence and the start of the repetition. Participants are meant to feel under pressure and are given a short period of time to produce the repetition.

As Bley-Vroman and Chaudron (1994) and Rebuschat and Mackey (2013) explain, it is assumed that accurate imitation is possible only if the structures being imitated have been acquired. Any inaccuracies can, thus, be useful to gain insights into the grammar of speakers. It is widely assumed that EI can tap into implicit (procedural, nonconscious linguistic competence) knowledge (Ellis 2005; Erlam 2009; Bowles 2011), as learners cannot solely rely on rote memorization or working memory to successfully complete the task (see Erlam 2009). As Lei and Yan (2022) argue, since the sentence that needs to be repeated exceeds the capacity of short-term memory, imitation would be difficult without actual comprehension that requires a speaker to draw on their long-term memory (and thus access stored grammatical knowledge). This argument is supported by Munnich et al. (1994), which attested to some convergence between EI tsks and Acceptability Judgment Tasks (AJT) (Flynn 1986). Using data from a group of bilingual children, Dosi, Papadopoulou and Tsimpli (2016) also argue that EI can reflect language ability and that more complex working memory skills, rather than simple memory, are needed to complete this task.

Bowles (2011) clearly demonstrates that EI can access learners' implicit knowledge. This is part of a wider study testing Ellis's (2005) battery of tasks examining implicit and explicit knowledge. Bowles asked both L2 and heritage speakers of Spanish to complete an imitation test, a narrative test, a metalinguistic knowledge task and two types of AJTs (one timed and one untimed). The results show that the L2 learner group achieved the highest scores on the two tests which measured explicit knowledge (the metalinguistic knowledge test (72.4%), followed by the untimed AJT (66.9%)). Interestingly, the heritage speakers' results showed the opposite pattern, as their lowest scores were found in the metalinguistic knowledge task. This pattern is consistent with the assumption that instructed learners perform better on tasks where they can use explicit knowledge. Since heritage speakers performed well in the EI task, we can assume that this is a task in which minimal explicit knowledge is required.

According to Rebuschat and Mackey (2013), researchers need to take into consideration the proficiency level of the participants when constructing a sentence which needs to be repeated. These authors also indicate that it is important that the pause between the end of the sentence and the start of the repetition is sufficiently long and that the target structure or form is in the appropriate position in the sentence, since the initial and final positions are typically more salient and easier to remember. Clear instructions should be provided to the participants with details of what the task will entail and when they will need to start speaking as the task is timed and there is limited time to repeat each sentence.

An example of the use of an EI to investigate grammatical acquisition is found in Chrabaszcz and Jiang (2014). The task was designed to investigate whether a group of Spanish speakers and a group of Russian speakers of English will show differences in their knowledge of the definite English article in non-generic contexts (e.g., *Fendi bought a car on Monday. On Wednesday he crashed the car*) (Chrabaszcz & Jiang 2014: 355). Spanish and English both use an article in this context, whereas Russian does not. The task was intended to show that the two learner groups would show differences due to the influence of their native language.

Participants saw a picture with a contextualizing sentence on a computer screen. After that, they heard the target sentence which sometimes agreed with the information depicted in the picture, but not always. After a pause of 30 ms, the participants had to do two tasks: say whether they agree or disagree with the target sentence they had just heard and repeat the sentence. The agreement/disagreement response was included to make the elicitation more meaning-focused and reconstructive and to ensure that implicit knowledge was being accessed. Each target sentence was the appropriate length so participants could not retain them in memory. Results showed differences between the learning groups, supporting the authors' prediction that L1 influence is relevant for this grammatical structure.

To investigate the acquisition of relative clauses, which are infrequent in the input, Bayram (2013) designed a task in which two almost identical pictures were presented to a group of Turkish heritage speakers in Germany. This task shares some features with EI tasks as the researcher plays an active role by asking specific questions which include the target structure, as in (10):

10 Researcher: "In your picture, is there a man who is watering the tree?"
    Participant: "Yes. In yours, is there a cat that is chasing the mouse?"

This method prompts the participant to use a relative clause, the target structure. Since the participant is engaged in conversation and is focusing on meaning, there is less focus on applying metalinguistic knowledge.

11.7 Find/spot the difference between pictures

This task presents the participant with a pair of pictures which are mostly identical, but which also show an obvious difference. The participant must describe what is different, mostly unaided, as the difference is clearly detectable. The investigator can engage with the participant to mimic natural conversation. The EI task used in Byram (2013) (see Section 11.6) was part of a spot-the-difference task in which participants had to describe the differences between two pictures in a conversation with the investigator.

Spinner (2013) also employed a spot-the-difference task but allowed the participants to answer freely. She investigated the acquisition of number and gender in Swahili by speakers of English. English does not show grammatical gender morphologically, whereas Swahili encodes both number and gender in one single nominal morpheme. The materials included pairs of cards depicting the same scene but with some clear differences with respect to color or size. Participants had to orally describe the difference between the pictures. Some pictures depicted people performing an action which prompted the elicitation of verbs. The responses were audio recorded and transcribed. The target nouns and adjectives were chosen from the textbooks which the students used in their Swahili classes and included all the gender classes in this language. The results indicated problems with plural marking rather than gender, which can be explained by Feature Reassembly (Lardiere 2009).

11.8 Conclusion

Oral and written production tasks have been widely used by generative second language researchers as they are extremely versatile and easily adaptable to test almost any structure. Tasks which take an open-ended format encourage learners to produce speech which they would produce naturally and can be valuable when investigating structures which are very frequent in the input. Production tasks can also be designed to elicit forms which are infrequent in the input. This is achieved by presenting the participants with contexts in which the target structure is expected to be used. The use of prompts and visual aids is a common way to achieve this.

In many studies, tasks which elicit production data are combined with tasks which elicit interpretation data (e.g., acceptability tasks), as this can provide more robust evidence for the same phenomenon. Although GenSLA research has mostly relied on introspective tasks to access grammatical

166 Methods typically used in GenSLA

representations, it is now assumed that some production tasks, such as EI, can also tap learner's implicit knowledge (nonconscious linguistic competence which relies on automatic processing) (see Ellis 2005; Bowles 2011). Since the application of explicit or implicit knowledge varies according to the demands imposed by the task (Bialystok 1982), careful consideration should be given to the actual task design. Many of the tasks described in this chapter show ways in which participants can engage in a task which focuses on semantic interpretation, rather than producing a particular form. The more controlled the production, the less naturalistic data will be elicited. Hence, researchers need to decide which design suits them better, also taking into consideration other factors such as the proficiency level of the learners and the properties of the structure being investigated.

11.9 Discussion questions

1 Imagine that you need to create a production task to examine the acquisition of the present tense in Spanish by a group of English speakers. This form can be used in two different contexts: with a progressive meaning (*Marta canta ahora en la ducha*/*Marta is singing in the shower right now) and with a habitual meaning (*Marta siempre canta en la ducha*/ Marta always sings in the shower). Only the habitual meaning is available in English. Discuss which types of production tasks would be most suitable to investigate the acquisition of this form and why.
2 Explain why open-ended tasks are more suitable to elicit naturalistic speech, compared to controlled tasks. Think of a study in which the elicited data should be close to what speakers produce in real-life contexts. What grammatical construction would you choose?
3 Think about how the L2 proficiency of the participants can impact the design of a controlled production task. Consider how you would design a spot-the-difference task for beginner and very advanced learners. What key changes would be required and why?

Notes

1 Chapter 12 explains this method of data elicitation in detail.
2 Other studies, e.g., Meisel (1997), Beck (1998), Eubank (1993/1994) and Vainikka and Young-Scholten (1994, 1996), have claimed that the production of uninflected forms can be the result of problems with syntax.
3 A full description of the SPLLOC database and the tasks used to elicit oral narratives can be found in Chapter 12.
4 Two other tasks included in the study (a self-paced reading acceptability task and a self-paced reading acceptability judgment task) are not described here.
5 Elicited imitation tasks are also used to evaluate L2 learners' proficiency. For a discussion on the validity of this talk as a language proficiency measure, see Yan et al. (2016); Lei and Yan (2002); Tracy-Ventura et al. (2014).

Further reading

Domínguez, L. (2019). A 'mixed methods' approach for investigating aspect in a second language: Evidence from the SPLLOC project. *Dutch Journal of Applied Linguistics, 8*(1), 41–66.

Faitaki, F., & Murphy, V. A. (2019). Oral language elicitation tasks in applied linguistics research. In J. McKinley and H. Rose (Eds.), *The Routledge handbook of research methods in applied linguistics* (pp. 360–369). Oxford: Routledge.

Perpiñán, S. (2013). Accounting for variability in L2 data: Type of knowledge, task effects, and linguistic structure. In J. W. Schwieter (Ed.), *Innovative research and practices in second language acquisition and bilingualism* (pp. 165–192). Amsterdam: John Benjamins.

Rebuschat, P., & Mackey, A. (2013). Prompted production. In C. A. Chapelle (Ed.), *The Encyclopedia of applied linguistics* (Vol. 5). Oxford: Wiley-Blackwell.

12
LEARNER CORPORA

12.1 Introduction

In this chapter, we overview how learner corpora can be used to address research questions from a generative second language acquisition lens. We describe the main characteristics of learner corpora, how they are constructed and what makes corpora a useful tool to investigate L2 language knowledge and use. We also provide concrete examples of how researchers have successfully employed this methodology to explain the L2 acquisition process and to test specific hypotheses.

Learner corpora are collections of data, put together for a specific purpose, and which are often analyzed using computerized tools (see Myles 2005, 2015; Callies & Paquot 2015). Researchers outside the field of corpus linguistics became interested in corpora in the early 1990s, since this methodology allowed them to investigate frequencies and compare between different groups (e.g., learners of different L1 backgrounds; learners vs native speakers), all while providing access to large amounts of data from which generalizations could be drawn (see Myles 2005).

An excellent example of the usefulness of computerized data is the Child Language Exchange System (CHILDES) database (https://childes.talkbank.org, MacWhinney & Snow 1990), which is the child data component of the TalkBank system (MacWhinney 2000).[1] TalkBank includes various sets of oral data contributed by researchers around the world investigating the development (i.e., grammatical knowledge, formulaic language, lexical and discourse development, etc.) of 34 languages. The main objective of TalkBank is easy data sharing among the research community, since this tool

DOI: 10.4324/9781003160762-14

provides free access to transcripts that are tagged for part of speech and include morphological analyses, often related to a corresponding audio/video file. CHILDES has set the agenda on how to use computerized analysis that can easily fit different research agendas.

L2 researchers have only recently begun to capitalize on research tools borrowed from corpus linguistics. One of the first and best well-known learner corpus is the International Corpus of Learner English (ICLE; https://uclouvain.be/en/research-institutes/ilc/cecl/icle.html) led by Sylviane Granger at the Catholic University of Louvain (Belgium). ICLE is a corpus of written learner language that has benefited the education and SLA research communities for decades. The corpus was first created in 2002 and comprises written texts from English learners from 25 different language backgrounds. It currently contains over 5.5 million words and it is machine readable so the data can be straightforwardly analyzed with computer tools (see Granger et al. 2002, 2015).

Currently, learner corpora from diverse populations, genres and learning contexts are available. These include CEDEL2, which is a written corpus of L2 English compositions produced by speakers of various native languages (Lozano 2022); LANGSNAP, which includes both spoken and written data produced by learners of French and Spanish during their year abroad component of a university language degree (Mitchell et al. 2017); and Spanish Learner Language Oral Corpus (SPLLOC), which contains oral data elicited by various tasks from L1-English learners of L2 Spanish (Mitchell et al. 2008).[2]

The use of learner corpora has not been as widespread in GenSLA, owing perhaps to the (false) belief that this type of data is not well-suited to provide useful explanations or test specific hypotheses. In this chapter, we show how generative researchers have changed this view by proposing new ways in which corpus data can benefit the generative agenda, specifically by designing purpose-built corpora and by combining corpus data with data elicited with other experimental means. Here, we also provide concrete examples of how researchers have used this methodology to answer questions about the nature of interlanguage grammars.

12.2 What are learner corpora?

Learner corpus research originally aimed to apply corpus linguistics research methods to the study of language learning, often with a pedagogical purpose. As McEnery et al. (2019: 74) explain,

> [C]orpus linguistics is a quantitative paradigm grounded in the empirical tradition of language analysis. It uses large quantities of observational data

compiled into data sets, called corpora, to provide evidence about language use by both first language (L1) and second language (L2) speakers.

Corpus-based SLA grew in popularity as researchers started to make the computer-based tools and techniques developed by corpus linguistics available to researchers in applied linguistics (see Granger 1993, 2021; McEnery & Hardie 2011). McEnery and Wilson (2001: 131) describe the four main advantages of corpora for language study, summarized as follows:

1. Sampling and quantification: Corpora are put together to be maximally representative of a particular population so that generalizations can be drawn.
2. Ease of access: Corpora can save time and effort because researchers do not need to collect their own data. Corpora are easily accessed and analyzed in machine-readable form.
3. Enriched data: Corpora often include part-of-speech annotation and grammatical parsing, which allow for useful grammatical analyses.
4. Naturalistic data: Data in public corpora are largely naturalistic and produced in real social contexts, which can be useful for researchers interested in investigating language use.

Corpus linguistics research methods were quickly adopted by usage-based and functionalist SLA researchers (e.g., Housen 2002; Gries & Wulff 2005, 2009). Having access to large-sized corpora was viewed as a methodological innovation because researchers could tally the frequency of use of both common and rare occurring forms. It also facilitated comparisons between learners from different linguistic backgrounds (McEnery et al. 2019). SLA researchers with a more formal focus, however, have only recently adopted corpus-based techniques (Myles 2005, 2015). For instance, using data from the Cambridge Learner Corpus (CLC), Murakami and Alexopoulou (2016) re-examined the dominant view that L2 learners follow a universal order of acquisition of morphemes. The CLC has been compiled by Cambridge University Press and contains 45 million words from 1,35,000 exam scripts from lower to advanced learners of English who took exams of Cambridge English Language Assessment. Murakami and Alexopoulou analyzed 11,893 scripts containing four million words to investigate six English morphemes (articles, past tense *-ed*, plural *-s*, possessive *'s*, progressive *-ing* and third person *-s*) with learners from seven L1 backgrounds (Japanese, Korean, Spanish, Russian, Turkish, German and French). Results showed that lacking the equivalent feature in the learners' L1 leads to lower accuracy in the use of the corresponding L2 form.

In other words, the order of morpheme acquisition was found to be influenced by the learners' L1.

This finding illustrates the usefulness of corpus-based methods to unveil key information about the frequency of use of target forms and the advantage of using learner corpora to tackle these types of issues (see Leech 2011; Gablasova et al. 2017).

Case Study Box 12.1: Murakami and Alexopoulou (2016)

Property: The authors focused on six of the most studied morphemes in the so-called morpheme studies which investigate the emergence and use of morphemes in learner speech (see Krashen 1977). The six forms are articles (both indefinite (*a, an*) and definite (*the*)), regular past tense *-ed*, plural *-s*, possessive *'s*, progressive *-ing* and third person *-s*. According to Krashen, learners acquire *-ing*, plural *-s* and copula *be* first; then they acquire auxiliary *be* and articles; third, they acquire irregular past tense; finally, regular past tense, third person *-s* and possessive *'s* are acquired.

Research questions: The authors set out to investigate whether the learners' L1 influenced the accuracy order of L2 English grammatical morphemes. They also wanted to determine the magnitude of influence of the L1, compared to factors such as general proficiency. Other research questions included determining whether grammatical morphemes were equally or differentially affected by L1 and whether the results unveiled a link between the L2 and the absence/presence of congruent morphemes in the L1.

Participants: Instructed learners of English from diverse L1 backgrounds (Japanese, Korean, Spanish, Russian, Turkish, German and French) at five proficiency levels corresponding to A2 to C2 of the Common European Framework of Reference levels.

Data: Approximately 10,000 written exam scripts from the CLC.

Data analysis: Obligatory contexts and errors with target morphemes were used to calculate accuracy scores per L1 group, proficiency group and morpheme. The authors calculated intragroup homogeneity, intergroup heterogeneity and cross-linguistic performance congruity using statistical analyses such as logistic regression analysis.

Results: The data only partially fit Krashen's natural order of acquisition. The most accurate morphemes are those with equivalent forms in the L1.

Interpretation of results: Corpus data provided strong evidence that the accuracy order of the target morphemes is influenced by the learners' L1.

12.3 Adapting corpus analysis tools to suit SLA research agendas

Despite the obvious benefits of corpus-based tools to investigate SLA, communication between corpus linguists and SLA researchers has not always been ideal (Granger 2021; Tono 2003). For corpus linguists, the data must represent authentic and spontaneous uses of language occurring in real life, so researchers should have little input in the design of the corpora. In contrast, many SLA researchers investigate language in classroom contexts and focus on learners who often do not use the L2 outside that environment (i.e., the real world).

A second difference is that for corpus linguistics, corpora should be representative, meaning that findings arising from the analysis should be generalizable to the whole language variety (Leech 1991). Biber (1993) contends that representative samples include the full range of variability in a population. This view of representativeness can easily apply to large corpora such as the British National Corpus, maintained by the University of Oxford (UK). This corpus is specifically designed "to represent a wide cross-section of British English, both spoken and written, from the late 20th century" (see http://www.natcorp.ox.ac.uk/) and includes 100 million words from a wide range of sources. However, representativeness is much more difficult to apply to L2 corpora because learner datasets tend to be smaller in size, since they tend to focus on one main genre or variety (e.g., exam scripts, written compositions, oral conversations etc.). Leech (1998) also noted that the way in which data are collected and sampled by SLA scholars can hide mediating variables which would render the dataset not completely authentic according to the prevalent views in corpus linguistics. Furthermore, many SLA researchers are interested in answering specific research questions, focusing on a set number of variables (proficiency, age, native language, L1 influence, etc.) rather than in discovering patterns that are representative of big cohorts of learners.

Thus, there exists a misalignment between the main goals and practices of corpus linguistics and SLA—a misalignment that has only recently been recognized and addressed (see Granger 2008, 2021; Römer 2019). This means that some adjustments are necessary for learner corpora to fully serve current SLA research agendas. For instance, many SLA researchers are concerned with obtaining good-quality data rather than with analyzing fully authentic uses of the language. Since speakers typically learn an L2 in "artificial" academic settings, that data can be authentic in the sense that it represents what learners can produce in those contexts (e.g., an exam, an interview or a short text) or as a response to a prompt. SLA researchers have also been more interested in using corpora to compare language production from learners from different backgrounds who are asked to perform the same task (e.g., writing an argumentative essay, orally describing a series of pictures to narrate a story).[3] It is also common for SLA researchers to work with purpose-built corpora (like ICLE) rather than with generic corpora (like the National British Corpus) because this better serves their research agenda—even if the data do not strictly occur naturalistically. This shows that a feature of learner corpora is to be representative in a different way when compared to large-scale native corpora (see Deshors & Gries 2021; Granger 2002).

Finally, it has been widely proposed that SLA researchers should consider using corpora in combination with experimental tasks to access a wide range of evidence (Egbert & Baker 2019; Callies 2013; Domínguez 2019; Ellis et al. 2016; Gilquin 2007; McEnery & Hardie 2011; Mendikoetxea & Lozano 2018; Mitchell et al. 2008; Myles 2005; McEnery et al. 2019). Likewise, learner corpora can better suit certain research agendas if the corpora is elicited using a variety of tasks ranging in the level of control (i.e., whether they are designed to provide evidence of what learners can use spontaneously or controlled to elicit the use of a specific structure) (Callies & Paquot 2015; Myles 2015; Tracy-Ventura & Myles 2015; Tracy-Ventura & Paquot 2021). The more control exercised by the researcher, the less authentic the data are. However, any loss in authenticity could result in a gain in explanatory power, which may suit specific research agendas, such as those aiming to test specific hypotheses.

These recent methodological developments show that SLA researchers have been able to adapt and improve methods borrowed from corpus linguistics to better suit their specific research goals.

12.4 Creation of a learner corpus

This section briefly summarizes the main steps to consider when creating a learner corpus. Since a corpus is built as a tool to be used by others, how the corpus will be accessed is as important as the data to be included. The first step in the creation of a corpus involves making key decisions regarding the design of the corpus, such as the type of data to be included (oral or written), the profile of the participants, whether data from control groups will be included and the type of tasks which will be used to elicit the data. The size of the corpus matters as well, and this depends on the research questions driving the construction of the dataset. Oral corpora tend to be smaller in size since the audio recordings need to be transcribed and this is a time-consuming task. A corpus of written texts which are already available (e.g., newspaper articles) tends to be bigger in size since the data collection process is minimized in this case.

When the data are elicited for the purpose of constructing a corpus, a questionnaire is often used to find out about the participants' age, the languages they speak and other relevant details regarding their experience as speakers and learners of various languages. These data will be included in the corpus and can be used as search parameters, to carry out analyses on subsets of the data (e.g., data from beginner learners only). Specific ethical protocols apply in the construction of a corpus, such as that the data included must be fully anonymized.

The next stage is to elicit the oral or written data using the tasks chosen or to compile the corpus from available sources (i.e., exams or essays written by learners). The oral data need to be transcribed and fully anonymized. If multiple transcribers are employed, checks need to be carried out to ensure consistency. There is no single protocol to transcribe audio or video recordings and different corpora use their own transcription conventions. The CHAT formatting conventions found in TalkBank are widely used, mainly because of its standardized format and because it is a free tool, easy to use and a good manual and resources already exist. CHAT files are compatible with CLAN (Computerized Language Analysis) programs, also part of TalkBank. This is an open-access analysis program (https://dali.talkbank.org/clan/) which is used to code and analyze the data in the CHAT format, including morphosyntactic analysis.

Transcriptions often include two parts: a series of header lines which provide information about the date of the recording, the age and name of the participants and other relevant information to understand the context of the interaction, as well as the transcription of the actual speech which appears as tier lines. In CHAT, the header lines begin with the symbol @ and the tier lines begin with an asterisk. Figure 12.1 shows a transcript in CHAT format from TalkBank (CHILDES). In this transcription, the child (CHI) and the mother (MOT)) are having a conversation in English. Speech from the investigator (COL) is part of the transcript as well.

This transcript provides useful information about the age of the child and who the participants are. It also explains the situation surrounding the interaction; in this case, it is a conversation between the child and the mother. Some transcriptions also include links to the audio and video recordings which can facilitate research carried out using those data.

There is not a single way or protocol to analyze the data in a corpus. The choice depends on the research agenda, the type of data elicited and the type of analytical tool available. However, all corpora are designed with the consideration that new users will access the (typically large) collection of electronic data using searching tools in a web program or application. It is important to provide a user-friendly interface which is easy to use and which can carry out string searches and other basic corpus analyses, such as frequencies.

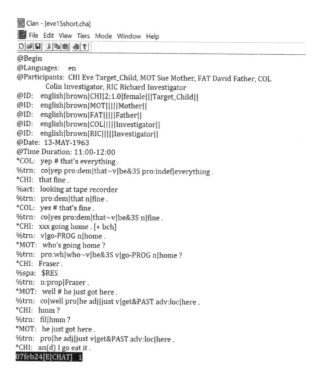

FIGURE 12.1 Sample of a CHAT transcript from TalkBank.

Some corpora focus on the acquisition of words and word collocations (the natural combination of certain words), whereas some other corpora are designed to investigate the acquisition of morphosyntax. For instance, the ICLE has a built-in concordance, a tool used to search for words and lemmas. The output produced presents the results according to the learner profile information. Corpora which are used to investigate morphosyntax provide a part of speech (POS) analysis using morphosyntactic tags. The most efficient and quicker way to achieve this is by using a tool already available, such as the MOR program in TalkBank, which is part of CLAN (the latter has over 20 built-in programs for analysis). MOR assigns a morphosyntactic tag to every word in a transcript (e.g., preposition, verb, noun, etc.) and provides extra grammatical information related to gender, number, tense, aspect and other information often carried by functional morphology, such as the *–s* morpheme attached to the verb in "She play-*s*." This analysis can also inform whether these forms are used correctly or incorrectly.

A MOR file which includes this extra grammatical information is ultimately created and added to the corpus. This is a process with various stages, some automatic and some manual. The investigator may need to manually add new words to the existing MOR vocabulary and manually check that the automated disambiguation has been carried out properly (i.e., when a form has two possible meanings, that the correct meaning has been chosen.) For instance, in English the morpheme –s can be either a marker of present tense on verbs or a marker of plural number on nouns. The investigator may need to check that the automated tagging has applied correctly in all instances of –s that appear in the corpus.

Example (1) shows an abstract from a MOR file from SPLLOC. It shows an exchange between two English learners of Spanish (D53 and D54). The %mor lines produced by the MOR program show the morphosyntactic analysis of the transcribed data. In this exchange, Speaker D54 asks "What did you put as number 1?" and speaker D53 answers "Um, I put number 1 like giving severe fines for arrests for violent acts."

1 *D54: vale qué pusiste para el número uno?
%mor: co|okay pro:int|qué=what vpret|pone-2S&PRET=put prep|para=for det:art|el&MASC&SG=the n|número&MASC=number vpres|uni-1S&PRES=unite?

*D53: um puse en número uno como poniendo multas severas por arrestos por actos violentos ehm.
%mor: co|um vpret|pone-1S&PRET=put prep|en=in n|número&MASC=number vpres|uni-1S&PRES=unite adv|como=like vger|pone-PROG=put n|multa-PL&FEM=fine adj|severo-FEM-PL=strict prep|por=for n|arresto-PL&MASC=arrest prep|por=for n|acto-PL&MASC=action adj|violento-MASC-PL=violent co|ehm.

Some of the most common commands in CLAN are FREQ (frequency counts), KWAL (Key Word and Line concordance) and COMBO (combined search for more than two words). FREQ shows the frequency of searched items, types (the total number of different words) and tokens (the total number of words) and can be used to tabulate type-token ratios.[4] The KWAL command searches for words and, crucially, shows the whole utterance in which they occur. These commands can be very useful in revealing when specific forms (articles, gender markers, prepositions, verbal endings, etc.) have been used by learners. They can provide this information in a quick and straightforward manner saving researchers a great deal of time. The list of programs available in CLAN is available from the commands window which is used to run those commands (see Figure 12.2). A full description of how to use the programs in CLAN can be found on the TalkBank website (https://talkbank.org/manuals/CLAN.pdf).

This section has briefly described the main considerations and key stages in creating a learner corpus. There is no single protocol to construct a

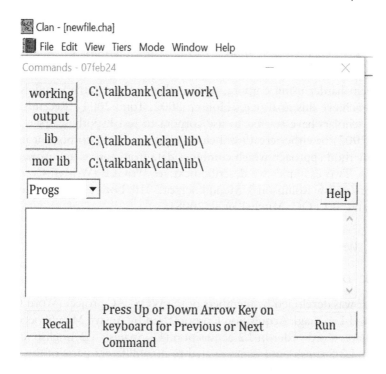

FIGURE 12.2 Access to the CLAN programs in the commands window.

corpus and to analyze data. We have shown one way of how a corpus could be analyzed using CLAN (TalkBank) as an illustration, as this is a widely used program which can suit the generative SLA agenda.

12.5 Learner corpora in generative SLA research

Although functional and usage-based SLA researchers have used learner corpora productively (see, e.g., Murakami & Ellis 2022), only recently have generative researchers started to use them (Myles 2005, 2007, 2015; Rankin 2009) because the paradigm has typically favored experimental data.[5] Early on, Granger (2002: 6) noted that the naturalistic contexts prevalent in learner corpora complicate controlling for variables—a key concern in generative SLA studies. Because generative SLA aims to tap into learner's competence (rather than language use), generative researchers lean toward experimental tasks focusing on a set of variables. These tasks are manipulated to expose L2 speakers to grammatical and, crucially, ungrammatical structures (e.g., using grammaticality/acceptability judgment tasks or truth-value judgment tasks). These tasks allow researchers to provide explanations on the nature of the acquisition process and to test theoretically grounded hypotheses (see Barlow 2005; Mitchell et al. 2008; Myles 2007, Mendikoetxea et al. 2009; or Tognini-Bonelli 2001, for discussion).

As Mendikoetxea et al. (2009) point out, although testing hypotheses may seem harder using corpora, some early (non-generative) studies were able to achieve this goal (e.g., Housen 2002; Tono 2004). Recently, generative scholars have started to use corpora to test hypotheses (see Myles 2005, 2007) by either creating their own purpose-built corpora or using a multi-method approach which combines data from corpus and experimental tasks. Two examples we describe next are WriCLE (Written Corpus of Learner English; Rollinson & Mendikoetxea 2010; Lozano & Mendikoetxea 2013; and SPLLOC; Mitchell et al. 2008).

12.5.1 WriCLE: written corpus of learner English

12.5.1.1 Description of the corpus

WriCLE was developed by members of the WOSLAC project (Word Order in Second Language Acquisition Corpora), led by Amaya Mendikoetxea. It investigates word order in L2 acquisition (L1 Spanish–L2 English and L1 English–L2 Spanish) and issues related to how different parts of the grammar (e.g., lexicon, phonology and discourse) interact with syntax. When WriCLE was created, these were central issues in GenSLA (see Sorace's Interface Hypothesis; Sorace 2011).[6] CEDEL2, mentioned above, was also created to address these research questions and includes control data from speakers from countries such as Spain and the USA.[7]

WriCLE and CEDEL2 were set up following the ICLE guidelines so they initially contained written essays produced by instructed learners. WriCLE comprises 52 essays containing around 750,000 words written by university students in their first and third year of an English degree at a Spanish university. The corpus includes the texts produced by the learners, relevant background information about the learners (e.g., proficiency scores in the Oxford Quick Placement Test, years of study and knowledge of other languages) and information about the types of texts produced.[8] The texts are annotated for target structures (e.g., passives, clefts, inversions, there-constructions, etc) in an exchangeable XML format (see Mendikoetxea et al. 2009). WriCLE can be accessed online (http://wricle.learnercorpora.com/) via a straightforward tool that allows users to search the corpus following desired criteria.

12.5.1.2 Data elicited by the corpus

Lozano and Mendikoetxea (2010) were the first to use corpora to investigate the role of linguistic interfaces in the acquisition of postverbal subjects

(WriCLE and ICLE).[9] The researchers tested three hypotheses focusing on unveiling the constraints on postverbal subject use, asking whether learners used more postverbal subjects with (a) unaccusative verbs, (b) heavy (long) subjects or (c) focused subjects (representing new information). All three hypotheses were confirmed. The authors concluded that learners use postverbal subjects in the same contexts as native speakers do, and that overuse was related to negative L1 transfer.

Their results also raised two interesting questions: why did learners not produce inversion with unergative verbs (a possible strategy in their native Spanish)? and why did learners use preverbal elements, some of which were ungrammatical (e.g., the use of null forms or expletives like *it*)? Because these questions could not be answered with corpus data alone, Mendikoetxea and Lozano (2018) designed a study to test learners' judgments of ungrammatical structures. Using an Acceptability Judgment Task administered to 367 Spanish learners and 50 English native controls, the task asked participants to evaluate the grammaticality of 32 sentences on a five-point Likert scale. The findings of this follow-up study showed that the experimental data largely converged with the corpus results since learners accepted postverbal subjects with unaccusative verbs and rejected them with unergative verbs. Learners also overused the expletive *it* inappropriately. The overuse of preverbal forms in the learner grammars, including *it* and null elements was related to L2 proficiency and language experience. Thus, thanks to the combination of corpus and experimental data, the authors provided full answers regarding the nature of postverbal subjects in L2 English.

12.5.2 SPLLOC: Spanish learner language oral corpora

12.5.2.1 Description of the corpus

SPLLOC is a small, cross-sectional corpus of L2 Spanish comprising oral narratives, paired discussion tasks and interviews with 120 English native speakers in the UK. It also includes a subcorpus of 30 native Spanish samples. SPLLOC was designed following the same principles guiding its sister corpus, FLLOC (French Learner Language Oral Corpus; Rule 2004; Rule et al. 2003). Overall, SPLLOC comprises 333,491 words (269,262 from learners and 64,229 from native speakers) and a total of 561 digital audio files (461 from learners and 100 from native speakers). Hosted by the University of Southampton (UK), the database is freely available (www.splloc.soton.ac.uk). Data can be searched through a tool which allows users to download audio recordings, transcripts and tagged files (for POS).

Like WriCLE, SPLLOC was created as part of a funded research project aiming to test hypotheses on the acquisition of structures in Spanish known to be problematic to English learners of Spanish (e.g., word order, postverbal subjects, gender marking, aspectual distinctions) and to test specific hypotheses. Although SPLLOC 1 was created to test Sorace's Interface Hypothesis (Sorace 2011) and SPLLOC2 to test the Lexical Aspect Hypothesis (Andersen 1989, 1991), these data can be used to investigate a wide range of research questions beyond those guiding their initial design.

As described by Mitchell et al. (2008), the principles underlying SPLLOC's design included a focus on collecting oral data from a variety of genres and balancing open-ended and focused tasks. The corpus includes various learner levels and uses CHILDES/TalkBank procedures to facilitate analyses and maximize data sharing and accessibility. Each corpus includes data from 60 learners who were learning Spanish students in a secondary school or at university. Participants were assigned to three proficiency levels (beginner, intermediate and advanced) according to their education level in the UK school system: lower secondary school (Year 10), final year of secondary school (Year 13) and university undergraduates (UG) during the final year of their Spanish degree. Data from native Spanish controls were also included.

The data included in the corpora were collected using a range of purposefully designed tasks covering a variety of genres and modes. Tasks were piloted with both native speakers and learners from each proficiency group. In SPLLOC 1, participants completed oral tasks aided by a researcher (a guided interview, two impersonal narrative tasks and a picture-based description task) or other participants (discussion task). In SPLLOC 2, tasks prompted participants to speak about past events and included an impersonal narrative (Cat Story), a controlled narrative (Las Hermanas), a picture-description task to elicit progressive events (Simultaneous actions task) and a personal narrative (semi-structured interview). See Table 12.1 for details.

For SPLLOC 2, it was important to include tasks in which participants had to use a range of verb types in a variety of contexts. This was addressed by including two types of impersonal narratives. Each study also collected introspective data by means of a sentence-matching acceptability task and a forced-choice clitic interpretation task in the case of SPLLOC 1 and a semantic interpretation task in the case of SPLLOC 2. Speech samples were recorded in schools and universities using portable digital equipment. The sound files generated were transcribed using CLAN programs following similar protocols as in previous projects (see Myles 2005, 2007, Mitchell, et al. 2008). Each transcript was fully anonymized and checked for accuracy. POS tagging of CHAT transcripts was then carried out on the anonymized files. In the case of SPLLOC 2, the oral data were also coded for lexical class (state, activity, accomplishment and achievement), discourse structure (background and foreground) forms produced (preterit, imperfect, present, etc.) and whether the form was appropriate or not. These parameters were

TABLE 12.1 Types of tasks used in SPLLOC 1 and SPLLOC 2

Task type	SPLLOC 1	SPLLOC 2
Free personal narrative	Semi-structured interview	Semi-structured interview
Free impersonal narrative	*Loch Ness:* picture-based story retell *Modern Times:* video-based story retell	
Semi-controlled impersonal narrative		*Cat Story:* picture-based story retell
Controlled impersonal narrative		*Las Hermanas:* picture-based story retell
Discussion task	Paired discussion task	
Controlled picture-description task	Clitic-production task	Simultaneous actions task

incorporated in each transcript as an extra layer of tagging which enables automatic analysis of aspectual and discursive features (e.g., lexical aspect class, obligatory context, morphological form and discourse structure).[10]

12.5.2.2 Data elicited by the corpus

The SPLLOC team set out to investigate learners' use of aspect-related verbal forms in Spanish which are difficult for English speakers (Arche 2014): preterit and imperfect. The difficulty resides in deciding which form is appropriate given the semantic context, such as habitual actions, progressive actions or actions which took place once. The Lexical Aspect Hypothesis (LAH) proposes that learners will use verb type (telic vs atelic) to decide between the imperfect and the preterit as per a universal congruent telic–preterit and atelic–imperfect correspondence. If true, these associations should be present from the outset. Domínguez et al. (2013) examined data from the two open-ended tasks in SPLLOC 2 (Cat Story and Interview) and showed that both learners and the native controls preferred the prototypical patterns (imperfect + atelic verbs, preterit + telic events), as predicted by the LAH. However, the authors noted that the absence of the opposite patterns (telic–imperfect and atelic–preterit) in the open-ended tasks should not be taken as evidence of learners' inability to use the preterit with atelic verbs and the imperfect with telic verbs.

To check whether learners used these non-prototypical pairings, data from the controlled narrative (Las Hermanas) was examined, since the contexts were manipulated so that participants were forced to choose between preterit and imperfect with both telic and atelic verbs. The results from this task revealed that learners were indeed able to use the preterit and the imperfect with both telic and atelic verbs. As Domínguez (2019) notes, the type of task used to elicit the oral data can affect the results obtained. While open-ended tasks favor the use of the imperfect in atelic contexts, this should not be presumed to be everything that learners know about the grammar of the imperfect and preterit.

Thus, Domínguez et al. (2013) showed how examining corpus data with a varying degree of control was instrumental in revealing that the LAH cannot fully explain the path of acquisition of the Spanish imperfect and preterit. Further, using data from the semantic acceptability judgment task, Domínguez et al. (2011; 2017) proposed an alternative explanation suggesting that L1 transfer of form–meaning associations can erroneously lead learners to choose the preterit when the imperfect should be used instead, particularly at the start of the acquisition of these forms.

12.6 Summary

In this chapter, we showed evidence of how SLA researchers have made use of research methods borrowed from corpus linguistics. We have also discussed how analyzing learner corpora can be useful for GenSLA scholars after some modifications and adjustments, which we summarize next:

- Focus on answering research questions, rather than obtaining authentic uses of the language;
- Include a diversity of tasks in the design of the corpus;
- Include focused tasks to have access to key evidence not easily obtained by open-ended tasks;
- Combine corpus data with data obtained with experimental tasks;
- Obtain proficiency measures and other relevant background data from the participants;
- Include a subcorpus of control data (from native speakers or others as appropriate);
- Prioritize automatization of the data analysis process and the facilitation of data sharing among users.

12.7 Discussion questions

1 What are the benefits of accessing evidence available from a corpus of oral or written data as opposed to a single focused task?
2 How can samples of language use, the type of evidence available through learner corpora, be useful to answer questions on learners' grammatical competence?

3 Think of one research question which could be answered using data from learner corpora combined with data collected through at least one experimental (acceptability) task, as shown in Mendikoetxea and Lozano (2018) and Domínguez et al. (2013).

Notes

1 See Rutherford and Thomas (2001), Marsden et al. (2002) and Myles (2005) for a discussion on how CHILDES and CHILDES-like databases are beneficial in SLA research.
2 Most existing corpora comprise written texts collected using one single task or a variety of tasks. For a discussion on the benefits of oral corpora to access learners' competence, see Myles (2005).
3 See the Contrastive Interlanguage Analysis proposed by Granger (2015) and Corpus-Based Contrastive Linguistics (Granger & Lefer 2020).
4 It is important to differentiate between types and tokens when analyzing a corpus as some learners may produce a large quantity of words, but this could be due to a repetition of the same words. The type-token ratio is obtained by dividing the types occurring in a text by the number of tokens. The higher the ratio, the higher degree of lexical variation. Advanced learners tend to show a higher type-token ratio than beginner learners.
5 This distinction has also been referred to as hypothesis-driven versus hypothesis-finding approaches (Granger 1998: 15) and as general corpus-based versus corpus-driven (Tognini-Bonelli 2001).
6 Rankin (2009), who used data from the ICLE corpus to test Sorace's (2011) Interface Hypothesis, argues that "the added value of learner corpora is that it allows the researcher to get an idea of what learners do in context" (Rankin 2009: 58), which is particularly relevant when testing the Interface Hypothesis.
7 Led by Cristóbal Lozano (Universidad de Granada), CEDEL2 comprises 1,105,936 words from 4,399 participants. The L2 subcorpus contains written and oral data from learners with 11 different native languages while a smaller subcorpus contains data from native speakers of Spanish, English, Arabic, Japanese, Portuguese and Greek. The corpus has been annotated using the UAM CorpusTool and it can be freely accessed via http://cedel2.learnercorpora.com/. For further details see Lozano (2022).
8 WriCLE also includes WriCLEinf(ormal), a subcorpus of over 1,000,000 words featuring L1Spanish-L2 English data from 1,140 non-academic texts of various genres such as poems, blogs, emails and narratives.
9 In Spanish, postverbal subjects are widely available while in English postverbal subjects are only possible with unaccusative verbs in certain contexts (e.g., *There arrived three men*).
10 See Diaz-Negrillo and Thompson (2013) for a discussion on what types of annotation are preferred in corpus-based SLA studies.

Further reading

Granger, S. (2021). Have learner corpus research and second language acquisition finally met? In B. Le Bruyn & M. Paquot (Eds.), *Learner corpus research meets second language acquisition* (pp. 243–257). Cambridge: Cambridge University Press.

Lozano, C. (2020). Generative approaches. In N. Tracy-Ventura & M. Paquot (Eds.), *The Routledge handbook of second language acquisition and corpora* (pp. 213–227). London: Routledge.

Myles, F. (2021). An SLA perspective on learner corpus research. In B. Le Bruyn & M. Paquot (Eds.), *Learner corpus research meets second language acquisition* (pp. 258–273). Cambridge: Cambridge University Press.

REFERENCES

Abate, M. L., McCabe, G. P., & Lynch, M. P. (1995). *Power as a function of reliability*. [Technical Report]. https://doi.org/10.2172/113946

Abdi, H. (2009). *Experimental design and analysis for psychology*. New York: Oxford University Press.

Abrahamsson, N., & Hyltenstam, K. (2009). Age of onset and nativelikeness in a second language: Listener perception versus linguistic scrutiny. *Language Learning, 59*, 249–306.

Adger, D., & Smith, J. (2005). Variation and the minimalist program. In L. Cornips & K. P. Corrigan (Eds.), *Syntax and variation: Reconciling the biological and the social* (pp. 149–178). Amsterdam: John Benjamins.

Albirini, A., & Benmamoun, E. (2014). Aspects of second-language transfer in the oral production of Egyptian and Palestinian heritage speakers. *International Journal of Bilingualism, 18*(3), 244–273.

Allopenna, P. D., Magnuson, J. S., & Tanenhaus, M. K. (1998). Tracking the time course of spoken word recognition using eye movements: Evidence for continuous mapping models. *Journal of Memory and Language, 38*(4), 419–439.

Altarriba, J., Kroll, J. F., Sholl, A., & Rayner, K. (1996). The influence of lexical and conceptual constraints on reading mixed-language sentences: Evidence from eye fixations and naming times. *Memory & Cognition, 24*, 477–492.

Andersen, R. (1989). *The acquisition of verbal morphology*. Los Angeles: University of California.

Andersen, R. (1991). Developmental sequences: The emergence of aspect marking in second language acquisition. In T. Huebner & C. Ferguson (Eds.), *Crosscurrents in SLA and linguistic theories* (pp. 305–324). Amsterdam: John Benjamins.

Arche, M. J. (2014). The construction of viewpoint aspect: The imperfective revisited. *Natural Language and Linguistic Theory, 32*(43), 791–831.

Arche, M. J., & Domínguez, L. (2024). Grammatical aspect. In T. Ionin, S. Montrul, & R. Slabakova (Eds.), *The Routledge handbook of second language acquisition* (pp. 284–296). New York: Routledge.

Archibald, J. (1997). The acquisition of English stress by speakers of nonaccentual languages: Lexical storage versus computation of stress. *Linguistics, 35*, 167–181.

Archibald, J. (1998). *Second language phonology*. Amsterdam: John Benjamins.

Archibald, J. (2009). Phonological feature re-assembly and the importance of phonetic cues. *Second Language Research, 25*, 231–233.

Bader, M., & Häussler, J. (2010). Toward a model of grammaticality judgments. *Journal of Linguistics, 46*, 273–330.

Bardovi-Harlig, K. (2000). Tense and aspect in second language acquisition: Form, meaning, and use. *Language Learning: A Journal of Research in Language Studies, 50*(suppl. 1).

Barlow, M. (2005). Computer-based analysis of learner language. In R. Ellis & G. Barkhuizen (Eds.), *Analysing learner language* (pp. 335–354). Oxford: Oxford University Press.

Bayram, F. (2013). Acquisition of Turkish by heritage speakers: A processability approach. Doctoral dissertation, Newcastle University.

Beck, M. L. (1998). L2 acquisition and obligatory head movement: English-speaking learners of German and the local impairment hypothesis. *Studies in Second Language Acquisition, 20*(3), 311–348.

Benders, T., Escudero, P., & Sjerps, M. J. (2012). The interrelation between acoustic context effects and available response categories in speech sound categorization. *Journal of the Acoustical Society of America, 131*, 3079–3087.

Berman, R. A., & Slobin, D. I. (1994). *Relating events in narrative: A cross-linguistic developmental study*. Hillsdale, NJ: L. Erlbaum.

Berwick, R. (1985). *The acquisition of syntactic knowledge*. Cambridge, MA: MIT Press.

Berwick, R. C., & Chomsky, N. (2011). The biolinguistic program: The current state of its development. In A. M. Di Sciullo & C. Boeckx (Eds.), *The biolinguistic enterprise: New perspectives on the evolution and nature of the human language faculty* (pp. 19–41). Oxford: Oxford University Press.

Best, C. T. (1995). A direct realist perspective on cross-language speech perception. In W. Strange (Ed.), *Speech perception and linguistic experience: Theoretical and methodological issues in cross-language speech research* (pp. 167–200). Timonium, MD: York Press.

Best, C. T., & Tyler, M. D. (2007). Nonnative and second-language speech perception: Commonalities and complementarities. In J. Munro & O.-S. Bohn (Eds.), *Language experience in second language speech learning: In honor of James Emil Flege* (pp. 13–34). Amsterdam/Philadelphia: John Benjamins.

Bialystok, E. (1982). On the relationship between knowing and using linguistic forms. *Applied Linguistics, 3*(3), 181–206.

Bialystok, E. (1997). The structure of age: In search of barriers to second language acquisition. *Second Language Research, 13*, 116–137.

Bialystok, E. (2001). *Bilingualism in development: Language, literacy, and cognition*. New York: Cambridge University Press.

Biber, D. (1993). Representativeness in corpus design. *Literary and Linguistic Computing, 8*(4), 243–257.

Biberauer, T. (2019). Factors 2 and 3: Towards a principled approach. *Catalan Journal of Linguistics,* 45–88, https://doi.org/10.5565/rev/catjl.219.
Biberauer, T., & Roberts, I. (2015). The clausal hierarchy, features and parameters. In Ur Shlonsky (Ed.), *Beyond functional sequence* (pp. 295–313). Oxford: Oxford University Press.
Bley-Vroman, R., & Chaudron, C. (1994). Elicited imitation as a measure of second-language competence. In A. Mackey & S. Gass (Eds.), *Research methodology in second-language acquisition* (pp. 245–261). Mahwah, NJ: Lawrence Erlbaum.
Bojko, A. (2013). *Eye tracking the user experience: A practical guide to research.* New York: Rosenfeld Media.
Boland, J. (2004). Linking eye movements to sentence comprehension in reading and listening. In M. Carreiras & C. Clifton Jr. (Eds.), *The on-line study of sentence comprehension: Eyetracking, ERP, and beyond* (pp. 51–76). Brighton, England: Psychology Press.
Bond, K., Gabriele, A., Fiorentino, R., & Aleman Bañón, J. (2011). Individual differences and the role of the L1 in L2 processing: An ERP investigation. In J. Herschensohn & D. Tanner (Eds.), *Proceedings of the 11th Generative Approaches to Second Language Acquisition conference (GASLA 2011)* (pp. 17–29). Somerville, MA: Cascadilla Proceedings Project.
Borer, H. (1984). *Parametric syntax: Case studies in semitic and romance languages.* Dordrecht: Foris.
Bornkessel-Schlesewsky, I., Staub, A., & Schlesewsky, M. (2016). The timecourse of sentence processing in the brain. In G. Hickok, & S. Small (Eds.), *Neurobiology of language* (pp. 607–620). Burlington: Academic Press.
Bowles, M. A. (2011). Measuring implicit and explicit linguistic knowledge. *Studies on Second Language Acquisition, 33,* 247–271.
Bradley, M. M., & Keil, A. (2012). Event-related potentials (ERPs). In V. S. Ramachandran (Ed.), *Encyclopedia of human behavior* (pp. 79–85). Burlington: Academic Press. https://doi.org/10.1016/B978-0-12-375000-6.00154-3
Broselow, E. (2004). Unmarked structures and emergent rankings in second language phonology. *International Journal of Bilingualism, 8,* 51–65.
Brown, C. (1998). The role of the L1 grammar in the L2 acquisition of segmental structure. *Second Language Research, 14,* 136–193.
Brown, J. D. (1980). Relative merits of four methods for scoring close tests. *Journal of Speech, Language, and Hearing Research, 50,* 940–967. https://doi.org/10.1111/j.1540-4781.1980.tb05198.x
Brysbaert, M., Drieghe, D., & Vitu, F. (2005). Word skipping: Implications for theories of eye movement control in reading. In G. Underwood (Ed.), *Cognitive processes in eye guidance* (pp. 53–77). Oxford: Oxford University Press.
Callies, M. (2013). Advancing the research agenda of interlanguage pragmatics: The role of learner corpora. In J. Romero Trillo (Ed.), *Yearbook of corpus linguistics and pragmatics 2013: New domains and methodologies* (pp. 9–36). New York: Springer.
Callies, M., & Paquot, M. (2015). Learner corpus research: An interdisciplinary field on the move. *International Journal of Learner Corpus Research, 1*(1), 1–6.
Carroll, S. E. (2017). Exposure and input in bilingual development. *Bilingualism: Language and Cognition, 20*(1), 3–16.

Carlson, K., Clifton Jr, C., & Frazier, L. (2001). Prosodic boundaries in adjunct attachment. *Journal of Memory and Language, 45*(1), 58–81.

Cebrian, J., Mora, J. C., & Aliaga-Garcia, C. (2010). Assessing crosslinguistic similarity by means of rated discrimination and perceptual assimilation tasks. In M. Wrembel, M. Kul, & K. Dziubalska-Kolaczyk (Eds.), *Achievements and perspectives in the acquisition of second language speech: New Sounds 2010. Vol. 1* (pp. 41–52). Frankfurt am Mein: Peter Lang.

Chapelle, C. (1999). Validity in language assessment. *Annual Review of Applied Linguistics, 19*, 254–272.

Chaplin, C. (Producer & Director). (1936). *Modern times* [Motion picture]. United Artists, USA.

Choi, S. H., Ionin, T., & Zhu, Y. (2018). L1 Korean and L1 Mandarin L2 English learners' acquisition of the count/mass distinction in English. *Second Language Research, 34*(2), 147–177. https://doi.org/10.1177/0267658317717581

Chomsky, N. (1959). A review of B. F. Skinner's verbal behaviour. *Language, 35*, 26–58.

Chomsky N. (1965). Aspects of the *theory* of *syntax*. Cambridge, MA: MIT Press.

Chomsky, N. (1975). *Reflections on language*. New York: Pantheon Books.

Chomsky, N. (1980). *Rules and representations*. Oxford: Blackwell.

Chomsky, N. (1981a). *Lectures on government and binding*. Dordrecht: Foris.

Chomsky, N. (1981b). Principles and parameters in syntactic theory. In N. Hornstein & D. Lightfoot (Eds.), *Explanation in linguistics: The logical problem of language acquisition* (pp. 32–75). London: Longman.

Chomsky, N. (1986a). *Barriers*. Cambridge, MA: MIT Press.

Chomsky, N. (1986b). *Knowledge of language: Its nature, origin, and use*. New York: Praeger.

Chomsky, N. (1995). *The minimalist program*. Cambridge, MA: MIT Press.

Chomsky, N. (2005) Three Factors in Language Design. *Linguistic Inquiry 36*(1), 1–22. doi: https://doi.org/10.1162/0024389052993655

Chomsky, N., & Lasnik, H. (1993). Principles and parameters theory. In J. Jacobs, A. von Stechow, W. Scernfeld & T. Vennenunn (Eds.), *Syntax: An international handbook of contemporary research* (pp. 13–127). Berlin: Walter de Gruyter.

Chondrogianni, V., & Marinis, T. (2011). Differential effects of internal and external factors on the development of vocabulary, tense morphology and morpho-syntax in successive bilingual children. *Linguistic Approaches to Bilingualism, 1*, 318–345.

Chrabaszcz, A., & Jiang, N. (2014). The role of the native language in the use of the English nongeneric definite article by L2 learners: A cross-linguistic comparison. *Second Language Research, 30*(3), 351–379.

Clahsen, H., & Felser, C. (2006). Grammatical processing in language learners. *Applied Psycholinguistics, 27*, 3–42.

Clahsen, H., & Muysken, P. (1989). The UG paradox in L2 acquisition. *Interlanguage Studies Bulletin (Utrecht), 5*(1), 1–29. https://doi.org/10.1177/026765838900500101

Cook, T. D., & Campbell, D. T. (1979). *Quasi-experimentation: Design & analysis issues for field settings*. Boston, MA: Houghton Mifflin Company.

Cowart, W. (1997). *Experimental syntax: Applying objective methods to sentence judgements*. Thousand Oaks, CA: Sage.

Crain, S., & McKee, C. (1985). The acquisition of structural restrictions on anaphora. In *Proceedings of NELS 16 vol. 15* (pp. 94–110). Amherst, MA: GLSA, University of Massachusetts.

Crain, S., & Thornton, R. (2000). *Investigations in universal grammar: A guide to experiments on the acquisition of syntax and semantics.* Cambridge, MA: MIT Press.

Cuza, A., & Frank, J. (2015). On the role of experience and age-related effects: Evidence from the Spanish CP. *Second Language Research, 31*(1), 3–28.

Dąbrowska, E., & Street, J. (2006). Individual differences in language attainment: Comprehension of passive sentences by native and non-native English speakers. *Language Sciences, 28*(6), 604–615.

Daidone, D. (2020). *How learners remember words in their second language: The impact of individual differences in perception, cognitive abilities, and vocabulary size.* Indiana University ProQuest Dissertations Publishing, open access. https://docs.google.com/viewer?url=http%3A%2F%2Fwww.ddaidone.com%2Fuploads%2F1%2F0%2F5%2F2%2F105292729%2Fdaidone__2020__dissertation.pdf

Daidone, D., & Darcy, I. (2021). Vocabulary size is a key factor in predicting second language lexical encoding accuracy. *Frontiers in Psychology, 12*, 688356. https://doi.org/10.3389/fpsyg.2021.688356

Davis, K. (2011). *Critical qualitative research in second language studies: Agency and advocacy.* Charlotte, NC: Information Age.

Dekydtspotter, L., & Renaud, C. (2014). On second language processing and grammatical development: The parser in second language acquisition. *Linguistic Approaches to Bilingualism, 4*(2), 131–165.

Derwing, T., & Munro, M. (1997). Accent, intelligibility, and comprehensibility: Evidence from four L1s. *Studies in Second Language Acquisition, 19*(1), 1–16.

Deshors, S. C., & Gries, S. Th. (2021). Comparing learner corpora. In N. Tracy-Ventura & M. Paquot (Eds.), *The Routledge Handbook of SLA and Corpora* (pp. 107–120). New York & London: Routledge.

Diaz-Negrillo, A., & Thompson, P. (2013). Learner corpora: Looking towards the future. In A. Diaz-Negrillo, N. Ballier & P. Thompson (Eds.), *Automatic treatment and analysis of learner corpus data: Studies in corpus linguistics* (pp. 9–20). Amsterdam: John Benjamins.

Domínguez, L. (2013). *Understanding interfaces: Understanding Interfaces.* Amsterdam: John Benjamins.

Domínguez, L. (2019). A "mixed methods" approach for investigating aspect in a second language: Evidence from the SPLLOC project. *Dutch Journal of Applied Linguistics, 8*(1), 41–66.

Domínguez, L., & Arche, M. J. (2021). The "comparative logic" and why we need to explain interlanguage grammars. *Frontiers in Psychology, 12*, 717635. https://doi.org/10.3389/fpsyg.2021.717635

Domínguez, L., & Arche, M. J. (2022). Early use of null and overt subjects in L2 Spanish: Evidence from two oral tasks. In K. McManus, & M. Schmid (Eds.), *How special are early birds? Foreign language teaching and learning* (EuroSLA Studies Series) (pp. 189–224). Berlin: Language Science Press.

Domínguez, L., Arche, M. J., & Myles, F. (2011). Testing the predictions of the feature-assembly hypothesis: Evidence from the L2 acquisition of Spanish aspect morphology. In N. Danis, K. Mesh, and H. Sung (Eds.), *Proceedings of the 35th annual Boston university conference on language development* (pp. 183–196). Somerville, MA: Cascadilla Press.

Domínguez, L., Arche, M. J., & Myles, F. (2017). Spanish Imperfect revisited: Exploring L1 influence in the reassembly of imperfective features onto new L2 forms. *Second Language Research, 33*(4), 431–457.

Domínguez, L., Tracy-Ventura, N., Arche, M. J., Mitchell, R., & Myles, F. (2013). The role of dynamic contrasts in the L2 acquisition of Spanish past tense morphology. *Bilingualism: Language and Cognition, 16*(3), 558–577.

Donchin, E., Ritter, W., & McCallum, W. C. (1978). Cognitive psychophysiology: The endogenous components of the ERP. In E. Callaway, P. Tueting, & S. H. Koslow (Eds.), *Event-related brain potentials in man* (pp. 349–441). New York: Academic Press.

Dörnyei, Z., & Csizér, K. (2012). How to design and analyze surveys in second language acquisition research. In A. Mackey, & S. Gass (Eds.), *Research methods in second language acquisition: A practical guide* (pp. 74–94). West Sussex: Wiley-Blackwell.

Dosi, I., Papadopoulou, D., & Tsimpli, I. M. (2016). Linguistic and cognitive factors in elicited imitation tasks: A study with mono-and biliterate Greek-Albanian bilingual children. In J. Scott & D. Waughtal (Eds.), *Proceedings of the 40th annual Boston University Conference on language development* (pp. 101–115). Somerville, MA: Cascadilla Press.

Douglas Fir Group. (2016). A transdisciplinary framework for SLA in a multilingual world. *The Modern Language Journal, 100*, 19–57.

Drieghe, D., Brysbaert, M., Desmet, T., & De Baecke, C. (2004). Word skipping in reading: On the interplay of linguistic and visual factors. *European Journal of Cognitive Psychology, 16*, 79–103

Drieghe, D., Rayner, K., & Pollatsek, A. (2005). Eye movements and word skipping during reading revisited. *Journal of Experimental Psychology: Human Perception and Performance, 31*(5), 954–969.

Duchowski, A. T. (2017). *Eye tracking methodology: Theory and practice*. Springer.

Duff, P. (2012). *Ethnographic research in applied linguistics: Exploring language teaching, learning, and use in diverse communities*. New York: Routledge.

Duffield, N., & Matsuo, A. (2009). Native speakers' vs. L2 learners' sensitivity to parallelism in VP-ellipsis. *Studies in Second Language Acquisition, 31*, 93–123.

Duffield, N., Matsuo, A., & Roberts, L. (2009). Factoring out the parallelism effect in VP-ellipsis: English vs. Dutch contrasts. *Second Language Research, 25*, 427–467.

Dussias, P. E., Valdés Kroff, J., & Gerfen, C. (2014). Visual wold eye-tracking. In J. Jegerski & B. VanPatten (Eds.), *Research methods in second language psycholinguistics* (pp. 93–126). New York/London: Routledge.

Eckman, F. (1977). Markedness and the contrastive analysis hypothesis. *Language Learning, 27*, 315–330.

Eckman, F. (2008). Typological markedness and second language phonology. In J. G. H. Edwards and M. L. Zampini (Eds.), *Phonology and second language acquisition* (pp. 95–115). Amsterdam: John Benjamins.

Egbert, J., & Baker, P. (Eds.). (2019). *Using corpus methods to triangulate linguistic analysis*. New York/London: Routledge.

Eimas, P. D., Siqueland, E. R., Jusczyk, P., & Vigorito, J. (1971). Speech perception in infants. *Science, 171*(3968), 303–306.
Ellis, N. C., & O'Donnell, M. B. (2012). Statistical construction learning: Does a Zipfian problem space ensure robust language learning? In J. Rebuschat & J. Williams (Eds.), *Statistical learning and language acquisition* (pp. 265–304). Berlin: Mouton de Gruyter.
Ellis, N. C., O'Donnell, M. B., & Römer, U. (2014). Second language verb-argument constructions are sensitive to form, function, frequency, contingency, and prototypicality. *Linguistic Approaches to Bilingualism, 4*, 405–431.
Ellis, N. C., Römer, U., & O'Donnell, M. B. (2016). *Usage-based approaches to language acquisition and processing: cognitive and corpus investigations of construction grammar* (Language Learning Monograph Series). Malden, MA: Wiley-Blackwell.
Ellis, N. C., & Sagarra, N. (2011). Learned attention in adult language acquisition: A replication and generalization study and meta-analysis. *Studies in Second Language Acquisition, 33*(4), 589–624. https://doi.org/10.1017/S0272263111000325
Ellis, N. C., & Wulff, S. (2018). Usage-based approaches to second language acquisition. In D. Miller, F. Bayram, J. Rothman & L. Serratrice (Eds.), *Bilingual cognition and language: The state of the science across its subfields* (pp. 37–56). Amsterdam: John Benjamins Publishing Company.
Ellis, R. (2005). Measuring implicit and explicit knowledge of a second language: A psychometric study. *Studies in Second Language Acquisition, 27*(2), 141–172.
Erlam, R. (2009). Elicited oral imitation as a measure of implicit knowledge. In R. Ellis, S. Loewen, C. Elder, R. Erlam, J. Philp & H. Reiders (Eds.), *Implicit and explicit knowledge in second language learning and teaching* (pp. 65–93). Bristol: Multilingual Matters.
Eskenazi, M. A., & Folk, J. R. (2017). Regressions during reading: The cost depends on the cause. *Psychonomic Bulletin & Review, 24*(4), 1211–1216.
Espírito Santo, A., Alexandre, N., & Perpiñán, S. (2023). The role of resumption in the acquisition of European Portuguese prepositional relative clauses by Chinese learners. *Second Language Research*, 02676583221137715.
Eubank, L. (1993/94). On the transfer of parametric values in L2 development. *Language Acquisition, 3*, 182–208.
Falk, Y., & Bardel, C. (2011). Object pronouns in German L3 syntax: Evidence for the L2 status factor. *Second Language Research, 27*, 59–82.
Felser, C., & Roberts, L. (2007). Processing wh-dependencies in a second language: A cross-modal priming study. *Second Language Research, 23*(1), 9–36.
Ferreira, F. (2003). The misinterpretation of noncanonical sentences. *Cognitive Psychology, 47*, 164–203.
Ferreira, F., Henderson, J. M., Anes, M. D., Weeks, P. A., & McFarlane, D. K. (1996). Effects of lexical frequency and syntactic complexity in spoken-language comprehension: Evidence from the auditory moving-window technique. *Journal of Experimental Psychology: Learning, Memory, and Cognition, 22*, 324–335.
Finer, D. L., & Broselow, E. I. (1986). Second language acquisition of reflexive binding. In S. Berman, J. McDonough, & J.-W. Choe (Eds.), *Proceedings of NELS 16* (pp. 154–168). Amherst, MA: GLSA, University of Massachusetts.
Flege, J. E. (1995). Second language speech learning: Theory, findings, and problems. In W. Strange (Ed.), *Speech perception and linguistic experience: Theoretical*

and methodological issues in cross-language speech research (pp. 233–277). Timonium, MD: York Press.

Flege, J. E., & Fletcher, K. L. (1992). Talker and listener effects on degree of perceived foreign accent. *Journal of the Acoustical Society of America, 91*(1), 370–389. https://doi.org/10.1121/1.402780

Flege, J. E., Birdsong, D., Bialystok, E., Mack, M., Sung, H., & Tsukada, K. (2006). Degree of foreign accent in English sentences produced by Korean children and adults. *Journal of Phonetics, 34*, 153–175.

Flege, J. E., Bohn, O.-S., & Jang, S. (1997). Effects of experience on nonnative speakers' production and perception of English vowels. *Journal of Phonetics, 25*, 437–470.

Flynn, S. (1986). Production vs. comprehension: Differences in underlying competences. *Studies in Second Language Acquisition, 8*(2), 135–164.

Fodor, J. D. (1998a). Learning to parse? *Journal of Psycholinguistic Research, 27*, 285–319.

Fodor, J. D. (1998b). Parsing to learn. *Journal of Psycholinguistic Research, 27*, 339–374.

Forster, K. I., Mohan, K., & Hector, J. (2003). The mechanics of masked priming. In S. Kinoshita & S. J. Lupker (Eds.), *Masked priming: The state of the art* (pp. 3–37). Hove: Psychology Press.

Franceschina, F. (2001). Morphological or syntactic deficits in near-native speakers? An assessment of some current proposals. *Second Language Research, 17*, 213–247.

Franceschina, F. (2005). *Fossilised second language grammars: The acquisition of grammatical gender*. Amsterdam: John Benjamins.

Francis, E. J. (2022). *Gradient acceptability and linguistic theory*. Oxford: Oxford University Press.

Frazier, L., & Clifton, C. (1996). *Construal*. MIT Press.

Friederici, A. D., Hahne, A., & Mecklinger, A. (1996). Temporal structure of syntactic parsing: Early and late event-related brain potential effects. *Journal of Experimental Psychology: Learning, Memory, and Cognition, 22*(5), 1219.

Friederici, A. D., Pfeifer, E., & Hahne, A. (1993). Event-related brain potentials during natural speech processing: Effects of semantic, morphological and syntactic violations. *Cognitive Brain Research, 1*(3), 183–192.

Gablasova, D., Brezina, V., & McEnery, T. (2017). Collocations in corpus-based language learning research: Identifying, comparing, and interpreting the evidence. *Language Learning, 67*(S1), 155–179.

Gabriele, A. (2009). Transfer and transition in the SLA of aspect: A bidirectional study of learners of English and Japanese. *Studies in Second Language Acquisition, 31*, 371–402.

Gabriele, A., Alemán Bañón, J., Hoffman, L., Covey, L., Rossomondo, A., & Fiorentino, R. (2021). Examining variability in the processing of agreement in novice learners: Evidence from event-related potentials. *Journal of Experimental Psychology: Learning, Memory, and Cognition, 47*(7), 1109–1140.

Gabryś-Barker, D., & Wojtaszek, A. (Eds.). (2014). *Studying second language acquisition from a qualitative perspective*. New York: Springer.

Gallego, A. (2011). Parameters. In C. Boeckx (Ed.), *Oxford handbook of linguistic minimalism* (pp. 523–550). Oxford: Oxford University Press.

García-Tejada, A., Cuza, A., & Lustres Alonso, E. G. (2023). The production and comprehension of Spanish se use in L2 and heritage Spanish. *Second Language Research, 39*(2), 301–331.

Garrett, M. F., Bever, T. G., & Fodor, J. A. (1966). The active use of grammar in speech perception. *Perception & Psychophysics, 1*, 30–32.

Gass, S. M., & Alvarez Torres, M. J. (2005). Attention when? An investigation of the ordering effect of input and interaction. *Studies in Second Language Acquisition, 27*(1), 1–31.

Gibson, E., & Warren, T. (2004). Reading-time evidence for intermediate linguistic structure in long-distance dependencies. *Syntax, 7*, 55–78

Gilquin, G. (2007). To err is not all: What corpus and elicitation can reveal about the use of collocations by learners. *Zeitschrift für Anglistik und Amerikanistik, 55*(3), 273–291.

Gliem, J. A., & Gliem, R. R. (2003). Calculating, interpreting, and reporting Cronbach's alpha reliability coefficient for Likert-type scales. In *Midwest research to practice conference in adult, continuing and community education* (pp. 82–88), Columbus, OH. https://scholarworks.iupui.edu/handle/1805/344

Goad, H., & White, L. (2006). Ultimate attainment in interlanguage grammars: A prosodic approach. *Second Language Research, 22*, 243–68.

Goad, H., & White, L. (2004). Ultimate attainment of L2 inflection: Effects of L1 prosodic structure. In S. Foster-Cohen, M. Sharwood Smith, A. Sorace, and M. Ota (Eds.), *Eurosla yearbook 4* (pp. 119–145). Amsterdam: Benjamins.

Godfroid, A. (2019). *Eye tracking in second language acquisition and bilingualism: A research synthesis and methodological guide.* New York: Routledge.

Goldberg, A. E. (2006). *Constructions at work: The nature of generalization in language.* Oxford: Oxford University Press.

Gordon, P. (1996). The truth-value judgment task. In D. McDaniel, C. McKee, & H. Smith Cairns (Eds.), *Methods for assessing children's syntax* (pp. 211–231). Cambridge, MA: MIT Press.

Granger, S., & Lefer, M.-A. (2020). Introduction: A two-pronged approach to corpus-based crosslinguistic studies. *Languages in Contrast, 20*(2), 167–183.

Granger, S. (1993). The International Corpus of Learner English. In J. Aarts, P. de Haan, & N. Oostdijk (Eds.), *English Language Corpora: Design, analysis and exploitation* (pp. 57–69). Amsterdam; Atlanta, GA: Rodopi.

Granger, S. (1998). *Learner English on computer.* London; New York: Addison Wesley Longman.

Granger, S. (2002). A bird's eye view of learner corpus research. In S. Granger, J. Hung, & S. Petch-Tyson (Eds.), *Computer Learner Corpora, second language acquisition and foreign language teaching* (pp. 3–36). Amsterdam: John Benjamins.

Granger, S. (2008). Learner Corpora. In A. Lüdeling & M. Kytö (Eds.), *Corpus linguistics: An international handbook* (pp. 259–275). Berlin; New York, NY: Walter de Gruyter.

Granger, S. (2015). Contrastive interlanguage analysis: A reappraisal. *International Journal of Learner Corpus Research, 1*(1), 7–24.

Granger, S. (2021). Have learner corpus research and second language acquisition finally met? In B. Le Bruyn & M. Paquot (Eds.), *Learner corpus research meets second language acquisition* (pp. 243–257). Cambridge: Cambridge University Press.

Granger, S., Dagneux, E., & Meunier, F. (2002). *The international corpus of learner English.* Louvain: Université Catholique de Louvain.

Granger, S., Gilquin, G., & Meunier, F. (Eds.) (2015). *The Cambridge handbook of learner corpus research.* Cambridge: Cambridge University Press.

Grant, D. A. (1948). The Latin square principle in the design and analysis of psychological experiments. *Psychological Bulletin, 45*(5), 427–442.

Gregg, K. (1993). Taking explanation seriously; or Let a couple of flowers bloom. *Applied Linguistics, 14*(3) 276–295.

Gries, St. Th., & Wulff, S. (2005). Do foreign language learners also have constructions? Evidence from priming, sorting, and corpora. *Annual Review of Cognitive Linguistics, 3,* 182–200.

Gries, St. Th., & Wulff, S. (2009). Psycholinguistic and corpus–linguistic evidence for L2 constructions. *Annual Review of Cognitive Linguistics, 7,* 164–187.

Grüter, T. (2005/2006). Another take on the L2 initial state: Evidence from comprehension in L2 German. *Language Acquisition, 13*(4), 287–317.

Grüter, T., Lieberman, M., & Gualmini, A. (2010). Acquiring the scope of disjunction and negation in L2: A bidirectional study of learners of Japanese and English. *Language Acquisition, 17,* 127–154.

Grüter, T., Rohde, H., & Schafer, A. (2014). The role of discourse-level expectations in non-native speakers' referential choices. In *Proceedings of the 38th annual Boston university conference on Language Development.* http://www.bu.edu/bucld/.

Gürel, A. (2006). L2 acquisition of pragmatic and syntactic constraints in the use of overt and null subject pronouns. In R. Slabakova, S. Montrul, & P. Prévost (Eds.), *Inquiries in linguistic development: Studies in honor of Lydia White* (pp. 259–282). Amsterdam: John Benjamins.

Hancin-Bhatt, B. (2000). Optimality in second language phonology: Codas in Thai ESL. *Second Language Research, 16,* 201–232.

Hancin-Bhatt, B. (2008). Second language phonology in optimality theory. In J. G. H. Edwards, & M. L. Zampini (Eds.), *Phonology and second language acquisition* (pp. 117–51). Amsterdam: John Benjamins.

Hawkins, R. (2001). The theoretical significance of universal grammar in second language acquisition. *Second Language Research, 17*(4), 345–367.

Hawkins, R. (2018). *How second languages are learned: An Introduction.* Cambridge: Cambridge University Press.

Hawkins, R., & Chan, C. (1997). The partial availability of Universal Grammar in second language acquisition: The "failed functional features hypothesis." *Second Language Research, 13,* 187–226.

Hawkins, R., & Liszka, S. (2003). Locating the source of defective past tense marking in advanced L2 English speakers. In R. Hout, A. Hulk, F. Kuiken, & R. Towell (Eds.), *The Lexicon-Syntax interface in second language acquisition* (pp. 21–44). Amsterdam: John Benjamins.

Haznedar, B., & Schwartz, B. D. (1997). Are there optional infinitives in child L2 acquisition? In E. Hughes, M. Hughes, & A. Greenhill (Eds.), *Proceedings of the 21st Annual Boston University conference on language development* (pp. 257–68). Somerville, MA: Cascadilla Press.

Heil, J., & López, L. (2020). Acquisition without evidence: English infinitives and poverty of stimulus in adult second language acquisition. *Second Language Research, 36*(4), 415–443. https://doi.org/10.1177/0267658319850611

Hirakawa, M. (1999). L2 acquisition of Japanese unaccusative verbs by speakers of English and Chinese. In K. Kanno (Ed.), *The acquisition of Japanese as a second language* (pp. 89–113). Amsterdam: John Benjamins.

Hoffman, J. E., & Subramaniam, B. (1995). The role of visual attention in saccadic eye movements. *Perception & Psychophysics, 57*(6), 787–795.

Hollenstein, N., Rotsztejn, J., Troendle, M., Pedroni, A., Zhang, C., & Langer, N. (2018). ZuCo, a simultaneous EEG and eye-tracking resource for natural sentence reading. *Scientific Data, 5*(1), 1–13.

Holmberg, A. (2010). Null subject parameters. In T. Biberauer, A. Holmberg, I. Roberts, & M. Sheehan (Eds.), *Parametric variation: Null subjects in minimalist theory* (pp. 88–124). Cambridge: Cambridge University Press.

Holmqvist, K., Nyström, M., Andersson, R., Dewhurst, R., Jarodzka, H., & Van de Weijer, J. (2011). *Eye tracking: A comprehensive guide to methods and measures*. Oxford: Oxford University Press.

Hoot, B., Leal, T., & Destruel, E. (2020). Object focus marking in Spanish: An investigation using three tasks. *Glossa: A Journal of General Linguistics, 5*(1), 70. https://doi.org/10.5334/gjgl.1160

Hopp, H. (2010). Ultimate attainment in L2 inflection: Performance similarities between non-native and native speakers. *Lingua, 120*(4), 901–931.

Hopp, H. (2013). Grammatical gender in adult L2 acquisition: Relations between lexical and syntactic variability. *Second Language Research, 29*(1), 33–56.

Hopp, H. (2022). Second language sentence processing. *Annual Review of Linguistics, 8*, 235–256.

Hopp, H., & Lemmerth, N. (2018). Lexical and syntactic congruency in L2 predictive gender processing. *Studies in Second Language Acquisition, 40*(1), 171–199.

Hopp, H., & Schmid, M. (2013). Perceived foreign accent in first language attrition and second language acquisition: The impact of age of acquisition and bilingualism. *Applied Psycholinguistics 34*(2), 361–394. https://doi.org/10.1017/S0142716411000737

Housen, A. (2002). A corpus-based study of the L2-acquisition of the English verb system. In S. Granger, J. Hung, & S. Petch-Tyson (Eds.), *Computer Learner Corpora, second language acquisition and foreign language teaching* (pp. 77–116). Amsterdam; Philadelphia, PA: John Benjamins.

Hulk, A., & Müller, N. (2000). Bilingual first language acquisition at the interface between syntax and pragmatics. *Bilingualism: Language and Cognition, 3* (3), 227–244.

Ibbotson, P. (2013). The scope of usage-based theory. *Frontiers in Psychology*. Epub ahead of print 8 May. https://doi.org/10.3389/fpsyg.2013.00255

Inagaki, S. (2001). Motion verbs with goal PPs in the L2 acquisition of English and Japanese. *Studies in Second Language Acquisition, 23*, 153–170.

Ionin, T., & Wexler, K. (2002). Why is 'is' easier than '-s'? Acquisition of tense/agreement morphology by child second language learners of English. *Second Language Research, 18*(2), 95–136.

Ionin, T., Ko, H., & Wexler, K. (2004). Article semantics in L2 acquisition: The role of specificity. *Language Acquisition, 12*(1), 3–69.

Ionin, T., Montrul, S., & Crivos, M. (2013). A bidirectional study on the acquisition of plural noun phrase interpretation in English and Spanish. *Applied Psycholinguistics, 34,* 483–518.

Isac, D., & Reiss, C. (2013). *I-language: An introduction to linguistics as cognitive science.* Oxford: Oxford University Press.

Ivanov, I. (2012). L2 acquisition of Bulgarian clitic doubling: A test case for the Interface Hypothesis. *Second Language Research, 28,* 345–368.

Jaeggli, O., & Safir, K. (1989). The null-subject parameter and parametric theory. In O. Jaeggli & K. Safir (Eds.), *The null-subject parameter* (pp. 1–44). Dordrecht: Kluwer Academic Publishers.

Jegerski, J. (2012). The processing of subject–object ambiguities in native and near-native Mexican Spanish. *Bilingualism: Language and Cognition, 15*(4), 721–735.

Jegerski, J. (2014). Self-paced reading. In J. Jegerski & B. VanPatten (Eds.), *Research methods in second language psycholinguistics* (pp. 36–65). New York/London: Routledge.

Jensen, I. N., Slabakova, R., Westergaard, M., & Lundquist, B. (2020). The Bottleneck Hypothesis in L2 acquisition: L1 Norwegian learners' knowledge of syntax and morphology in L2 English. *Second Language Research, 36*(1), 3–29. https://doi.org/10.1177/0267658318825067

Jesney, K. (2004). The use of global foreign accent rating in studies of L2 acquisition. Unpublished master's dissertation, University of Calgary, Language Research Centre.

Johnson, J., & Newport E. (1989). Critical period effects in second language learning: The influence of maturational state on the acquisition of English as a second language. *Cognitive Psychology, 21*(1), 60–99.

Judy, T., Puig-Mayenco, E., Chaouch-Orozco, A., Martín-Villena, F., & Miller, D. (2023). Testing the competing systems hypothesis: Further evidence from aspect in tutored L1-English–L2-Spanish. *Second Language Research, 39*(4), 1165–1189. https://doi.org/10.1177/02676583221123954

Juffs, A., & Harrington, M. (1995). Parsing effects in second language sentence processing: Subject and object asymmetries in wh-extraction. *Studies in Second Language Acquisition, 17*(4), 483–516.

Juffs, A., & Rodríguez, G. A. (2014). *Second language sentence processing.* New York; London: Routledge.

Just, M. A., & Carpenter, P. A. (1980). A theory of reading: From eye fixations to comprehension. *Psychological Review, 87,* 329–354.

Just, M. A., Carpenter, P. A., & Woolley, J. D. (1982). Paradigms and processes in reading comprehension. *Journal of Experimental Psychology: General, 111*(2), 228–238.

Kaan, E. (2014). Predictive sentence processing in L2 and L1: What is different? *Linguistic Approaches to Bilingualism, 4*(2), 257–282.

Kaan, E., Harris, A., Gibson, E., & Holcomb, P. (2000). The P600 as an index of syntactic integration difficulty. *Language and Cognitive Processes, 15*(2), 159–201.

Kamide, Y., Altmann, G. T., & Haywood, S. L. (2003). The time-course of prediction in incremental sentence processing: Evidence from anticipatory eye movements. *Journal of Memory and Language, 49*(1), 133–156.

Kanno, K. (1997). The acquisition of null and overt pronominals in Japanese by English speakers. *Second Language Research, 13*, 299–321.

Kaushanskaya, M., Blumenfeld, H. K., & Marian, V. (2018). The Language Experience and Proficiency Questionnaire (LEAP-Q): Ten years later. *Bilingualism: Language and Cognition, 23*(5), 945–950. https://doi.org/10.1017/S1366728919000038

Keating, G. D., & Jegerski, J. (2015). Experimental designs in sentence processing research: A methodological review and user's guide. *Studies in Second Language Acquisition, 37*(1), 1–32.

Kijak, A. (2009). *How stressful is L2 stress? A cross-linguistic study of L2 perception and production of metrical systems*. Utrecht: LOT publishing.

Klein, W., & Perdue, C. (1992). *Utterance structure: Developing grammars again* (Vol. 5). Amsterdam: John Benjamins Publishing.

Kliegl, R., & Laubrock, J. (2017). Eye-movement tracking during reading. In A. M. de Groot & P. Hagoort (Eds.), *Research methods in psycholinguistics and the neurobiology of language: A practical guide* (pp. 68–88). Hoboken, NJ: Wiley-Blackwell.

Krashen, S. (1977). The Monitor Model for adult second language performance. In M. Burt, H. Dulay, & M. Finocchiaro (Eds.), *Viewpoints on English as a Second Language* (pp. 152–161). New York: Regents.

Kruger, J. L., & Steyn, F. (2014). Subtitles and eye tracking: Reading and performance. *Reading Research Quarterly, 49*(1), 105–120.

Kuhl, P. K., & Iverson, P. (1995). Linguistic experience and the "perceptual magnet effect." In W. Strange (Ed.), *Speech Perception and Linguistic Experience: Issues in Cross-language Research* (pp. 121–154). Baltimore: York Press.

Kutas, M., & Federmeier, K. D. (2011). Thirty years and counting: Finding meaning in the N400 component of the event-related brain potential (ERP). *Annual Review of Psychology, 62*, 621–647.

Kutas, M., & Hillyard, S. A. (1980). Reading senseless sentences: Brain potentials reflect semantic incongruity. *Science, 207*(4427), 203–205.

Kutas, M., & Van Petten, C. (1988). ERP studies of language. In P. K. Ackles, J. R. Jennings, & M. G. H. Coles (Eds.), *Advances in psychophysiology* (pp. 139–188). Greenwich, CT: JAI Press.

Kutner, M. H., Nachtsheim, C. J., Neter, J., & Li, W. (2005). *Applied linear statistical models* (5th ed.). Irwin, NY: McGraw-Hill.

Labov, W. (1972). Some principles of linguistic methodology. *Language in Society, 1*(1), 97–120.

Lado, R. (1957). *Linguistics across cultures: Applied linguistics and language teachers*. Ann Arbor, MI: University of Michigan Press.

Lardiere, D. (1998a). Dissociating syntax from morphology in a divergent L2 end-state grammar. *Second Language Research, 14*(4), 359–375.

Lardiere, D. (1998b). Case and tense in the "fossilized" steady state. *Second Language Research, 14*(1), 1–26.

Lardiere, D. (2000). Mapping features to forms in second language acquisition. In J. Archibald (Ed.), *Second language acquisition and linguistic theory* (pp. 103–129). Oxford: Blackwell.

Lardiere, D. (2005) On morphological competence. In L. Dekydtspotter et al. (Eds.), *Proceedings of the 7th Generative Approaches to Second Language Acquisition Conference (GASLA 2004)*, (pp. 178–192). Somerville, MA: Cascadilla Proceedings Project.

Lardiere, D. (2007). *Ultimate attainment in second language acquisition*. London: Routledge.

Lardiere, D. (2009). Some thoughts on the contrastive analysis of features in second language acquisition. *Second Language Research, 25*(2), 173–227.

Leal Méndez, T., & Slabakova, R. (2014). The interpretability hypothesis again: A partial replication of Tsimpli and Dimitrakopoulou (2007). *International Journal of Bilingualism, 18*(6), 537–557. https://doi.org/10.1177/1367006912448125

Leal Méndez, T., Rothman, J., & Slabakova, R. (2015). Discourse-sensitive clitic-doubled dislocations in heritage Spanish. *Lingua, 155*, 85–97.

Leal, T. (2018). Data analysis and sampling: Methodological issues concerning proficiency in SLA research. In A. Edmonds & A. Gudmestad (Eds.), *Critical reflections on data in second language acquisition* (pp. 63–88). Amsterdam: John Benjamins. https://doi.org/10.1075/lllt.51.04lea

Leal, T. (2024). Information structure: Topic and focus. In T. Ionin, S. Montrul, & R. Slabakova (Eds.), *The Routledge handbook of second language acquisition, morphosyntax and semantics* (pp. 502–517). New York: Routledge.

Leal, T., Destruel, E., & Hoot, B. (2018). The realization of information focus in monolingual and bilingual native Spanish. *Linguistic Approaches to Bilingualism, 8*(2), 217–251.

Leal, T., & Hoot, B. (2022). L2 representation and processing of Spanish focus. *Language Acquisition, 29*(4), 410–440.

Leal, T., & Shea, C. E. (2018). Psycholinguistic approaches to Hispanic linguistics. In K. Geeslin (Ed.), *The Cambridge handbook of Spanish linguistics* (pp. 95–120). Cambridge: Cambridge University Press.

Leal, T., Destruel, E., & Hoot, B. (2019). The acquisition of focus in L2 Spanish. *Second Language Research, 35*(4), 449–477.

Leech, G. (1991). The state of the art in corpus linguistics. In K. Aijmer & B. Altenberg (Eds.), *English corpus linguistics: Studies in honour of Jan Svartvik* (pp. 8–29). London: Longman.

Leech, G. (1998). Preface: Learner corpora: What they are and what can be done with them. In S. Granger (Ed.), *Learner English on computer* (pp. xiv–xx). London; New York: Addison Wesley Longman.

Leech, G. (2011). Frequency, corpora and language learning. In F. Meunier, S. Cock, & G. Gilquin (Eds.), *A taste for corpora. In honour of Sylviane Granger* (pp. 7– 31). Amsterdam: John Benjamins.

Leeser, M., Brandl, A., & Weissglass, C. (2011). Task effects in second language sentence processing. In P. Trofimovich & K. McDonough (Eds.), *Applying priming methods to L2 learning, teaching, and research: Insights from psycholinguistics* (pp. 179–198). Amsterdam: Benjamins.

Lei, Y., & Yan, X. (2022). An exploratory study of strategy use on elicited imitation tasks. *Frontiers in Psychology, 13*, 917168.

Lemhöfer, K., & Broersma, M. (2012). Introducing LexTALE: A quick and valid Lexical test for advanced learners of English. *Behavior Research Methods, 44*, 325–343.

Liceras, J. (1989). On some properties of the "pro-drop" parameter: Looking for missing subjects in non-native Spanish. In S. Gass & J. Schachter (Eds.), *Linguistic perspectives on second-language acquisition* (pp. 109–33). Cambridge: Cambridge University Press.

Lozano, C. (2022). CEDEL2: Design, compilation and web interface of an online corpus for L2 Spanish acquisition research. *Second Language Research, 38*(4), 965–983.

Lozano, C., & Mendikoetxea, A. (2010). Interface conditions on postverbal subjects: A corpus study of L2 English. *Bilingualism: Language and cognition, 13*(4), 475–497.

Lozano, C., & Mendikoetxea, A. (2013). Learner corpora and second language acquisition: The design and collection of CEDEL2. In A. Díaz-Negrillo, N. Ballier & P. Thompson (Eds.), *Automatic treatment and analysis of learner corpus data* (pp. 65–100). Amsterdam: John Benjamins.

Luck, S. J. (2005). *An introduction to the event-related potential technique*. Cambridge, MA: MIT Press.

Luchkina, T., Ionin, T., Lysenko, N., Stoops A., & Suvorkina, N. (2021). Evaluating the Russian language proficiency of bilingual and second language learners of Russian. *Languages, 6*(2), 83. https://doi.org/10.3390/languages6020083

MacDonald, M. C., Pearlmutter, N. J., & Seidenberg, M. S. (1994). The lexical nature of syntactic ambiguity resolution. *Psychological Review, 101*(4), 676.

Mackey, A., & Gass, S. M. (Eds.) (2012). *Research methods in second language acquisition: A practical guide*. Chichester: Wiley-Blackwell.

MacWhinney, B. (2000). *The CHILDES project: Tools for analyzing talk: Volume I: Transcription format and programs. Volume II: The database*. Mahwah, NJ: Erlbaum.

MacWhinney, B., & Snow, C. (1990). The child language data exchange system: An update. *Journal of Child Language, 17*(2), 457–472.

Major, R. C., & Kim, E. (1996). The similarity differential rate hypothesis. *Language Learning, 46*(3), 465–496.

Marian, V., Blumenfeld, H. K., & Kaushanskaya, M. (2007). The Language Experience and Proficiency Questionnaire (LEAP-Q): Assessing language profiles in bilinguals and multilinguals. *Journal of Speech, Language, and Hearing Research, 50*, 940–967.

Marinis, T. (2007). On-line processing of passives in L1 and L2 children. In A. Belikova, L. Meroni, & M. Umeda (Eds.), *Proceedings of the 2nd conference on generative approaches to language acquisition North America* (pp. 265–276). Somerville, MA: Cascadilla Proceedings Project.

Marinis, T. (2013). Online methods in second language acquisition. In C. Chapelle (Ed.), *The encyclopedia of applied linguistics* (pp. 4307–4315). Oxford: Wiley Blackwell.

Marsden, E. (2019). Methodological transparency and its consequences for the quality and scope of research. In J. McKinley & H. Rose (Eds.), *The Routledge handbook of research methods in applied linguistics* (pp. 15–28). New York: Routledge.

Marsden, E., & Morgan-Short, K. (2023). (Why) are open research practices the future for the study of language learning? https://doi.org/10.1111/lang.12568

Marsden, E., Thompson, S., & Plonsky, L. (2018). A methodological synthesis of self-paced reading in second language research. *Applied Psycholinguistics, 39*(5), 861–904.

Marsden, H. (2009). Distributive quantifier scope in English–Japanese and Korean–Japanese interlanguage. *Language Acquisition, 16*, 135–177.

Marsden, H. (2009). Distributive quantifier scope in English-Japanese and Korean-Japanese interlanguage. *Language Acquisition, 16*(3), 135–177.

Martohardjono, G. (1993). Wh-Movement in the acquisition of a second language: A cross-linguistic study of three languages with and without movement. Unpublished PhD dissertation, Cornell University.

Mayer, M. (1969). *Frog, where are you?* New York: Dial Press.

McDonald, J. L. (2006). Beyond the critical period: Processing-based explanations for poor grammaticality judgment performance by late second language learners. *Journal of Memory and Language, 55*(3), 381–401.

McDonald, S. A. (2006). Effects of number-of-letters on eye movements during reading are independent from effects of spatial word length. *Visual Cognition, 13*, 89–98.

McEnery, T., & Hardie, A. (2011). *Corpus linguistics: Method, theory and practice.* Cambridge: Cambridge University Press.

McEnery, T., & Wilson, A. (2001). *Corpus linguistics: An introduction.* Edinburgh: Edinburgh University Press.

McEnery, T., Brezina, V., Gablasova, D., & Banerjee, J. (2019). Corpus linguistics, learner corpora, and SLA: Employing technology to analyze language use. *Annual Review of Applied Linguistics, 39*, 74–92.

Meisel, J. M. (1997). The acquisition of the syntax of negation in French and German: Contrasting first and second language development. *Second Language Research, 13*(3), 227–263.

Mendikoetxea, A., & Lozano, C. (2018). From corpora to experiments: Methodological triangulation in the study of word order at the interfaces in adult late bilinguals (L2 learners). *Journal of Psycholinguistic Research, 47*, 871–98.

Mendikoetxea, A., O'Donell, M., & Rollinson, P. (2009). WriCLE: A learner corpus for second language acquisition research. In Proceedings of the Fifth Corpus Linguistics, Liverpool.

Miller, D., & Rothman, J. (2020). You win some, you lose some: Comprehension and event-related potential evidence for L1 attrition. *Bilingualism: Language and Cognition, 23*(4), 869–883.

Minakata, K., & Beier, S. (2021). The effect of font width on eye movements during reading. *Applied Ergonomics, 97*, 103523.

Mitchell, R., Domínguez, L., Arche, M., Myles, F., & Marsden E (2008). SPLLOC: A new database for Spanish second language acquisition research. In L. Roberts, F. Myles, & A. David (Eds.), *EUROSLA yearbook 8* (pp. 287–304). Amsterdam: John Benjamins.

Mitchell, D. C. (2004). On-line methods in language processing: Introduction and historical review. In M. Carreiras & C. J. Clifton (Eds.), *The on-line study of sentence comprehension* (pp. 15–32). Brighton, UK: Routledge.

Mitchell, R., Tracy-Ventura, N., & McManus, K. (2017). *Anglophone students abroad: Identity, social relationships and language learning*. Abingdon: Routledge.

Montalbetti, M. (1984). After binding. On the interpretation of pronouns. PhD dissertation, MIT, Cambridge, MA.

Montrul, S. (2000). Transitivity alternations in L2 acquisition: Toward a modular view of transfer. *Studies in Second Language Acquisition, 22*, 229–273.

Montrul, S., & Slabakova, R. (2003). Competence similarities between native and near-native speakers: An investigation of the preterite-imperfect contrast in Spanish. *Studies in Second Language Acquisition, 25*(3), 351–398.

Montrul, S., De La Fuente, I., Davidson, J., & Foote, R. (2013). The role of experience in the acquisition and production of diminutives and gender in Spanish: Evidence from L2 learners and heritage speakers. *Second Language Research, 29*(1), 87–118.

Morgan-Short, K., & Tanner, D. (2013). Event-related potentials (ERPs). In J. Jegerski & B. VanPatten (Eds.), *Research methods in second language psycholinguistics* (pp. 127–152). New York: Routledge.

Morgan, J. L., & Demuth, K. (eds.) (1996). *Signal to syntax: Bootstrapping from speech to grammar in early acquisition*. Hillsdale, NJ: Erlbaum.

Müller, N., & Hulk, A. (2001). Crosslinguistic influence in bilingual language acquisition: Italian and French as recipient languages. *Bilingualism: Language and Cognition, 4*(1), 1–21.

Munnich, E., Flynn, S., & Martohardjono, G. (1994). Elicited imitation and grammaticality judgment tasks: What they measure and how they relate to each other. In E. Tarone, S. Gass, & A. Cohen (Eds.), *Research methodology in second-language acquisition* (pp. 227–245). Hillsdale, NJ: Lawrence Erlbaum.

Munro, M. J., & Derwing, T. M. (1995). Foreign accent, comprehensibility and intelligibility in the speech of second language learners. *Language Learning, 45*, 73–97.

Murakami, A., & Ellis, N. C. (2022). Effects of availability, contingency, and formulaicity on the accuracy of English grammatical morphemes in second language writing. *Language Learning, 72*, 899–940.

Murakami, A., & Alexopoulou, T. (2016). L1 influence on the acquisition order of English grammatical morphemes: A Learner Corpus Study. *Studies in Second Language Acquisition, 38*(3), 365–401.

Murphy, V. A. (1997). The effect of modality on a grammaticality judgement task. *Second Language Research, 13*, 34–65.

Myles, F. (2005). Interlanguage corpora and second language acquisition research. *Second Language Research, 21*, 373–391.

Myles, F. (2007). Using electronic corpora in SLA research. In D. Ayoun (Ed.), *French applied linguistics* (pp. 377–400). Amsterdam: John Benjamins.

Myles, F. (2015). Second language acquisition theory and learner corpus research. In S. Granger, G. Gilquin, & F. Meunier (Eds.), *The Cambridge handbook of learner corpus research* (pp. 309–331). Cambridge: Cambridge University Press.

Naigles, L. R. (1990). Children use syntax to learn verb meanings. *Journal of Child Language, 17*, 357–374.

References

Nicol, J., Swinney, D., Love, T., & Hald, L. (2006). The on-line study of sentence comprehension: An examination of dual task paradigms. *Journal of Psycholinguistic Research, 35,* 215–231.

Norris, J. M. (2018). *Developing C-tests for estimating proficiency in foreign language research.* New York, NY: Peter Lang.

Optican, L. M., & Pretegiani, E. (2017). What stops a saccade? *Philosophical Transactions of the Royal Society B: Biological Sciences, 372*(1718), 20160194.

Osterhout, L., Mclaughlin, J., & Bersick, M. (1997). Event-related brain potentials and human language. *Trends in Cognitive Sciences, 1,* 203–209.

Osterhout, L. (2023). http://faculty.washington.edu/losterho/erp_tutorial.htm

Osterhout, L., & Holcomb, P. J. (1993). Event-related potentials and syntactic anomaly: Evidence of anomaly detection during the perception of continuous speech. *Language and Cognitive Processes, 8,* 413–437.

Osterhout, L., Kim, A., & Kuperberg, G. R. (2012). The neurobiology of sentence comprehension. In: M. Spivey, M. Joannisse, & K. McCrae (Eds.), *The Cambridge handbook of psycholinguistics* (pp. 365–389). Cambridge: Cambridge University Press.

Özçelik, Ö., & Sprouse, R. (2017). Emergent knowledge of a universal phonological principle in the L2 acquisition of vowel harmony in Turkish: A 'four'-fold poverty of the stimulus in L2 acquisition. *Second Language Research, 33*(2), 179–206.

Pallotti, G. (2015). A simple view of linguistic complexity. *Second Language Research 31*(1), 117–134. https://doi.org/10.1177/0267658314536435

Papadopoulou, D., Tsimpli, I. M., & Amvrazis, N. (2013). Self-paced listening. In J. Jegerski & B. VanPatten (Eds.), *Research methods in second language psycholinguistics* (pp. 50–68). New York: Routledge.

Papadopoulou, D., Varlokosta, S., Spyropoulos, V., Kaili, H., Prokou, S., & Revithiadou, A. (2011). Case morphology and word order in second language Turkish: Evidence from Greek learners. *Second Language Research, 27,* 173–205.

Patino, C. M., & Carvalho Ferreira, J. (2018). Internal and external validity: Can you apply research study results to your patients? *Jornal Brasileiro de Pneumologia, 44,* 183.

Payne, B. R., & Stine-Morrow, E. A. L. (2012). Aging, parafoveal preview, and semantic integration in sentence processing: Testing the cognitive workload of wrap-up. *Psychology and Aging, 27*(3), 638–649.

Pelli, D. G., Palomares, M., & Majaj, N. J. (2004). Crowding is unlike ordinary masking: Distinguishing feature integration from detection. *Journal of Vision, 4*(12), 12–12.

Pérez-Leroux, A. T., & Glass, W. R. (1999). Null anaphora in Spanish second language acquisition: Probabilistic versus generative approaches. *Second Language Research, 15*(2), 220–249.

Perpiñán, S., Marín, R., & Moreno Villamar, I. (2020). The role of aspect in the acquisition of *ser* and *estar* in locative contexts by English-speaking learners of Spanish. *Language Acquisition, 27*(1), 35–67.

Perpiñán, S. (2013). Accounting for variability in L2 data: Type of knowledge, task effects and linguistic structure. In J. Schwieter (Ed.), *Innovative research and practices in second language acquisition and bilingualism* (pp. 1–25). Amsterdam/ Philadelphia, PA: John Benjamins.

Phinney, M. (1987). The pro-drop parameter in second-language acquisition. In T. Roeper & E. Williams (Eds.), *Parameter setting* (pp. 221–246). Boston: D. Reidel Publishing Company.

Pica, T. (1983). Methods of morpheme quantification: Their effect on the interpretation of second language data. *Studies in Second Language Acquisition*, 6(1), 69–78.

Pinker, S. (1994). *The language instinct: How the mind creates language*. London: Penguin UK.

Plonsky, L., Marsden, E., Crowther, D., Gass, S. M., & Spinner, P. (2020). A methodological synthesis and meta-analysis of judgment tasks in second language research. *Second Language Research*, 36(4), 583–621. https://doi.org/10.1177/0267658319828413

Politzer-Ahles, S. (2020). What can electrophysiology tell us about the cognitive processing of scalar implicatures? *Language and Linguistics Compass*, 14(10), 1–22.

Pollatsek, A., Bolozky, S., Well, A. D., & Rayner, K. (1981). Asymmetries in the perceptual span for Israeli readers. *Brain and Language*, 14, 174–180.

Prévost, P., & White, L. (2000). Missing surface inflection or impairment in second language acquisition? Evidence from tense and agreement. *Second Language Research*, 16, 103–133.

Prévost, P., & White, L. (2000). Missing surface inflection or impairment in second language acquisition? Evidence from tense and agreement. *Second Language Research*, 16(2), 103–133.

Prince, A., & Smolensky, P. (2004). *Optimality Theory: Constraint interaction in generative grammar*. Malden, MA/Oxford: Blackwell Publishing.

Rankin, T. (2009). Verb second in advanced L2 English: A learner corpus study. In M. Bowles (Ed.), *Proceedings of the 10th generative approaches to second language acquisition conference* (pp. 46–59). Somerville, MA: Cascadilla Proceedings Project.

Rayner, K. (2009). The thirty fifth Sir Frederick Bartlett lecture: Eye movements and attention in reading, scene perception, and visual search. *Quarterly Journal of Experimental Psychology*, 62, 1457–1506.

Rayner, K., & Castelhano, M. (2007). Eye movements. *Scholarpedia*, 2(10), 3649.

Rayner, K., Well, A. D., & Pollatsek, A. (1980). Asymmetry of the effective visual field in reading. *Perception & Psychophysics*, 27(6), 537–544.

Rebuschat, P., & Mackey, A. (2013). Prompted production. In C. A. Chappelle (Ed.), *The encyclopedia of applied linguistics*, vol. 5. Oxford: Wiley-Blackwell.

Rehman, I., Mahabadi, N., Motlagh, M., et al. (2022). Anatomy, head and neck, eye fovea [Updated 2022 August 30]. In *StatPearls* [Internet]. Treasure Island, FL: StatPearls Publishing. https://www.ncbi.nlm.nih.gov/books/NBK482301/

Reichle, E. D., & Reingold, E. M. (2013). Neurophysiological constraints on the eye-mind link. *Frontiers in Human Neuroscience*, 7, 361.

Riazi, A. M. (2016). *The Routledge encyclopedia of research methods in applied linguistics*. New York: Routledge.

Rispens, J., & Krikhaar, E. (2010). Using event-related potentials in language acquisition research. In E. Bloom, & S. Unsworth (Eds.), *Experimental methods in language acquisition research* (pp. 95–114). Hillsdale, NJ: Benjamins.

Rizzi, L. (1982). *Issues in Italian Syntax*. Dordrecht: Foris.

Roberts, L. (2014). Cross-modal priming with sentences. In J. Jegerski & B. VanPatten (Eds.), *Research methods in second language psycholinguistics* (pp. 212–230). New York/London: Routledge.

Roberts, L., Gullberg, M., & Indefrey, P. (2008). Online pronoun resolution in L2 discourse: L1 influence and general learner effects. *Studies in Second Language Acquisition*, *30*(3), 333–357.

Roberts, L., Marinis, T., Felser, C., & Clahsen, H. (2007). Antecedent priming at trace positions in children's sentence processing. *Journal of Psycholinguistic Research*, *36*(2), 175–188.

Rocha-Hidalgo, J., & Barr, R. (2022). Defining bilingualism in infancy and toddlerhood: A scoping review. *International Journal of Bilingualism*. https://doi.org/10.1177/13670069211069067

Rogers, J., & Révész, A. (2019). Experimental and quasi-experimental designs. In J. McKinley, & H. Rose (Eds.), *The Routledge handbook of research methods in applied linguistics* (pp. 133–143). New York: Routledge.

Rohde, H., Kehler, A., & Elman, J. L. (2006). Event structure and discourse coherence biases in pronoun interpretation. In Ron Sun (Ed.), *Proceedings of the 28th annual conference of the cognitive science society* (pp. 617–622). Mahwah, NJ: Lawrence Erlbaum Associates.

Rollinson, P., & Mendikoetxea, A. (2010). Learner corpora and second language acquisition: Introducing WriCLE. In J. L. Bueno Alonso, D. González Álvarez, U. Kirsten Torrado, A. E. Martínez Insua, J. Pérez-Guerra, E. Rama Martínez & R. Rodríguez Vázquez (Eds.), *Analizar datos>Describir variación/Analysing data>Describing variation* (pp. 1–12). Vigo: Universidade de Vigo (Servizo de Publicacións).

Römer, U. (2019). Corpus research for SLA: The importance of mixing methods. In V. Wiegand & M. Mahlberg (Eds.), *Corpus linguistics, context and culture* (pp. 467–482). Berlin; Boston, MA: De Gruyter.

Rommers, J., & Federmeier, K. D. (2018). Electrophysiological methods. In A. M. B. de Groot, & P. Hagoort (Eds.), *Research methods in psycholinguistics and the neurobiology of language: A practical guide* (pp. 247–265). Oxford: Wiley Blackwell.

Rothman, J., & Iverson, M. (2007). On parameter clustering and resetting the null-subject parameter in L2 Spanish: Implications and observations. *Hispania*, *90*(2), 328–341.

Rothman, J. (2008). Aspect selection in adult L2 Spanish and the competing systems hypothesis: When pedagogical and linguistic rules conflict. *Languages in Contrast*, *8*(1), 74–106.

Rothman, J., & Slabakova, R. (2018). The generative approach to SLA and its place in modern second language studies. *Studies in Second Language Acquisition*, *40*(2), 417–442.

Rule, S. (2004). French interlanguage oral corpora: Recent developments. In F. Myles & R. Towell (Eds.), The acquisition of French as a second language. *Journal of French Language Studies*, *14*(3), 343–356.

Rule, S., Marsden, E., Myles, F., & Mitchell, R. (2003). Constructing a database of French interlanguage oral corpora. In D. Archer, P. Rayson, E. Wilson, & T. McEnery (Eds.), *Proceedings of the corpus linguistics 2003 conference*, UCREL Technical Papers no. 16 (pp. 669–77). University of Lancaster.

Rutherford, W., & Thomas, M. (2001). The child language data exchange system in research on second language acquisition. *Second Language Research, 17*(2), 195–212.
Safir, K. (1985). *Syntactic chains*. New York: Cambridge University Press.
Sani, F., & Todman, J. (2006). *Experimental design and statistics for psychology: A first course*. Malden, MA: Blackwell Publishing.
Sanz, C. (1997). Experimental tasks in SLA research: Amount of production, modality, memory, and production processes. In A. Pérez-Leroux & W. Glass (Eds.), *Contemporary perspectives on the acquisition of Spanish: Vol. 2 production, processing and comprehension* (pp. 41–56). Somerville, MA: Cascadilla.
Schotter, E. R., Angele, B., & Rayner, K. (2012). Parafoveal processing in reading. *Attention, Perception, & Psychophysics, 74*(1), 5–35.
Schütze, C. (1996). *The empirical base of linguistics: Grammaticality judgments and linguistic methodology*. Chicago, IL: University of Chicago Press.
Schütze, C. & Sprouse, J. (2014). Judgment data. In R. Podesva & D. Sharma (Eds.), *Research methods in linguistics* (pp. 27–51). Cambridge: Cambridge University Press.
Schwartz, B. D. & Sprouse, R. A. (1996). L2 cognitive states and the full transfer/full access hypothesis. *Second Language Research, 12*, 40–72.
Schwartz, B. D., & Sprouse, R. A. (2013). Generative approaches and the poverty of the stimulus. In J. Herschensohn & M. Young Scholten (Eds.), *The Cambridge handbook of second language acquisition* (pp. 137–158). Cambridge: Cambridge University Press.
Shehata, A. (2018). Native English speakers' perception and production of Arabic consonants. In M. T. Alhawary (Ed.), *The Routledge handbook of Arabic second language acquisition* (pp. 56–69). Abingdon: Routledge.
Shimanskaya, E., & Slabakova, R. (2017). Re-assembling objects: A new look at the L2 acquisition of pronominal clitics. *Bilingualism: Language and Cognition, 20*(3), 512–529.
Singh, H., & Singh, J. (2012). Human eye tracking and related issues: A review. *International Journal of Scientific and Research Publications, 2*(9), 1–9.
Slabakova, R. (2000). L1 transfer revisited: The L2 acquisition of telicity marking in English by Spanish and Bulgarian native speakers. *Linguistics, 38*(4), 739–770.
Slabakova, R. (2001). *Telicity in the second language*. Amsterdam: John Benjamins.
Slabakova, R. (2003). Semantic evidence for functional categories in interlanguage grammars. *Second Language Research, 19*, 76–109.
Slabakova, R. (2005). What is so difficult about telicity marking in L2 Russian? *Bilingualism: Language and Cognition, 8*(1), 63–77.
Slabakova, R. (2006). Learnability in the second language acquisition of semantics: A bidirectional study of a semantic parameter. *Second Language Research, 22*(4), 498–523. https://doi.org/10.1191/0267658306sr277oa
Slabakova, R. (2008). *Meaning in the second language*. Berlin: Mouton de Gruyter.
Slabakova, R. (2013). What is easy and what is hard to acquire in a second language: A generative perspective. In M. García Mayo, M. J. Gutiérrez Mangado, & M. Martínez-Adrián (Eds.), *Contemporary approaches to second language acquisition* (pp. 5–28). Amsterdam: John Benjamins.
Slabakova, R. (2016). *Second language acquisition*. Oxford: Oxford University Press.
Slabakova, R. (2019a). "L" stands for language. *The Modern Language Journal, 103*, 152–160. https://doi.org/10.1111/modl.12528

Slabakova, R. (2019b). The Bottleneck hypothesis updated. In T. Ionin & M. Rispoli (Eds.), *Three streams of generative language acquisition research* (pp. 319–345). Amsterdam: John Benjamins.

Slabakova, R., Kempchinsky, P., & Rothman, J. (2012). Clitic-doubled left dislocation and focus fronting in L2 Spanish: A case of successful acquisition at the syntax-discourse interface. *Second Language Research, 28*, 319–343.

Slabakova, R., White, L., & Brambatti Guzzo, N. (2017). Pronoun interpretation in the second language: Effects of computational complexity. *Frontiers in Psychology*, 8, 1236.

Slabakova, R., Leal, T., Dudley, A., & Stack, M. (2020). *Generative second language acquisition*. Cambridge University Press.

Sorace A., & Filiaci, F. (2006). Anaphora resolution in near-native speakers of Italian. *Second Language Research, 22*, 339–368.

Sorace, A. (1996): The use of acceptability judgments in L2 acquisition research. In W. Ritchie & T. Bhatia (Eds.), *The Handbook of second language* acquisition (pp. 375–409). New York: Academic Press.

Sorace, A. (2005). Syntactic optionality at interfaces. In L. Cornips & K. Corrigan (Eds.), *Syntax and variation: Reconciling the biological and the social* (pp. 46–111). Amsterdam: John Benjamins.

Sorace, A. (2011). Pinning down the concept of "interface" in bilingualism. *Linguistic Approaches to Bilingualism, 1*(1), 1–33.

Sorace, A., & Keller, F. (2005). Gradience in linguistic data. *Lingua, 115*(11), 1497–1524.

Souza, C., Garrido, M. V., & Carmo, J. C. (2020). A systematic review of normative studies using images of common objects. *Frontiers in Psychology, 11*, 573314.

Spinner, P. (2013). The second language acquisition of number and gender in Swahili: A feature reassembly approach. *Second Language Research, 29*(4), 455–479.

Spivey, M. J., & Tanenhaus, M. K. (1998). Syntactic ambiguity resolution in discourse: Modeling the effects of referential context and lexical frequency. *Journal of Experimental Psychology: Learning, Memory, and Cognition, 24*(6), 1521.

Sprouse, J. (2011). A test of the cognitive assumptions of magnitude estimation: Commutativity does not hold for acceptability judgments. *Language, 87*(2), 274–288.

Sprouse, J. (2018). Acceptability judgments and grammaticality, prospects and revolution in linguistics. In N. Hornstein, C. Yang, & P. Patel-Grosz (Eds.), *Syntactic structures after 60* (pp. 195–224). Berlin: Mouton de Gruyter.

Sprouse, J. (2023). Acceptability judgments. In J. Sprouse (Ed.), *The Oxford handbook of experimental syntax* (pp. 3–28). Oxford: Oxford University Press.

Sprouse, J., Yankama, B., Indurkhya, S., Fong, S., & Berwick, R. C. (2018). Colorless green ideas do sleep furiously: Gradient acceptability and the nature of the grammar. *The Linguistic Review, 35*(3), 575–599.

Steinhauer, K. (2014). Event-related potentials (ERPs) in second language research: A brief introduction to the technique, a selected review, and an invitation to reconsider critical periods in L2. *Applied Linguistics, 35*(4), 393–417.

Stowe, L., & Kaan, E. (2006). *Developing an experiment: Techniques and design*. http://ufdc.ufl.edu/IR00005517/00001

Tanenhaus, M. K., & Trueswell, J. C. (1995). Sentence comprehension. In J. L. Miller & P. D. Eimas (Eds.), *Speech, language, and communication* (pp. 217–262). San Diego, CA: Academic Press. https://doi.org/10.1016/B978-012497770-9.50009-1

Tanenhaus, M. K., Magnuson, J. S., Dahan, D., & Chambers, C. (2000). Eye movements and lexical access in spoken-language comprehension: Evaluating a linking hypothesis between fixations and linguistic processing. *Journal of Psycholinguistic Research, 29*, 557–580.

Tang, W., Fiorentino, R., & Gabriele, A. (2023). Examining transfer in the acquisition of the count/mass distinction in L2 English. *Second Language Research, 39*(1), 231–257. https://doi.org/10.1177/02676583211023729

Tatler, B. W., Kirtley, C., Macdonald, R. G., Mitchell, K., & Savage, S. W. (2014). The active eye: Perspectives on eye movement research. In M. Horsley, M. Eliot, B. A. Knight, & R. Reilly (Eds.), *Current trends in eye tracking research* (pp. 3–16). Cham: Springer.

Tognini-Bonelli, E. (2001). *Corpus linguistics at work: Studies in corpus linguistics.* Amsterdam: John Benjamins.

Tokowicz, N., & MacWhinney, B. (2005). Implicit and explicit measures of sensitivity to violations in second language grammar: An event-related potential investigation. *Studies in Second Language Acquisition, 27*(2), 173–204.

Tono, Y. (2003). Learner corpora: Design, development and applications. In D. Archer, P. Rayson, A. Wilson & T. McEnery (Eds.), *Proceedings of the 2003 corpus linguistics conference* (pp. 800–809). UCREL: Lancaster University.

Tono, Y. (2004). Multiple comparisons of IL, L1 and TL corpora: The case of L2 acquisition of verb subcategorization patterns by Japanese learners of English. In G. Aston, S. Bernardini & D. Stewart (Eds.), *Corpora and language learners* (pp. 45–66). Amsterdam: John Benjamins.

Torregrossa, J., Andreou, M., Bongartz, C., & Tsimpli, I. M. (2021). Bilingual acquisition of reference: The role of language experience, executive functions and crosslinguistic effects. *Bilingualism: Language and Cognition, 24*(4), 694–706. https://doi.org/10.1017/S1366728920000826

Townsend, D. J., & Bever, T. G. (2001). *Sentence comprehension: The integration of habits and rules.* MIT Press.

Tracy-Ventura, N., McManus, K., Ortega, L., & Norris, J. M. (2014). "Repeat as much as you can": Elicited imitation as a measure of global proficiency in L2 French. In P. Leclercq, H. Hilton, and A. Edmonds (Eds.), *Proficiency assessment issues in SLA research: Measures and practices* (pp.143–166). Bristol: Multilingual Matters.

Tracy-Ventura, N., & Myles, F. (2015). The importance of task variability in the design of learner corpora for SLA research. *International Journal of Learner Corpus Research, 1*(1), 58–95.

Tracy-Ventura, N., & Paquot, M. (2021). *The Routledge handbook of SLA and corpus linguistics.* New York: Routledge.

Tremblay, A. (2011). Proficiency assessment standards in Second Language Acquisition Research: "Clozing" the Gap. *Studies in Second Language Acquisition, 33*(3), 339–372.

Trofimovich, P., & McDonough, K. (Eds.). (2011). *Applying priming methods to L2 learning, teaching and research: Insights from psycholinguistics.* Amsterdam: John Benjamins.

Trueswell, J. C., Sekerina, I., Hill, N., & Logrip, M. (1999). The kindergarten-path effect: Studying on-line sentence processing in young children. *Cognition, 73,* 89–134.

Tsimpli, I. M. (2003). Interrogatives in the Greek/English interlanguage: A minimalist account. In E. Mela-Athanasopoulou (Ed.), *Selected papers on theoretical and applied linguistics* (pp. 214–225). Thessaloniki: Aristotle University.

Tsimpli, I. M., & Dimitrakopoulou, M. (2007). The interpretability hypothesis: Evidence from wh-interrogatives in second language acquisition. *Second Language Research, 23*(2), 215–242. https://doi.org/10.1177/0267658307076546

Tsimpli, I. M., & Mastropavlou, M. (2007). Feature interpretability in L2 acquisition and SLI: Greek clitics and determiners. In H. Goodluck, J. Liceras, & H. Zobl (Eds.), *The role of formal features in second language acquisition* (pp. 143–183). London: Routledge.

Tsimpli, I., Sorace, A., Heycock, C., & Filiaci, F. (2004). First language attrition and syntactic subjects: A study of Greek and Italian near-native speakers of English. *International Journal of Bilingualism, 8*(3), 257–277.

Tuniyan, E. (2018). *Second language acquisition of definiteness: A feature-based contrastive approach to second language learnability*. Doctoral dissertation, University of Southampton.

Vainikka, A., & Young-Scholten, M. (1994). Direct access to x'-theory. In T. Hoekstra & B. D. Schwartz (Eds.), *Language acquisition studies in generative grammar* (pp. 265–315). Amsterdam: John Benjamins.

Vainikka, A., & Young-Scholten, M. (1996). Gradual development of L2 phrase structure. *Second Language Research, 12*(1), 7–39.

van Berkum, J. J. A. (2009). The neuropragmatics of "simple" utterance comprehension: An ERP review. In U. Sauerland, & K. Yatsushiro (Eds.), *Semantics and pragmatics: From experiment to theory* (pp. 276–316). Basingstoke: Palgrave Macmillan.

van Gompel, R. P. (2013). Sentence processing: An introduction. In R. P. van Gompel (Ed.), *Sentence processing* (pp. 13–32). London: Psychology Press, Taylor & Francis Group.

VanPatten & Cadierno (1993). Input Processing and second language acquisition: A role for instruction. *The Modern Language Journal, 77*(1), 45–57.

Walker, C. (2021). Eye-tracking the reader experience. In *An eye-tracking study of equivalent effect in translation*. Cham: Palgrave Macmillan. https://doi.org/10.1007/978-3-030-55769-0_6

Werker, J. F., & Tees, R. C. (1999). Influences on infant speech processing: Toward a new synthesis. *Annual Review of Psychology, 50*(1), 509–535.

White, E. J., Genesee, F., & Steinhauer, K. (2012). Brain responses before and after intensive second language learning: Proficiency based changes and first language background effects in adult learners. *PloS One, 7*(12), e52318.

White, L (1985a). The pro-drop parameter in adult second-language acquisition. *Language Learning, 35,* 47–62.

White, L. (1985b). The acquisition of parameterized grammars: Subjacency in second language acquisition. *Second Language Research, 1,* 1–17.

White, L. (1986). Implications of parametric variation for adult second-language acquisition: An investigation of the "pro-drop" parameter. In V. Cook (Ed.),

Experimental approaches to second-language acquisition (pp. 55–72). Oxford: Pergamon.

White, L. (1988). Island effects in second language acquisition. In S. Flynn & W. O'Neill (Eds.), *Linguistic theory in second language acquisition* (pp. 144–172). Dordrecht: Reidel.

White, L. (1989). *Universal grammar and second language acquisition*. Amsterdam: John Benjamins.

White, L. (1990). Second language acquisition and Universal Grammar. *Studies in Second Language Acquisition, 12,* 121–133.

White, L. (1990/1991). The Verb-Movement Parameter in Second Language Acquisition. *Language Acquisition 1*(4), 337–360.

White, L. (2003). *Second language acquisition and universal grammar*. Cambridge: Cambridge University Press.

White, L., & Juffs, A. (1998). Constraints on Wh-movement in two different contexts of non-native language acquisition: Competence and processing. In S. Flynn, G. Martohardjono, & W. O'Neill (Eds.), *The generative study of second language acquisition* (pp. 111–130). Hillsdale, NJ: Lawrence Erlbaum Associates.

White, L., Brown, C., Bruhn de Graravito, J., Chen, D., Hirakawa, M., & Montrul, S. (1999). Psych verbs in second language acquisition. In G. Martohardjono & E. Klein (Eds.), *The development of second language grammars: A generative approach* (pp. 173–199). Amsterdam: John Benjamins.

White, L., Bruhn-Garavito, J., Kawasaki, T., Pater, J., & Prévost, P. (1997). The researcher gave the subject a test about himself: Problems of ambiguity and preference in the investigation of reflexive binding. *Language Learning, 47,* 145–172.

Yan, X., Maeda, Y., Lv, J., & Ginther, A. (2016). Elicited imitation as a measure of second language proficiency: A narrative review and meta-analysis. *Language Testing, 33*(4), 497–528.

Zipf, G. K. (1949). *Human behavior and the principle of least effort*. Cambridge, MA: Addison-Wesley Press.

Zyzik, E. C. (2008). Null objects in second language acquisition: Grammatical vs. performance models. *Second Language Research, 24*(1), 65–110.

AUTHOR INDEX

Note: *Italic* page numbers refer to figures and page numbers followed by "n" refer to end notes.

Albirini, A. 152
Alexopoulou, T. 170–171
Aliaga-García, C. 91
Allopenna, P. D. 126
Arche, M. J. 23, 150

Bader, M. 69n1
Bardovi-Harlig, K. 157
Bayram, F. 155, 164–165
Beck, M. L. 166n2
Benders, T. 93
Benmamoun, E. 152
Biber, D. 172
Bley-Vroman, R. 163
Boland, J. 130
Bongartz, C. 19
Borer, H. 9
Bornkessel-Schlesewsky, I. 138, 144, 147n1
Bowles, M. A. 163
Bradley, M. M. 138
Broselow, E. 88, 98
Brown, C. 93

Cadierno, T. 79
Campbell, D. T. 34–35
Carlson, K. 113

Carroll, S. E. 13, 19
Cebrian, J. 91
Chapelle, C. 36
Chaudron, C. 163
Choi, S. H. 64
Chomsky, N. 6–8, 17–18, 23–24
Chrabaszcz, A. 164
Cook, T. D. 34–35
Cowart, W. 23, 56
Crain, S. 14, 71, 73, 75
Cuza, A. 159

Daidone, D. 95
Darcy, I. 95
Derwing, T. M. 87
Díaz-Negrillo, A. 183n10
Dimitrakopoulou, M. 63, 67
Domínguez, L. 23, 150, 153, 181–182
Donchin, E. 140
Dosi, I. 163
Duffield, N. 81, 82
Dussias, P. E. 121

Ellis, N. C. 20, 21, 163
Escudero, P. 93
Espírito Santo, A. 161–162
Eubank, L. 166n2

Felser, C. 115–117
Ferreira, F. 111
Fiorentino, R. 64
Fodor, J. D. 19
Francis, E. J. 18
Frank, J. 159
Friederici, A. D. 143–144

Gabriele, A. 64, 73, 145–146
García-Tejada, A. 158
Gibson, E. 115
Glass, W. 41
Goad, H. 89–90
Godfroid, A. 125, 129–131, 133
Granger, S. 177, 183n3
Gregg, K. 29
Grüter, T. 159
Gullberg, M. 131
Gürel, A. 80, 81

Hancin-Bhatt, B. 89
Haüssler, J. 69n1
Heil, J. 15
Hillyard, S. A. 142
Hoffman, J. E. 119
Holcomb, P. J. 143
Holmqvist, K. 125
Hoot, B. 105, 107
Hopp, H. 58, 87, 102, 126, 127

Indefrey, P. 131
Ionin, T. 59, 64, 74–75, 153
Ivanov, I. 77
Iverson, M. 15, 42, 47

Jaeggli, O. 43
Jegerski, J. 101–102, 110
Jiang, N. 164
Judy, T. 157
Juffs, A. 47, 101
Just, M. A. 105, 109

Kaan, E. 104, 109, 143
Kamide, Y. 128
Kang, Y. 88, 98
Kanno, K. 41, 80
Keating, G. D. 110
Keil, A. 138
Kijak, A. 92
Klein, W. 151
Kliegl, R. 125
Ko, H. 153

Krashen, S. 171
Krikhaar, E. 137
Kutas, M. 142

Lado, R. 22, 88
Lardiere, D. 29, 43, 49, 149
Laubrock, J. 125
Leal, T. 31, 105, 107, 161
Leech, G. 172
Lei, Y. 163, 166n5
Lemmerth, N. 126–127
López, L. 15
Lozano, C. 178, 179
Luck, S. J. 140, 144

Mackey, A. 163, 164
MacWhinney, B. 107–108
Marinis, T. 111–112
Marsden, E. 76, *76,* 79, 110, 125, 183n1
Martohardjono, G. 23
Mastropavlou, M. 145
Matsuo, A. 81–82
Mayer, Mercer: *Frog, Where Are You?* 154–155
McDonough, K. 114
McEnery, T. 169, 170
Meisel, J. M. 166n2
Méndez, L. T. 67
Mendikoetxea, A. 178, 179
Miller, D. 142
Mitchell, R. 180
Montrul, S. 74–75, 160
Mora, J. C. 91
Morgan-Short, K. 125, 141, 144
Munnich, E. 163
Munro, M. J. 87
Murakami, A. 170–171
Murphy, V. A. 58
Myles, F. 183n1, 183n2

Nicol, J. 101

O'Donnell, M. B. 20, 21
Osterhout, L. 141, 143
Özçelik, Ö. 97–98

Pallotti, G. 46
Papadopoulou, D. 163
Perdue, C. 151
Pérez-Leroux, A. 41
Perpiñán, S. 162

Pinker, S. 136
Plonsky, L. 58
Politzer-Ahles, S. 140

Rankin, T. 183n6
Rebuschat, P. 163, 164
Reichle, E. D. 134n1
Reingold, E. M. 134n1
Revesz, A. 35, 37n2
Rispens, J. 137
Rizzi, L. 43
Roberts, L. 81, 114, 115–117, 131–132
Rodriguez, G. A. 101
Rogers, J. 35, 37n2
Rohde, H. 159
Romer, U. 21
Rothman, J. 4, 15, 42, 47, 103, 142
Rutherford, W. 183n1

Safir, K. 43
Sagarra, N. 21
Sani, F. 33
Schmid, M. 87
Schotter, E. R. 123
Schütze, C. T. 5, 23, 61
Schwartz, B. D. 15–16
Shehata, A. 94
Shimanskaya, E. 45
Sjerps, M. J. 93
Slabakova, R. 4, 6, 15, 45–46, 62, 67, 72, 80, 81, 83n1, 103
Sorace, A. 183n6

Souza, C. 135n3
Spinner, P. 165
Sprouse, R. A. 15–16, 61, 97–98
Stowe, L. 104, 109
Subramaniam, B. 119

Tang, W. 64
Tanner, D. 141, 144
Thomas, M. 183n1
Thompson, P. 183n10
Thornton, R. 14, 71, 73
Todman, J. 33
Tokowicz, N. 107–108
Tremblay, A. 50
Trofimovich, P. 114
Tsimpli, I. M. 19, 63, 67, 145, 163
Tuniyan, E. 160

Vainikka, A. 166n2
VanPatten, B. 79

Walker, C. 134
Warren, T. 115
Werker, J. 90
Wexler, K. 153
White, L. 15, 43, 47, 79, 80, 83n1, 89–90, 98

Yan, X. 163, 166n5
Young-Scholten, M. 166n2

Zhu, Y. 64

SUBJECT INDEX

Note: **Bold** page numbers refer to tables, *italic* page numbers refer to figures and page numbers followed by "n" refer to end notes.

Acceptability Judgment Tasks (AJTs) 5–6, 22, 55–57, 66, 67, 74, 106; advantages 55–56; AJT in context 75–78; aural presentation 57–58; conditions 64–66; with corrections 59; description of the method 57–61; design 61–66; factorial design 63–64; factors affecting 56–57; fillers 66; gradient acceptability 16–18, 23; instructions 61–62; mode of presentation 57–58; practice items 62; response types 59–61; timed/untimed AJTs 58; written presentation 57–58
acquisition context 47–48; classroom (instructed) acquisition 47; naturalistic acquisition 47–48
action-based studies 121
age of acquisition (AoA) 86–87
age of arrival (AoA) 99n1
ambiguity resolution 131
anomaly paradigms 131
anonymization 174, 180
aspect: telicity 46
atomicity 64
attention 106, 119, 129
auditory stimuli 110–111, 113–114, 121
auditory window technique 110
authentic data 172–173

binding 40, 74, 80, 82
Bottleneck Hypothesis 9, 29
British National Corpus (BNC) 15, 172
built-in concordance 175

Cambridge Learner Corpus (CLC) 170, 171
categorical variables 31
category change task 95
causal relationships 30, 33–35
CHAT 174, *175*, 180
CHILDES (Child Language Exchange System) database 168–169, 174, 180, 183n1
CLAN (Computerized Language Analysis) programs 174–177, *177*, 180
cloze tests 157–159
COMBO (combined search for more than two words) 176
competence *see* grammatical competence
comprehension 11, 19, 50, 66, 73, 77, 101–106, 119, 122, 130, 157, 163

conditions 31–32; AJTs 64–66; control conditions 32, 106–107, 129, 142; as element of experimental design 30–32; experimental conditions 32, 59, 64
construction frequency 48–49
construct validity 11, 58
continuous variables 31
contrast (linguistic) 22, 41, 91–94
Contrastive Analysis Hypothesis 22, 88
control conditions 32, 106–107, 129, 142
control groups 21–23
convenience sampling 34
cornea 120
corpus analysis tools 172–173
Corpus Escrito del Español como L2 (CEDEL2) 169, 178, 183n7
corpus linguistics 168–173, 182
Corpus of Contemporary American English (COCA) 49
corrections: AJT with 59
Critical Period Hypothesis 87–88, 104
cross-modal priming 113–117
C-tests 50–51

dependency paradigms 131
dependent variables 31
discrete variables 31
discrimination tasks 91; ABX discrimination task 94–95; AXB discrimination task 94; AX discrimination task 94–95; Oddball (category change) task 94–95; Oddity task 94–95; speech perception 93–96

E-language 3, 25n3
electrical potentials 137
electroencephalogram (EEG) 137
electrophysiological methods 139
elicitation tasks: contextualized 159–160; controlled elicitation task 151; picture-based 154–156, 156; picture/video 160–163; targeting sentences 159–160; silent film 156–15
elicited imitation (EI) 163–165
Empty Category Principle 25n2
ethical protocols 174
European Science Foundation (ESF) oral corpus 151

event-related potentials (ERPs): data elicited with 136–146; electrical potentials 137, 139; ERP components 140–144; ERP effects 142; experimental conditions 32, 59, 64; overview 136
evidence: in the input 48–49; lexical/construction frequency 48–49; negative 47–48; positive 15, 17, 39, 48–49
experience *see* exposure
experimental conditions 32, 59, 64
experimental design: elements of 30–32; formulating hypotheses 27–30; life cycle of 26–37; quality of (quasi-)experimental design 34–36; quasi-experimental research 33–34; scientific method 27; validity and reliability 34–36; variables and conditions 30–32
explicit knowledge 47, 58, 104, 163–164
exposure: to language 13, 18–20, 48–50; language exposure and global proficiency 49–51 *see also* input; research issues 18–20
external validity 34–35
Eye-Mind Hypothesis 119
eye movements 119, 121–122, 125–127, 134
eye-tracking 119–134; data collected by 121–125; overview 119–121; with text (Reading paradigm) 130–134; Visual World paradigm 125–130

"false alarms" 96, 99n2
feature(s): encoding parametric variation 43–45; functional 43–44; in Minimalism 8–10
Feature Reassembly Hypothesis 29–30, 43
fillers: AJTs 66
film-based narrative 156
find/spot the difference between pictures 165; *see also* spot-the-difference task
first pass time 124
fixations 121; first fixation duration 124–125, 130–132; fixation proportions 121, 124
form-meaning mapping 14; form-meaning relationship 70, 182

Subject Index

formulating hypotheses 27–30
fovea 123
free narrative task 149
French Learner Language Oral Corpus (FLLOC) 179
FREQ (frequency word count) 176
Frog, Where Are You? (Mayer) 154–155
functional categories 47, 89, 150–151
functional features 43–44; animacy 43–44; case 43–44; gender 43–44; number 43–44; person 43–44
functionalist SLA 85, 170

gaze duration 105, 124–125, 130
generative SLA (GenSLA) 3–6, 10, 38, 48; designing experiments in 38–52; features encoding parametric variation 43–45
global foreign accent 86–88
gradient acceptability 16–18, 23
grammatical competence 11n2, 21, 71, 149, 163
Grammaticality Judgment Task *see* Acceptability Judgment Task

heritage speaker 152, 155, 158–161, 163–164
hypotheses: formulating 27–30; hypothesis generation 26, 36; sources of 28–29; types of hypotheses 29–30

identification tasks 91–93
I-grammar *see* I-language
I-language 5–6, 11n2, 25n3; and role of Universal Grammar in SLA 3–4
impersonal narrative 180, **181**
implicit knowledge 4, 11, 23, 49, 58, 149, 163–164, 166
implicit measure 102, 119
incremental processing 113, 144
independent variable 31
individual differences 13, 94
input and exposure 13, 18–20
input (for language acquisition) 4, 7, 12n4, 13–16, 18–21, 27–28, 39, 42, 47–49, 51, 52, 85, 88, 97–98, 101, 128, 163–165, 172
instruction (language) 47, 61–62
Interface Hypothesis 103, 183n6
interlanguage 4, 9, 56, 152–153
internal validity 34–35

International Corpus of Learner English (ICLE) 169
Interpretability Hypothesis 9, 145, 147n3
interpretation (reading) 14, 70–75
interpretation tasks 70–82; acceptability judgment in context 75–78; described 70–71; interpretation choice task 80–81; Picture Matching Task (PMT) 78–80; Sentence Conjunction Judgment Task (SCT) 81–82; Truth Value Judgment Task (TVJT) 71–75
interval scale 61, 74
interview 149–154, 179–181

KWAL (Key Word and Line concordance) 176

L1 influence 132, 164, 171, 172; *see also* transfer from the native language
language: exposure and global proficiency 49–51; exposure to 13, 18–20, 48–50
language exposure questionnaire 50
language processing 49, 101, 114, 119, 141, 143, 147
Languages and Social Networks Abroad Project (LANGSNAP) 169
latency-based measures: cross-modal priming 113–117; latency 100–104, 113–117; latency-based methods and L2/GenSLA studies 103–104; overview 100–103; self-paced listening 110–113; self-paced reading 104–110, *105*
Latent Semantic Analysis 143, 147n2
learner corpora: corpus analysis tools and SLA research agendas 172–173; creation of 173–177; described 169–171; in generative SLA research 177–182; overview 168–169; SPLLOC 179–182; WriCLE 178–179
learning task 7, 10, 22, 38, 44–45, 76
Lexical Aspect Hypothesis 181–182
lexical decision task 114
lexical frequency 48–49
life cycle of an experimental design 26–37
linguistic complexity 46–47

linguistic universals in phonology 97–98
listening: comprehension measures 128, 130; self-paced 110–113
looking-while-listening studies 121

markedness 88
metalinguistic knowledge 58, 73, 163–165
Minimalist Program 8–9, 102
Minimalist view of language and acquisition 8–10
Missing Surface Inflection Hypothesis 9, 151
"Modern Times" film 156
morpheme acquisition studies 171
morphosyntactic tags 175
MOR 175–176

N400 component 141, 142
narrative (controlled) 180–181
native language 45–46
Native Language Magnet Theory 86
native speaker, construct of 23–25
naturalistic contexts 177
naturalistic measure 119
naturalistic production tasks 150–151
naturalistic speech 151, 154–155
natural order of acquisition 171
neural activity: non-cumulative 137
neurolinguistics 10, 13, 24, 147
non-violation paradigm 131
Null Subject Parameter 41–42, 46

obligatory contexts 152–153
oddball task 95 *see also* discrimination tasks
open-ended task 150–151
optionality 10, 17
Overt Pronoun Constraint 40–41
Oxford English Dictionary 30

P600 component 141, 143
parafoveal region 123
parameter (linguistic): Null Subject Parameter 41–42, 46; parameter-setting 7–9; parametric cluster 41–42
parametric variation: features encoding 43–45; functional features 43–44; test feature reassembly 44
participant selection 26

pass: first pass time 124; second pass time 124
perceptional assimilation task 91
Perceptual Assimilation Model 86, 91
perceptual span 123, 135n2
performance 11n2, 23, 47–48
phonetics 84–85
phonology: linguistic universals in 97–98; and phonetics 84–85; second language 85–86
picture-based elicitation 154–156, *156*
picture-based narrative 150–151, 154, 156
picture description task 157
Picture Matching Task (PMT) 78–80
Picture Selection Task (PST) 71; *see also* Picture Matching Task
picture/video elicitation tasks 160–163
POS (part of speech) 169, 175
Poverty of the Stimulus 13–16
presentation: cumulative 105; non-cumulative 104–105
principle (linguistic) 7–8
Principles and Parameters theory 7–8
processing models 101–103
production tasks 149–166; coding and analysis 152–153; controlled 157–163; elicited imitation (EI) 163–165; find/spot the difference between pictures 165; open-ended/ naturalistic 150–151; repetition tasks 163–165; semi-controlled elicited narratives 154–157; speech production 88–90
proficiency: global proficiency 49–51; linguistic 31, 49–50
prompt 155–159
pronouns: null pronoun 40, 41, 70, 131; overt 40, 70, 153; reflexive 4, 6, 158–159; resumptive 49, 63–64, 162
property theory 29
purpose-built corpora 168, 169, 173–174, 178

quasi-experimental research design 33–34: quality of 34–36; validity and reliability 34–36
questionnaire 19, 50–51, 174

random assignment 33–34, 37n1
reaction times 100, 106, 108, 116–117

reading: self-paced 104–110, *105*
Reading Studies: creating stimuli 132–134; types of eye-tracking while 131–132
regressions 121; regression path duration 124–125
reliability 35–36; (quasi-)experimental design 34–36
repetition tasks 163–165
Representational Deficit Hypothesis 9
research design: control groups 21–23; input, exposure and experience 18–20; native speaker, construct of 23–25; Poverty of the Stimulus 13–16; research methods from other frameworks 20–21; variability and gradient acceptability 16–18
research questions/models: in 1980s 38–39; in 1990s 38–39; in second language phonology 85–86
root infinitives 151
rote memorization 163

saccades 121, 122
scalp topography 140, 144
scientific method 27
second pass time 124
self-paced listening 110–113; creating stimuli 113
self-paced reading 104–110, *105*; creating stimuli 108–110; data that is elicited with 106–108
semantic anomaly 141, 144
semantic priming 114
semi-controlled elicited narratives 154–157; overview 154; picture-based elicitation 154–156, *156*; silent film elicitation 156–157
sentence conjunction task (SCT) 81–82
Shallow Structure Hypothesis 103, 131
silent film elicitation 156–157
sources of hypotheses 28–29
Spanish Learner Language Oral Corpus (SPLLOC) 153, 155, 166n3, 169, 176, 179–182, **181**; data elicited by 181–182; description of 179–181; types of tasks used in **181**
speech: perception 90–96; production 88–90; spontaneous speech 149–150
Speech Learning Model 86

speech perception 90–96; creating stimuli 96; discrimination tasks 93–96; identification tasks 91–93
speech production 88–90
speech tasks 84–99; global foreign accent 86–88; linguistic universals in phonology 97–98; phonetics and phonology 84–85; research questions/models in second language phonology 85–86; speech perception 90–96; speech production 88–90
spot-the-difference task 165
statistical analysis 61, 93
stimuli: in self-paced listening 113; in self-paced reading 108–110; speech perception 96; in Visual World studies 128–130
stimulus presentation 95
story-retelling task 87, 156
syntactic priming 114

TalkBank system 168, 174
temporal resolution 136–137, 144
tense 6, 9, 73–74, 155, 158
threats to validity 34–35, 37
timed AJTs 58 *see* Acceptability Judgment Task
transfer (native language transfer) 55; *see also* L1 influence
transition theory 29
Truth Value Judgment Tasks (TVJTs) 12n3, 22, 71–75, 81

unacceptability 14, 23, 57
Universal Grammar (UG) 4, 13, 38–39; full access 39; L2 knowledge of principles 39–41; L2 parameter knowledge 41–43; Minimalist view of language and acquisition 8–10; parameters, features, and role of 6–10; partial access 39; principles and parameters 38–43; Principles and Parameters theory 7–8; research questions in 1980s/1990s 38–39; in SLA 3–4; Universal Grammar principles and parameters 38–43
universals (linguistic): in comprehension 86; in phonology 97–98; in production 88, 90
usage-based SLA 20–21

validity: (quasi-)experimental design 34–36; external 34–35; internal 34–35; threats to 34–35
variability 16–18
variables: categorical variables 31; continuous variables 31; dependent variables 31; as element of experimental design 30–32; independent variables 31; types of 30–31
variation: among individual speakers of the same language 17; individual variation 19; linguistic variation 17; register variation 18; *see also* variability
video clip 147, 154, 157, 160–161
video-elicitation task 160–163
violation paradigms 131

Visual World studies: creating stimuli 128–130; eye-tracking in 125–130; paradigm studies 121; representative studies 126–128
vocabulary list 154

Word Order in Second Language Acquisition Corpora (WOSLAC) 178
working memory 103, 104, 117, 146, 163
wrap-up effects 109, 133
Written Corpus of Learner English (WriCLE) 178–179, 183n8; data elicited by 178–179; description of 178

Zipfian distribution 21, 25n1